P9-CJC-266

THE PREHISTORIC EXPLORATION AND COLONISATION OF THE PACIFIC

A small Vanikoro canoe with D'urville's ship *L'Astrolab* on its voyage of 1826–29.

THE

PREHISTORIC EXPLORATION

AND

COLONISATION

OF THE

PACIFIC

Geoffrey Irwin

Professor of Archaeology,
University of Auckland

CAMBRIDGE
UNIVERSITY PRESS

Riverside Community College
Library
4800 Magnolia Avenue
Riverside, California 92506

APR '95

Published by the Press Syndicate of the University of Cambridge
The Pitt Building, Trumpington Street, Cambridge CB2 1RP, UK
40 West 20th Street, New York, NY 10011-4211, USA
10 Stamford Road, Oakleigh, Victoria 3166, Australia

© Cambridge University Press 1992
First published 1992

Printed in Hong Kong by Colorcraft

National Library of Australia cataloguing in publication data
Irwin, Geoffrey.
Prehistoric exploration and colonisation of the Pacific.
Bibliography.
Includes index.
ISBN 0 521 40371 5.
1. Pacific Area—Discovery and exploration.
I. Title.
910.91

Library of Congress cataloguing in publication data
Irwin, Geoffrey.
The prehistoric exploration and colonisation of the Pacific/Geoffrey Irwin.
Includes bibliographical references and index.
ISBN 0-521-40371-5
1. Navigation, Prehistoric—Pacific Area. 2. Trade routes—
Pacific Area—Computer simulation. 3. Pacific Area—Discovery and
exploration. 4. Pacific Area—Colonization. 5. Pacific Area—
Antiquities. I. Title.
GN871.I78 1992
990—dc20   91-23105
                                                                              CIP

A catalogue record for this book is available from the British Library

ISBN 0 521 40371 5 hardback

CONTENTS

LIST OF FIGURES

LIST OF TABLES

1

AN INTRODUCTION TO THE PACIFIC AND THE THEORY OF ITS SETTLEMENT

The exploration of the vast Pacific Ocean and the settlement of its hundreds of remote islands were remarkable episodes in human prehistory. They seem all the more so because the methods and motives of the first Pacific settlers are not well understood. Early sea-going explorers had no prior knowledge of Pacific geography, no documents to record their route, no metal, no instruments for measuring time and evidently none for navigation. But this book, which reviews indigenous navigation and the archaeology of early settlement, suggests that the first exploration of the remote Pacific was rapid and purposeful; that it was more systematic and involved less loss of human life than conventionally thought; that navigation methods continued to improve as colonisation spread to more distant islands.

There are rich ethnographic and historic accounts of traditional navigation methods, but these have had millennia in which to elaborate and change. Sailing in a sea that is mapped in the mind is very different from sailing in an unknown one. There have been many experimental voyages by various rafts, replica canoes and Western vessels, but they cannot fully duplicate conditions of the first voyages. There have been computer simulations. Added to this are the results of 40 years of modern archaeology.

After more than 200 years of debate about how the Pacific was settled, the literature on the subject is now very large and, interestingly, many of the early themes are still alive. In all of this discussion, most attention has been given to whether voyaging was accidental or deliberate, what routes it took through the regions and islands of the ocean, when it happened, and who did it. In popular belief, the people involved have ranged from mythical hero navigators able to sail the ocean, discover new land and return home with sailing directions to find it again, to accidental travellers or exiles who made lucky (and unlucky) one-way passages in an ocean they could not map, leaving behind islands to which they could not return. The modern view is that they were competent sailors. However, many prehistorians believe they may have suffered high losses at sea, that their range of return voyaging was restricted, that they may have harboured unrealistic ideas about their island world, and may have been transported across parts of the ocean by conditions beyond their understanding or control. These views follow from uncertainty about the methods and circumstances of colonisation.

There are many other issues of interest to prehistorians. One concerns the kind of ancient navigation needed to settle the chains of large and often intervisible islands between mainland Southeast Asia, the Pleistocene continent of New Guinea and Australia (Greater Australia or Sahul), and its near neighbours in the west of Melanesia, which are known to have been reached by 40,000 to 30,000 years ago.

Other questions concern the much later, very rapid, exploration of the vast expanse of the remote Pacific farther to the east, which began after 3500 years ago. For instance, what was the origin of the first deep-sea navigators? To what extent was navigation a matter of chance or technological competence? Was discovery by one-way or return voyaging? How could navigators fix the positions of new islands in order to find them again? How many explorers may have survived or died at sea? Was there anything systematic about the order of colonisation and the elapsed time it took? How did navigation change as colonisation proceeded? How and why did the main thrust of colonisation take place against the prevailing easterly winds when that was the most difficult way to go?

Current models of early voyaging confuse issues of method with motive. Romantic notions about early navigators are often a sign that gaps in the argument are glossed over. A common assumption is that people did not choose to go, they were forced to, but there is no evidence as yet which says so. Another example is the presumption that explorers were so set on finding new land that they were equally willing to die at sea in the attempt. One objective of this book is to avoid much of the mystery by looking carefully at what was feasible in navigation, and then inspecting archaeological data for evidence of what happened.

A review of theories of voyaging and Pacific settlement (Irwin 1989) and a yacht voyage across its western part have led to the suggestion that the general pattern of colonisation implies developing methods of directed exploration, which allowed, not the fastest rate of advance, but the highest chance of survival. This predicts in a general way the order in which island groups should be settled and variations in the time this should take and, as such, it can be weighed against archaeological evidence. As a second level of testing, and also to find out about the detail of changes to navigation methods, a new computer simulation of voyaging is described.

Many difficulties arise. Firstly, while there is a wealth of information on surviving traditional navigation systems in parts of the Pacific, in crucial respects they do not represent the original ones. While there are many unknowns about navigation, there is a set of parallel issues in the archaeology of early settlement. The evidence itself is patchy, subject to sampling error and subject to change. Experience has shown that theories that are closely data-driven change as quickly as the data. Much can be gained from considering wider probabilities as well. Secondly, while archaeology and historical linguistics have been of mutual assistance in tracking prehistoric settlement, the expectations of the one have sometimes unnecessarily restricted the other, and biological data are still too few to produce detailed patterns. A third general problem is that some diversity in culture, language and biology, which has been attributed to colonisation, may result instead from the contacts of post-settlement voyaging, and it seems there were systematic patterns in both. Such difficulties have resulted in particular disputes in prehistory, concerned with the time and order of island settlement, the location and nature of 'homelands' for settlers, and the extent to which there were pauses in colonisation to allow cultural changes to take place.

Perhaps the most unsatisfactory thing about the current view of Pacific settlement is its context. It is not concerned with the practicalities of deep-sea sailing, with details of weather and the relative accessibility of different island targets. It has little to say about how new communities might be established. At the core of the problem is the lack of an explicit navigational theory of colonisation. The consequence is that, in reconstructions of past events, colonising populations have not been moved by considerations that might have made sense to them, but by the exigencies of a rather narrow prehistory of artifacts, settlement patterns, proto-languages and biological traits, which retrospectively require them to go, sometimes to stop, and then to take one route rather than another. This context is actually more suited to the end of prehistory, when the age of discovery was long past, ocean voyaging had declined, and when island populations had changed.

THE SCOPE OF THIS BOOK

This book is concerned with two distinct episodes of voyaging and colonisation. The first began some 50,000 years ago in the tropical region of Island Southeast Asia, the continent of Australia and its Pleistocene outliers. This was the first voyaging of its kind in the world. The second episode began after 3500 years ago and was a burst of sophisticated maritime and neolithic settle.nent in the remote Pacific. Apart from some isolated islands in other oceans which were left to be discovered much later by Europeans, this virtually completed the human settlement of the world apart from its ice-caps. Interestingly, the origins of the second episode are to be found in the region of the first.

Pleistocene voyaging was remote in time, and no navigational materials or methods survive for our inspection. Our knowledge of early island and coastal archaeology is fragmentary, and much of what can be said about colonisation is circumstantial and follows from investigation of the navigational and geographical conditions of the region. The first part of the book offers a view of Pleistocene voyaging realities and is largely a background to what follows.

The evidence of Pacific prehistory fills out with time and has a rich context of ethnography at the end. There is much more to be said about navigation in the remote Pacific and a new theory of colonisation is presented. The ancestors of the people involved appear to be identifiable as an archaeological category. The cultural sequences of many of the islands settled are substantially known, and the colonists themselves approach an ethnic entity as they go.

The emphasis of this book follows available information, such as it is. Archaeological evidence is presented in detail in so far as it relates to colonisation. The book is not intended to be a general work on Pacific prehistory, but is rather concerned with Pacific navigation and the archaeology of early settlement. However, in two important respects its scope goes beyond that. The final chapters present results of the computer simulation designed to examine previous conclusions about the settlement of the remote Pacific. It tells us more about people's methods and motives in exploration. There is also a study of the pattern of inter-island voyaging in the remote Pacific, after colonisation, and how this contact systematically affected the patterns of development that followed. We learn something about the context of cultural and biological diversification.

The rest of this chapter provides a background sketch of Pacific islands and the prehistory of their settlement, a summary of arguments about navigation, exploration and colonisation, a description of Pacific weather patterns, and a brief account of the main themes of 200 years of previous debate on these matters. It ends with a description of the contents of the chapters which follow.

A SKETCH OF THE PACIFIC AND ITS SETTLEMENT

Full accounts are available elsewhere (e.g. Bellwood 1978; Jennings 1979; Irwin 1980; Kirch 1984b; Terrell 1986), but to summarise briefly, the islands of the Pacific offer diverse habitats for humans. One distinction is between the islands of the continental regions in the western Pacific and those on the Pacific Plate, east of the 'Andesite Line', where volcanic mountains penetrate the surface to form volcanic islands or show their presence underwater with a crown of coral (Fig .1). Large high islands in the west are geologically diverse and rich in resources for settlement; on the Pacific Plate there are many high, basaltic islands, which offer a rather more restricted range. Sometimes these have a windward/leeward distinction in rainfall; large, deep valleys with alluvial soils; fringing reefs or barrier reefs offshore. There are many low islands on coral reefs near sea-level and others raised by volcanic activity; some are short of good soil and water. The most extreme habitats are atolls, which have a reef enclosing a lagoon without a central island; along it are islets of sand and coral rarely more than a few metres above the sea, but people have lived successfully on some for 2000 years or more. Pacific settlement accommodated tropical, sub-tropical, temperate and near sub-Antarctic climates. There were seasonal changes and natural hazards, such as droughts, cyclones and *tsunami*. Human settlements, although constrained by their environments, actually transformed them, sometimes again and again.

Pacific islands occur alone and in groups. They become more isolated, with distance east in the Pacific, and their natural flora and fauna increasingly impoverished, although marine food remains abundant where there are reefs. Traditional economies included a diverse range of portable

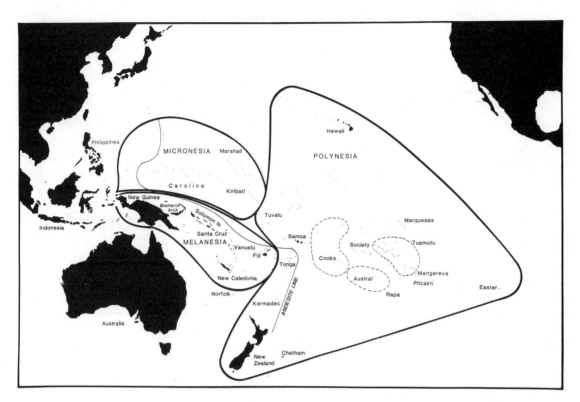

1. The regions and island groups of the Pacific. The background to Pacific colonisation lies in mainland and Island Southeast Asia, which includes Indonesia and the Philippines. Melanesia, Micronesia and Polynesia are the conventional divisions of Oceania. The Andesite Line marks a geological division between continental islands in the west from the volcanic islands of the Pacific Plate.

garden plants and tree crops. Pigs, dogs and fowls were sometimes kept, and seafood was important. In many islands, agriculture, aboriculture and even aquaculture were intensified. Traditional settlement patterns ranged from dispersed households to socially differentiated villages. Society was integrated by exchange relations, which occurred locally and over wider areas. There was a great variety of forms of leadership. Society ranged from small-scale and egalitarian, without much formal hierarchy, to large-scale, stratified and with hereditary chieftainship, which was especially developed in parts of Polynesia.

To turn to the question of first settlement. Greater Australia (Sahul), the Pleistocene continent of Australia and New Guinea, was already colonised 40,000 years ago. By 30,000 B.C., the Bismarck Archipelago was settled, and the then-larger islands of the Solomons either already settled or about to be. Early inhabitants were diverse hunter-gatherers in varied habitats. There is evidence for emerging agriculture in New Guinea even before its separation from Australia by rising seas in the early Holocene.

An easy 'voyaging corridor' stretched from mainland Southeast Asia to the end of the Solomon Islands. Seasonal and often sheltered conditions favoured early movement of simple craft, and the routes they took were influenced by the distance and size of island targets, patterns of intervisibility and favourable winds and currents.

Beyond the Solomons, islands are much farther apart and usually smaller, too, and conditions were different enough to arrest further settlement for 25,000 years, or for as long as it took people to learn how to sail offshore and survive. However, the voyaging corridor offered safe sailing conditions

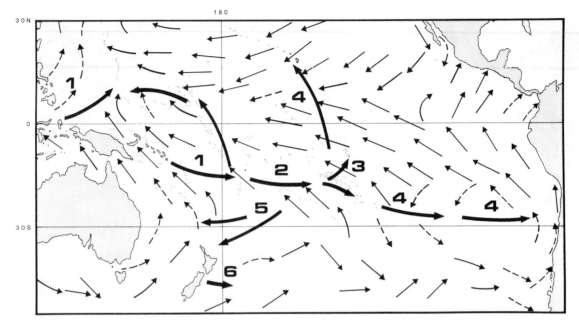

APPROXIMATE YEARS BEFORE PRESENT

(**1**) 3500–3000 (**2**) 3000–2500 (**3**) 2500–2000 (**4**) 2000–1500 (**5**) 1000 (**6**) 500

2. The colonisation of the remote Pacific led first against the prevailing winds, then across and down them and, finally, beyond the tropics. The direction of advance offered the highest chance of survival.

for such skills to be learned and to which the first, tentative offshore trips could return.

The broad pattern of settlement of the remote Pacific is shown in Figure 2, together with the prevailing winds of the southern winter. Deep-sea colonisation began after 3500 years ago probably with the rapid spread of an archaeological culture called Lapita through the islands of Melanesia to reach Fiji and West Polynesia by 1000 B.C., or before. This coastal and maritime adaptation carried its own portable economy of plants and animals, and engaged in long-distance exchange. Available radiocarbon dates now indicate that the Marquesas Islands in far East Polynesia may have been settled by A.D. 0, and some prehistorians hold the view that earlier sites, between 3000 and 2000 years old, are still to be found among closer groups such as the Cook and Society islands. In the centuries following A.D. 0, settlement reached Hawaii, distant Easter Island and probably South America. Cool and more difficult sailing conditions delayed settlement south of the tropics, but by approximately A.D. 1000, colonists reached New Zealand. The very remote Chatham Islands to the southeast appear to have been the final settlement of Polynesia.

At much the same time as Lapita left the east of the voyaging corridor, other groups with a different archaeological signature, but probably with some element of contact in their histories, sailed out from somewhere to the west of New Guinea into the high islands of western Micronesia. The Mariana Islands were settled c.1000 B.C. and the much closer islands of Belau and Yap were possibly discovered at much the same time, although there is no evidence for this. The eastern groups of Micronesia, which are nearly all atolls, were settled by A.D. 0, but a longer period of settlement is a distinct possibility. The source of eastern Micronesian settlement, somewhere between eastern Melanesia and West Polynesia, is as vague as that for western Micronesian settlement, somewhere in the Philippines or eastern Indonesia.

NAVIGATION

We know colonisation was deliberate, because explorers took with them the plants and animals, women and men necessary to establish viable settlements. As for navigation, it has been shown by a major computer simulation by Levison, Ward and Webb (1973), which took account of actual conditions of wind and current in the Pacific, that the major voyages of settlement could not have occurred by drift and were the result of some kind of directed navigation. Detailed ethnographic research on traditional Pacific canoes and navigation, which included experimental voyages at sea (Gladwin 1970; Lewis 1972; Finney 1977; Siers 1977), established that voyaging canoes were large, fast and safe, with double hulls (like catamarans) or with single hull and outrigger. Practical skills widespread in the Pacific were to steer an accurate course at sea, to maintain a running fix of position by dead-reckoning, and to detect destination islands from beyond sighting range by the use of sea-signs and, where possible, create broad overlapping target-island screens. Esoteric skills most probably included estimating a conceptual equivalent of latitude by the night sky without instruments. While longitude could not be controlled as such without time-pieces, it is both possible and likely that the position of new islands could be fixed by a combination of astronomy and an extension of geographical knowledge by dead-reckoning (Irwin 1989). In just a few millennia a large part of the world's surface was explored, but what remains to be inferred, here, are the kinds of sailing methods that were used by these oceanic explorers as the Pacific was crossed.

Exploration and survival

No sailing boat can sail into the wind, and the problem is that the prevailing wind in the tropical Pacific is from the east, against the direction of settlement. The similarities of Oceanic people, especially in language, with others to the west was obvious from early historical times, but did not always match the force of the contrary wind in theories of origin. An American source for Polynesians was an early idea, and its modern exponent is Thor Heyerdahl. Yet, in spite of the difficulty, eastward voyages were recorded in the tropics from early historic times, and it was understood then that the means to do so arise from seasonal interruptions in the easterly trade winds.

Sailing between known and unknown islands has its risks, but sailing into empty ocean is fatal. Some theories of Pacific colonisation prefer many explorers to die at sea, but there is nothing to show Pacific explorers were unconcerned about their lives. Without a doubt, it is safest to sail first in the direction that is normally upwind because one can expect the fastest trip back. The hard way is really the easy or safe way and this simple paradox is one of the keys to explaining the trajectory of human settlement. Practically every radiocarbon date in the remote Pacific supports the view that colonisation went first against the prevailing winds and only then across and down them.

Sailing upwind also provides the means to find the way home by latitude sailing. This was probably developed at some point in the settlement of the Pacific, and simply involves returning to the latitude of one's origin island, while still upwind of it, and then running with the wind along the latitude. Experimental evidence shows that the error in estimating latitude from the stars, without instruments, is matched by the ability to detect the presence of land from offshore.

To sail with some safety across the prevailing wind requires a knowledge of islands to leeward of the starting island, in case that cannot be reached on the return journey. Sailing downwind, on the other hand, usually requires returning by a different route. The circumstances of exploration changed in the remote Pacific as geographical knowledge was added to navigational knowledge, and the range of feasible options increased. Increasing experience and skill were needed to manage the long exploratory probes eventually made into the difficult higher-latitude extremities of Polynesia, and to South America.

In the southern winter of 1985, with four others, I took my 11.2 m yacht *Rhumbline* from New Zealand north to Fiji, and then across the island groups of the western Pacific to New Guinea. The trip was to survey the Louisiade Archipelago, but at the same time I was nursing my dissatisfaction with the subject of Pacific colonisation. All the way to the west I was noting conditions as they would have been for a canoe sailing without charts in the opposite direction, and checking the progress of yachts going that way. We slipped easily downwind with the rhythm of trade wind sailing. There was usually a clear view of much of the sky at night and, relying as we were on sextant and satellite navigation, it was still easy to tell by eye from the altitude of the stars that we were maintaining our approximate latitude. We could see clouds overtake us from behind knowing they could bring more wind. We usually saw line squalls before they arrived. It was hard to get weather forecasts, and when low pressure troughs arrived they took us as much by surprise as an early voyager would have been. But it was just a question of reducing sail and waiting for them to pass through, which in the trade wind season they do fairly quickly.

What we were experiencing was the other side of the coin of colonisation. It was what any canoe could choose to do, which had sailed upwind, whether it found land or not. The ease of sailing west is what made sailing east possible! *Rhumbline* is about as fast as a sailing canoe off the wind. It took us under six days to cross the 500 sea miles from Fiji to Vanuatu. We had the *Pacific Pilot* and charts to show us what lay ahead, whereas a returning early navigator would have had known seamarks and landmarks of another kind. Not even we could miss the peak of Erromanga, more than 50 nautical miles south of us, when our destination, Efate, still lay below the horizon but closer ahead. The trip to the Solomon Islands took another six days, and so did the voyage across the Solomon Sea to New Guinea. Later on, it took just three and a half days to cross the

Coral Sea to the Queensland coast, on a broad reach across the wind. Australia and America are implicated in Pacific colonisation, as we shall discuss later.

Return voyaging is a natural and conventional part of any maritime settlement, and just because people were involved in an episode of colonisation, they were not restricted to one-way traffic. Strategic use of weather systems is conventional too. I have been lucky enough to sail with Mailu people in southeast coastal New Guinea in essentially the same 11–15 m long, stable, seaworthy and fast, double-hulled sailing canoes as were used in prehistory. Traditional trading still takes them some hundreds of kilometres into the Massim region; they sail east with the monsoon and return at the beginning of the trade wind season. If they go west, they take the last of the trades and have variables or monsoonal north-westerlies to come home on. On short trips along the Papuan coast, even during the trade wind season, a canoe can make some progress east in the early morning, when wind from the land holds the trades a mile or so offshore; but later in the day there is always a fresh southeasterly to return on. In the Louisiade Archipelago, small and medium-sized outrigger canoes can often be seen coming and going about their inter-island business, and people watch the weather and use it to advantage. The situation is typical of the parts of the Pacific where sailing survives.

A number of issues arise from this discussion of navigation, and several propositions require further investigation (Irwin 1989). One is that there was a general direction of exploration, which led first upwind. Secondly, the order of discovery was generally in the order of ease of return, and voyages were conventionally two-way. Thirdly, methods that began the settlement of the remote Pacific did not complete it as inter-island distances increased, areas of ocean expanded, and sailing outside of the tropics became harder. Further, there may have been geographical reasons for variations in the order and elapsed time of island settlement, but we should be wary of pauses that follow from the hindsight of prehistorians' reasoning.

WEATHER PATTERNS IN THE PACIFIC

Details of the weather are important to some of the arguments that follow, so a general outline is provided here. The weather in the Pacific is affected by global patterns of air movement. Warmed air rises at the equator, flows poleward and cools, descending to the surface in the regions of latitude 30°N. and 30°S., and some flows back towards the lower pressure tropics. Cold, dense air from the poles flows towards the equator, meets the air flowing from around latitude 30°, and there is another ascendance, which occurs around latitude 60°. The Coriolus Force, caused by the earth's rotation, deflects air flow to the left in the Southern Hemisphere, so air flowing towards the pole gives winds from the west and air flowing towards the equator gives winds from the east. In the Northern Hemisphere air is deflected to the right giving similar east and west winds (Brierly 1985:17–18). The general flow of air around the earth is divided into

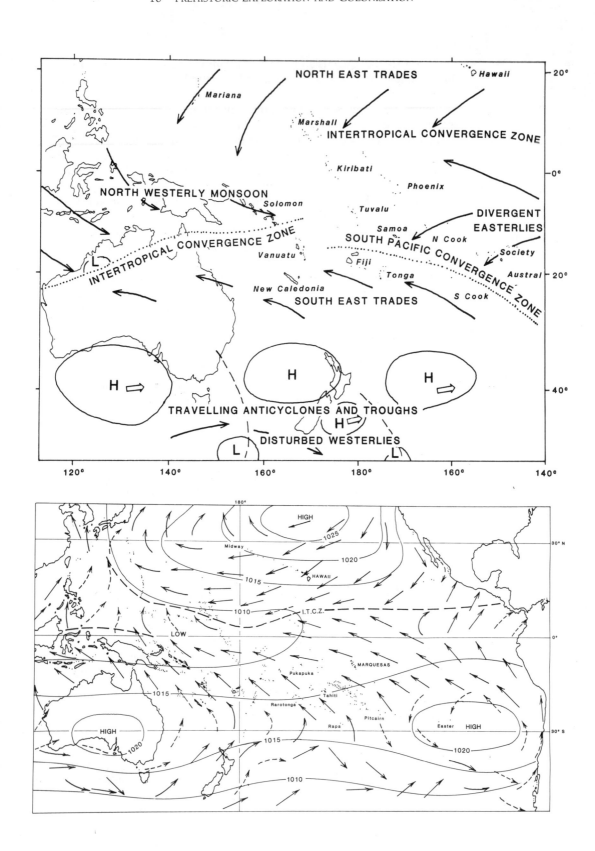

3 (opposite). The weather
systems of the southern
summer. (Adapted from
Hessell 1981,
Appendix 3B.)

bands, which change their boundaries with the seasonal passage of the
sun. Within each band other climatic systems build and die, giving the
patterns we call the weather. The heating and cooling of air over large
land masses modifies the pattern, and there are other local effects (Coutts
1981:98-9). The various climatic zones of the equator and South Pacific
Ocean, which are of most concern, are described below and illustrated
in Figures 3-5, summarised largely from *Ocean Passages for the World* (1973).

The Doldrums

Also known as the Equatorial Trough or the Intertropical Convergence
Zone (ITCZ), this area lies permanently north of the equator in the eastern
Pacific, east of about longitude 160°W. To the west of there, it moves
south in the southern summer and north in the northern summer. Typically,
it is about 150 miles wide, but both width and position vary. The weather
is light, variable winds, calms, squalls, heavy showers and thunderstorms.

4 (opposite). Prevailing
winds in the Pacific Ocean
in the southern
hemisphere winter and
northern summer.
(Adapted from *Ocean
Passages for the World* 1973;
reproduced by permission
of the editor from Irwin,
1989.)

5. Pacific Ocean currents
and islands mentioned in
the text. (Adapted from
Ocean Passages for the World
1973.)

Southeast trade winds

These blow on the equatorial side of a semi-stationary high pressure area
situated in the eastern ocean at about 30°S., and, west of there, of migratory
anticyclones, which travel east from Australia. The northern limit is the
ITCZ, and the southern limit is about 20°-25°S. in summer and 15°-20°S.
in winter. Winds are generally steady and reach the strength of a near-
gale on only one or two days a month in most of the region. The typical
weather is fair, with small cumulus cloud over about half the sky. The
wind tends to freshen with increased cloud and showers. Between the
South Pacific Convergence Zone (SPCZ) and the ITCZ, in the eastern Pacific,
rainfall reduces and the sky is more cloudy.

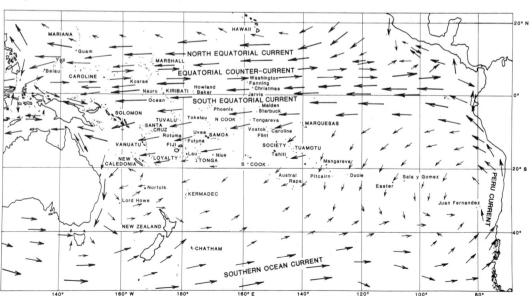

Northwest monsoon

In the southern summer, the ITCZ is situated near a low pressure area over the north of Australia; the northeast trades of the western side of the North Pacific are drawn across the equator and deflected to the left to produce northwesterly winds. These monsoonal northwest winds particularly affect the Queensland coast and Island Melanesia, but they become more intermittent with distance east. Winds are generally light to moderate, but strong squalls and heavy showers are common.

Cyclones

The cyclone season in the Southern Hemisphere coincides with the summer monsoon, from November to March, although they are not unknown at other times of the year. Cyclones form at about 8°S. and typically track to the west, swing south, and often re-curve to the east. They most affect an area north of New Zealand.

Variables

South of the trades is a belt of variable winds of mainly moderate strength. It can extend as far as 40°S. in summer and about 30°S. in winter; average wind strengths increase with latitude. The weather here is affected by eastward-moving high pressure systems separated by troughs of low pressure, which respectively bring alternating fine and bad weather.

Westerlies

Westerly winds predominate in a belt of low pressure south of the variables. There is a continuous passage of depressions, wind direction and strength vary, and gales are common. Of the areas of prehistoric settlement in the Pacific, only New Zealand and the Chatham Islands were affected by these conditions, and especially in winter.

Currents

The main circulation in the Southern Hemisphere is anticlockwise and the details are shown in Figure 5 (which also shows many island place names).

Westerly winds for sailing east

In spite of the prevailing easterly winds in the tropical Pacific there are variations that make it possible, but usually not easy, to make progress to the east. A number of methods have been suggested, and these will be discussed in greater detail below with reference to the settlement of particular parts of the ocean. Firstly, while the doldrums are a zone of variables, the problem here seems to be sailing in any direction, let alone east. A more obvious possibility is the monsoonal reversal of the southern summer in the western Pacific, which brings westerlies and northerlies into Melanesia and intermittently farther east, but with decreasing effect. Lewis (1972:297) notes that they are felt every few weeks as far as Tahiti, but that north and east of there trades are virtually continuous.

Another source of westerly winds are the rotational weather systems, which move from west to east south of the tropics and affect its southern reaches (Ferdon 1963, Irwin 1987, Finney 1988), and which have been shown to be usable for strategic sailing in canoes (Finney *et al.* 1989). Troughs associated with low pressure systems reach northward into the tropics and bring a predictable pattern of wind shifts, and they extend deeper into the tropics in the southern winter with the movement north of the SPCZ.

More unusual conditions, such as El Niño, which brings sustained anomalous westerlies to the southern tropics have been invoked as well, but their role in prehistory is problematical.

THEMES IN THE HISTORY OF THEORIES OF VOYAGING

Observations by European voyagers in the South Pacific more than 200 years ago had recognised many issues on the subject of origins, which have remained until this day. A few of the more significant examples are reviewed here as background to the discussion which follows. In 1770 Sir Joseph Banks wrote:

> From the similarity of customs, the still greater of traditions and the almost identical sameness of Language between these people [Maori] and those of the Islands of the South Seas there remains little doubt that they came originaly [sic] from the same source; but where that source is future experience may teach us, at Present I can say no more than I firmly beleive [sic] that it is to the Westward and by no means to the East. [Banks 1962, 2:37]

As well as the questions of unity and direction of origins, there was the question of dispersal, and Captain James Cook asked in 1778, in Hawaii:

> How shall we account for this Nation spreading itself so far over this Vast ocean? We find them from New Zealand to the South, to these islands to the North and from Easter Island to the Hebrides. [Beaglehole 1967:279]

Cook was already aware, from the time of his first voyage to the South Pacific, of the wide geographic knowledge of Polynesians, as revealed especially by the map made from information given by the Raiatean navigator, Tupaia, at Tahiti, which showed most of the islands of Polynesia, with the exception of those at the margins, including Easter Island, Hawaii and New Zealand. Their knowledge of other matters was known too. The Polynesians' knowledge of the stars was very detailed.

> Of these they know a very large part by their Names and the clever ones among them will tell in what part of the heavens they are to be seen in any month when they are above their horizon; they know also the time of their annual appearing and disappearing to a great nicety, far greater than would be easily beleivd [sic] by an European astronomer. [Banks 1962, 1:368]

Banks and others also agreed that Polynesians were able to forecast the weather with general accuracy for three days ahead, and had far more ability in this than Europeans (Dening 1963:117).

On the question of winds, Cook noted in his Journal account of Tahiti that the east wind was not constant, but subject to variation, there often being a fresh gale from the southwest for two to three days, but very seldom from the northwest. He considered that these westerlies could be due to the movement north and south of the boundary zone between the easterly trade winds and the belt of westerlies he knew to lie south of them, and that this latitudinal shift occurred within and between seasons (Beaglehole 1968:137). In fact sub-tropical westerlies are even now assuming more importance in arguments about voyaging. Cook also notes that Tupaia had informed them of westerly winds (probably of monsoonal origin) with rain from November to January 'and they know very well how to take the Advantage of these in their Navigations' (Beaglehole 1968:139). It is not really surprising that Cook, at this time, saw the possibility of deliberate voyaging:

> In these Proes or Pahee's . . . these people sail in those seas from Island to Island for several hundred Leagues, the Sun serving them for a compass by day and the moon and Stars by night. When this comes to be prov'd we Shall be no longer at a loss to know how the Islands lying in those seas came to be people'd, for if the inhabitants of Uleitea [in the Society Islands] have been at Islands laying 2 or 300 Leagues to the westward of them it cannot be doubted but that the inhabitants of those western Islands may have been at others as far to the westward of them and so we may trace them from Island to Island quite to the East Indias. [Beaglehole 1968:154]

According to Dening:

> Bougainville was willing to allow the Polynesians the skill to perform voyages of over three hundred leagues, and so was Cook till the influence first of the Forsters and later Anderson suggested to him that the story of Pacific migrations was to be told in terms of accidental voyages which peopled the scattered islands. [1963:111]

It is recorded that in 1777, at Atiu in the Southern Cook Islands, Omai, Cook's Tahitian companion, discovered three other Tahitians, who had been blown away while on a voyage from Tahiti to Raiatea, both in the Society Islands, and Cook wrote that the incident

> will serve to explain, better than the thousand conjectures of speculative reasoners, how the detached parts of the earth, and, in particular, how the South Seas, may have been peopled; particularly those that lie remote from any inhabited continent, or from each other. [Cook and King 1785a: 200-2]

These few examples (and there are others) show that some 200 years ago it was already realised that many Pacific islanders were related and probably had an origin in the west, not the east; that the prevailing easterly winds were interrupted, especially in some months, and that westerly winds could be used strategically for sailing east; that Polynesian specialists had wide geographical knowledge as well as a detailed understanding of astronomy, tides, weather and other matters; that navigators could maintain their sense of direction at sea, as shown by Tupaia on his voyage with Cook; that the means of colonisation of Pacific islands could range from systematic and intentional voyaging to unintended and largely undirected accidents.

Information and theories accumulated through the nineteenth century. The possibility of an American origin was raised, not for the first time, by Ellis, a Hawaiian missionary (Ellis 1831). John Williams, who was head of the London Missionary Society (LMS) mission at Raiatea, in the Society islands, from 1817–39, explicitly disagreed, and it is interesting to note some details of his argument. He was 'convinced . . . of the practicality' of west to east colonisation (1837:512). He acknowledged that among the objections to an Asian origin were 'the prevalence of the easterly trade winds within the tropics', and the great distance from the Malay coast, and that 'it is thought to have been impossible for the natives to perform such a voyage with their vessels and imperfect knowledge of navigation' (1837:506). But, he suggested, 'if we can show that such a voyage may be performed by very short stages, the difficulty will disappear' (1837:506). On the question of the trade winds, he said, 'after some observation, I am satisfied that the direction of the wind is not so uniform as to prevent the Malays from reaching the various islands and groups, in which their descendants are, I believe, now found' (1837:509). Williams continues with an explicit account of westerly winds that were known, including their Tahitian names, the months they blew, and their typical duration and patterns of change. He also described various of his own voyages, including one from Rarotonga to Tahiti: 'although it blows from the E. almost constantly in those latitudes, we were favoured, during our voyage of 800 miles, with a fair wind' – which is decribed as light and the sea smooth (1837:169).

At the same time, however, evidence was accumulating of voyages of a different kind. In 1797 Wilson of the *Duff* made a very explicit case about migrations that occurred under stress of weather when canoes were driven from island to island and from one group to another (Parsonson 1963:18). Many others mentioned involuntary voyages of an unsophisticated kind as well as one-way voyages of exile. In 1866 W. Pritchard said:

> It cannot be doubted that the early migrations of the ancestors of these islanders were involuntary rather than the result of roving dispositions, or of the pressure of limited and over-populated homes; that, in fact, they were blown away from their earlier homes in their frail canoes. [Pritchard 1866:402]

Pritchard, however, noticed an anomaly in that the pattern of recorded drift voyages was from east to west (1866:402) which, of course, was against the direction of colonisation. J. D. Lang, who sailed in the Pacific in the mid-nineteenth century, emphasised accidental storm drifts and believed Polynesians might have reached America; however, he did allow adventurous spirits and forced voyages of exile as possibilities, as well (Lang 1877).

Towards the end of the century the theory of deliberate voyaging was more widely accepted. For the origins of Polynesians, most writers looked to the west to Asia, and some looked even beyond. Fornander, in Hawaii, and Tregear and Smith, in New Zealand, developed grandiose migration theories, which drew uncritically on voyaging traditions (Finney 1979a:323). However, not all were willing to take this kind of view (Sorrenson 1979:45).

This century has continued to favour a western origin, with Heyerdahl (1952) providing another American diversion. It began with the view held by scholars such as Smith (1921) and Best (1923) that the Pacific was explored by navigators able to discover new land and return to their homes with sailing directions that others could follow. Buck's (1938) view was similar, but his idea of voyaging more realistic, and he allowed some centuries for settlement to take place.

Andrew Sharp over-reacted to the excesses of this position by arguing that voyaging was one-way and discoveries were accidental (1957, 1963). In many respects his argument restated an earlier position. While there was ethnographic evidence for return voyaging of up to about 300 miles in a few surviving contact areas in Micronesia, Fiji/West Polynesia and between the Society and northwestern Tuamotu islands, Sharp believed that prehistoric navigation methods were not good enough to allow returns over greater distances. A considerable debate followed. Some authorities, such as Hilder (1963) and Akerblom, (1968), took a position similar to Sharp's, while others, such as Heyen (1963), took a more positive stance.

Two major developments followed. The first was a computer simulation by Levison, Ward and Webb (1973), which took account of recorded weather conditions, and persuaded most scholars that the major colonising voyages of the Pacific could not have occurred by drift, even if the methods that had been used were unknown. At the same time, other scholars, including Alkire (1965), Gladwin (1970), Lewis (1972), Finney (1977, 1979b), Siers (1977) and others, have re-established the reputation of ancient voyagers by historical and ethnographic studies, and many experimental voyages in replica canoes and other craft have made successful landfalls (although not all). This position does not exclude the possibility of some accidental colonisation, but no longer sees it as necessary.

PROBLEMS FOR THIS BOOK

Many questions remain, including some mentioned already. What systematic methods or strategies of ocean exploration were used, if any, and how did they change? What evidence is there of a concern for survival? How did colonists fix the position of new land? To what extent was voyaging one-way or two-way and what was the effective range of return voyages? How did factors of geography and weather influence the time and order of island settlement? Why did voyaging decrease in much of the Pacific after it was settled, and in some places disappear completely? Should the colonisation of the remote Pacific be seen as a coherent whole or was it a series of unrelated episodes? What does the evidence say about the culture of the people concerned, or of their motives for what they did?

These questions are addressed in this book. Chapter 2 discusses the Pleistocene background, and deals with the colonisation of the voyaging corridor between mainland Southeast Asia and the Solomon Islands. Chapter 3 considers the origins, many thousands of years later, of the first groups of deep-sea sailors, who settled western Micronesia and eastern Melanesia/West Polynesia. Chapter 4 is a detailed discussion of indigenous navigation and the theory of position-fixing without instruments; it also outlines a general theory of survival sailing and systematic exploration, which offers a predictive model for archaeology. The next chapters of the book deal with the archaeological evidence for early settlement and weighs it against the various theories on that subject. Chapter 5 covers upwind colonisation of eastern Melanesia and West Polynesia, on to central East Polynesia and, finally, South America. Chapter 6 deals with the settlement of Hawaii and New Zealand, which entailed voyages across the wind and out of the tropics. It also considers the evidence from smaller island neighbours of these two great archipelagos, to see if they contribute to a coherent pattern. Chapter 7 is about the settlement of Micronesia, the least-well understood part of the remote Pacific. The final chapters are concerned with other approaches, and begin with Chapter 8, a computer simulation of settlement. That chapter attempts, firstly, to test some of the arguments of this book, and, secondly, to explore the kinds of navigational techniques that were used in prehistory, by comparing particular strategies and their different outcomes with archaeological evidence. Chapter 9 distinguishes patterns of language, material culture and biology, which have been attributed to colonisation, but which may result partly from the diversification that followed post-settlement contact. It is concluded that rather different, but equally coherent, patterns can be found in both. The final chapter, Chapter 10, summarises the issues that have been raised, and considers some cultural implications and questions, such as why voyages of exploration began and ended. It ends with a discussion of how navigation changed in the post-discovery period, and a description of traditional methods at the time of Western contact.

2

PLEISTOCENE VOYAGING AND THE SETTLEMENT OF GREATER AUSTRALIA AND ITS NEAR OCEANIC NEIGHBOURS

When the sea-level was lower, *Homo erectus* walked into an extended Pleistocene land mass of mainland Southeast Asia. At no stage of the Pleistocene was this connected to the former continent of Greater Australia and there is no evidence yet for a water crossing beyond Wallace's Line, although the continuing mystery of *Stegadons* (elephantids) in Sulawesi, the Philippines, Timor and Flores suggests these islands were once more accessible than now. *Homo sapiens* entered the island chains of Wallacea to reach Greater Australia, and beyond to the Bismarck Archipelago and the Solomon Islands. When and how this happened, and what routes it took, have been matters of investigation, speculation and even simulation. This chapter reviews the main arguments.

The suggestion has long been made that the penetration of the tropical belt of this new region would have been assisted by continuity of marine and plant environments (Golson 1971; White and O'Connell 1982:51), although by New Guinea there was a change to a mainly Australian fauna, which, from a hunter's point of view, became sharply attenuated in the archipelagos farther east (Thorne 1963; Green in press).

The archaeological evidence of settlement now approaches 40,000 years. One site of that age on the Huon Peninsula of the north coast of New Guinea had access to local lagoons and fringing reefs and a forested hinterland. There were flaked, probably hafted, axes, which have been interpreted as for forest-edge manipulation (Groube *et al.* 1986) on this island, which by the early Holocene had evidence for early, and probably indigenous, plant domestication (Golson 1977).

By 30,000 years ago there were continental adaptations as diverse as to the periglacial interior of Tasmania (Cosgrove 1989) and possibly even

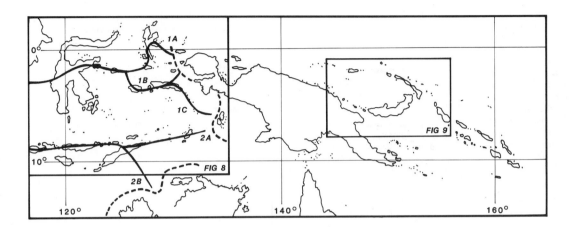

6. A voyaging corridor of large, often-intervisible islands joins Southeast Asia to Melanesia. Conditions allowed Pleistocene settlement as far east as the Solomon Islands, which involved the earliest documented voyages in the World. Possible routes shown between the continents of Asia and Greater Australia are those suggested by Birdsell (1977). No leg on any route was greater than approximately 100 km in Pleistocene times.

arid parts of Australia (Allen 1989). A New Ireland (Bismarck Archipelago) cave site, Matenkupkum, of about 33,000 years ago, indicates use of coastal marine and lowland tropical forest resources (Allen, Gosden and White 1989) and possibly initial settlement at least of the immediate area.

The pattern of dates does not show much delay before a successful crossing was made to the Solomon Islands farther east. A cave on Buka that dates from c.26,000 B.C. contained mammal, lizard and fish bone, marine shell and flaked stone throughout its sequence (Wickler and Spriggs 1988). This island was then joined to a string of others stretching farther south to Nggela. On Guadalcanal, which was separated by a very narrow strait, there have been surface finds of waisted axes similar to those dated on the Huon Peninsula, which suggests a considerable antiquity in the south of the Solomons too.

Distance and angle of island target

Birdsell (1977) examined in some detail the possible routes to Greater Australia. He noted that the sea between the Sunda and Sahul shelves was island-studded, and that the majority of islands were high, although a few chains of low ones existed as well. He identified two sizeable chains of large islands, which extend between the two emergent shelves as the basis for his major Routes 1 and 2, the former in the north and trending towards the island of New Guinea and the other in the south and directed closer to the northwest coast of Australia. Birdsell specified five likely sub-routes – three in the north, two in the south – which contained between 8 and 17 stages (Fig. 6). At times of glacial maximum no stage was greater than about 100 km, and for the rest of the Pleistocene, when the sea generally stood about 40–70 m below current levels, the water gaps between high islands remained much the same, although there were appreciable changes of distance on the emergent shelves (Birdsell 1977:128).

Figure 7 plots inter-island distances and angles of island target as taken from British Admiralty Charts numbers. 941B, 942A and 942B, between the islands on the northern Route 1, which is shown here because it

7. A graph showing the relative accessibility of islands in the voyaging corridor by distance from their neighbours – calculated for a minus-50 m shoreline – and by angle of target. In general, island accessibility and the nature of intervisibility relate systematically to the archaelogical age of island settlement.

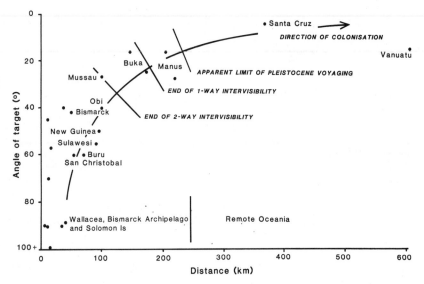

was also intervisible all the way. Distances are calculated for the minus-50 m shoreline and angles of island target are similar to those shown by Birdsell (1977:124–5), although here they are directed only generally towards visible land ahead and do not necessarily distinguish every stepping-stone in between. These target angles do not allow for any expanded radii, as it is not assumed here that colonists were able to detect the presence of land from beyond the range of sight offshore, using, for example, cloud formations, drifting smoke from fires, flotsam patterns, or sea bird behaviour – at this early time – although they had become part of the repertoire of purposeful navigation in the remote Pacific by the time of Western contact.

It is interesting to note that the first voyage between the shelves, to Sulawesi, was much the same distance as the last, to New Guinea (Fig. 7) and that some voyages farther east to reach the Bismarck Archipelago and others, within the main Solomon Islands chain were no greater. Beyond the larger islands of the Bismarck Archipelago, circumstances gradually began to change. The island of Mussau lies some 98 km north of New Hanover at a distance no greater than others crossed already. However, the angle of target (23°) is rather less. No Pleistocene dates are reported yet from Mussau in spite of field work efforts (Kirch 1987) but the island appears to be within range of the voyaging technology. Whether such a relatively small island was able to sustain early settlement is another matter.

The distance from the Bismarck Archipelago to Buka, the closest of the Solomon Islands, was effectively greater than those before. Figure 7 shows a distance of approximately 140 km via Feni and of 175 km direct from New Ireland. Because the shorter distance offers the smaller target, there may not be much to choose between two routes. The Green Islands offered a possible but rather unlikely stepping-stone, because they were small and low and could not have been detected except from close by. At all events, the greater distance to the Solomon Islands was not enough to delay settlement appreciably, according to the current dates.

8. Details of intervisibility eastward along Birdsell's (1977) postulated routes to Greater Australia (including New Guinea). Sighting arcs show the ranges of visibility of high land standing at the apex of each arc. In the north, Birdsell's Route 1A is intervisible all the way from mainland Asia, while his Route 1B is intervisible on a westward journey. In the south, Birdsell's routes run blind. Fluctuations in Pleistocene sea-level did not materially affect sighting ranges.

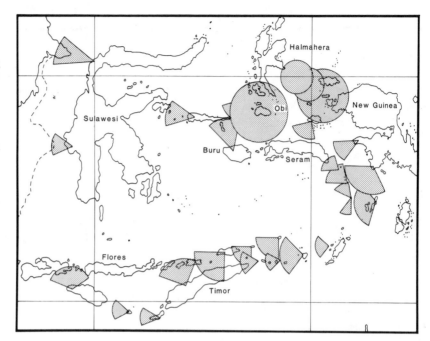

The island of Manus is still farther. The then-larger Pleistocene outlier lay at similar distances from Mussau (200 km) and New Hanover (230 km) in the Bismarck Archipelago and also from mainland New Guinea (220 km from Karkar Island). The approximate target arcs from Mussau (17°) and New Hanover (15°) were less than from New Guinea (28°). Whether the greater distance to Manus delayed its successful settlement is still to be resolved. Distance and target angle are factors that are mediated by other factors, including intervisibility, the pattern of winds and currents and island size, but, certainly, Pleistocene settlement of Manus has been regarded as most likely (Irwin 1989:168–9 and Fig. 1), because the first significant navigational threshold occurs farther east between the main Solomon Islands chain and Santa Cruz (Fig. 7). This break has long been recognised as a biogeographic divide (Thorne 1963), and Pawley and Green (1973) have stressed the influence on human colonisation of fewer resources. The marked difference in accessibility, as measured here by angle and distance of island target, helps explain why this navigational divide was more difficult for humans to cross, just as it had been for other animals and plants.

Intervisibility

While Birdsell (1977) noted modern island heights, he did not translate this into specific distances from which they could be seen ahead, but he did correctly identify intervisibility as an important variable as did Pawley and Green (1973). In fact it is (and probably was) possible to see from mainland Asia to the end of the Bismarck Archipelago (Fig. 8). One of Birdsell's (1977) five hypothetical sub-routes (1A) provides intervisibility along an unbroken chain of islands. His other northern sub-routes (1B and 1C) are at the margins of intervisibility, but the two southern

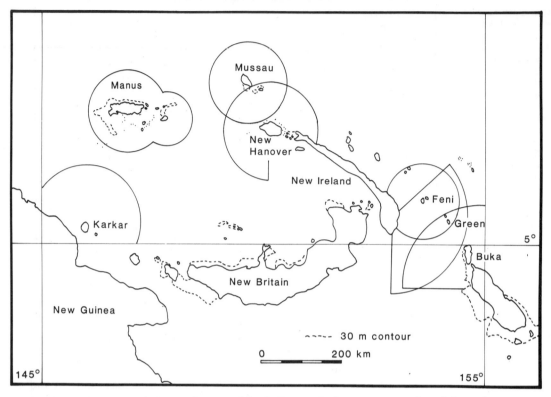

9. Land was visible in both directions from New Guinea to New Britain and New Ireland. On a crossing to the northern Solomons, land cannot be seen ahead until New Ireland is at least 55 km behind. However, New Ireland remains in sight for most of the journey across. Manus requires a passage with a blind portion of at least 60–90 km. Such differences may have affected the age of first settlement.

sub-routes become blind. Figure 8 shows ranges of visibility of a passive kind, which refer to high land that can be seen ahead from sea-level and does not require a person to climb higher with the intention of seeing farther. (Even if one stood on the highest point of Timor, it would not have been possible to discern the shore of Australia when the sea was at its lowest stand in the Pleistocene.) The apex of each sighting arc in Figure 8 is positioned on a high point, which can be seen from anywhere within the arc. It is interesting that the difference between lower or higher Pleistocene sea-levels does not alter the drawing, because the difference in sighting distance is accommodated by the thickness of the line representing the arc. Times of low sea-level were no better than any others in this respect.

In terms of travelling in the reverse direction from New Guinea, Birdsell's Route 1A is now just beyond the limits of intervisibility, whereas his Route 1B becomes clearly intervisible, which it was not the other way. However, it was not possible to see from Sulawesi back across the Strait of Malacca to what was then mainland Southeast Asia unless one travelled south from Sulawesi to islands from which Flores, in Route 2, is visible today, but whether it was in the late Pleistocene is unknown.

In ideal conditions one can see as far as the curvature of the earth will allow, allowing for refraction of light by the atmosphere. If one is living on an island, at times conditions will be good enough to see what other land there is to be seen, and people could acquire an habitual knowledge of neighbouring islands within sight. Visibility at sea is a very different case, because conditions are variable, and cloud, haze, etc., severely restrict it. Sometimes one can see high land from a long way away, at sea, but cannot depend on it.

Two-way intervisibility by land extends into the Bismarck Archipelago, and Mussau lies approximately at the margins of it (Figure 9). Crossing to the Solomon Islands involved a change to one-way intervisibility by sea - in which land appeared ahead before it was lost from sight behind. Feni can be seen today from New Ireland but the Solomon Islands do not come into view until one is at least 40 km south of Feni. The Solomon Islands can be seen some time after 55 km on a voyage from New Ireland. However, on voyages from both Feni and New Ireland the mountains of New Ireland can be seen behind, in ideal conditions, almost all the way across to Buka and, in most conditions, until the Solomons are in clear view ahead. Reaching the Solomons did not require losing sight of land, but it is clear that Buka was not found, because people already knew it was there before they left. However, the pattern of radiocarbon dates does not show that these conditions constituted a new navigational threshold here. Indeed, the same conditions could have been met already in Wallacea.

Manus is farther offshore and lower in elevation than the northern Solomons, which necessitated a blind crossing, and voyagers would have been out of sight of land for a minimum distance of from 60 to 90 km, depending on the line of approach taken (Figure 9), and on most occasions longer. Given that the Bismarck Archipelago was settled at least 30,000 years ago and the northern Solomons shortly afterwards, it is navigationally plausible that Mussau was reached at much the same time, even if it was not settled then. However, Manus can only have been discovered by people already out of sight of known land, which could have led to delayed settlement, but the length of any such delay remains to be seen. The recent terminal Pleistocene dates obtained for Manus by Ambrose and Spriggs (pers. comm. 1989) are in keeping with the aceramic but younger evidence previously published by Kennedy (1983) and with the proposed navigational context for Manus (Irwin 1989).

All of these calculations of sighting distance depend, of course, on substantial geological stability for the last 30,000 years or more in a region of known tectonic and volcanic activity (Birdsell 1977:133). Geological information suggests that the high points along Birdsell's Route 1 to New Guinea were likely to have been in existence during the time in question (R. W. Johnston pers. comm. 1988), while most uncertainty relates to the east of New Guinea. Southern New Ireland was probably already high, but Karkar, Feni and the northern Solomons are volcanic and could have been still rising, and, if so, intervisibility would have been less than now.

Climate and weather

Assessment of the settlement of this region is similarly influenced by changes in climate. However, the assertion has been made that equatorial climates changed relatively little (Wild 1985:66-7), and there can be expected to be several points of similarity between the late Pleistocene and now. The

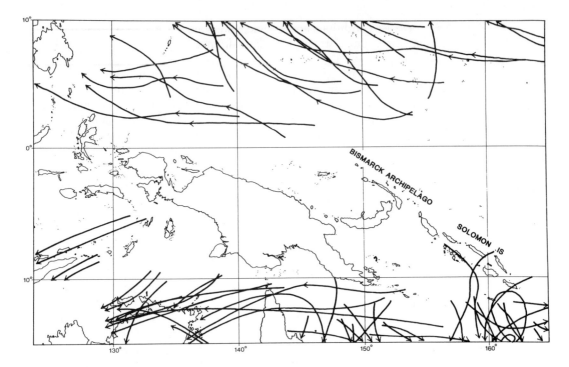

10. The voyaging corridor lies in a band of shelter between northern and southern tropical cyclone belts. In terms of colonisation, it represented (1) a region of easy Pleistocene island-hopping, (2) a voyaging 'nursery', in which maritime technology was able to develop for 50,000 years, and (3) a large safety-net to which the first tentative voyages of deep-ocean exploration could return. (Adapted from the *Indonesia Pilot* and *Pacific Islands Pilot;* reproduced by permission of the editor from Irwin, 1989.)

temperature then was some five or so degrees cooler, sea-levels were lower, and shorelines were different. However, because the area is equatorial, there would have been no wholesale latitudinal displacement of tropical weather systems. With respect to seasonality, the ITCZ would still have moved north and south with the sun. The ITCZ, today, is the breeding ground of cyclones, and whatever ones blew in the Pleistocene they probably left a band of shelter between the northern and southern cyclone belts not unlike that shown in Figure 10. Warmed air still rose over the climatic equator, creating a wind flow north and south towards it, while the earth's rotation and the Coriolus Force gave it the same easterly slant as today's trade winds. If the land mass of northern Australia warmed in summer, as it does now, the monsoon of the southern summer would have existed in some form, but it may have been affected by the larger exposed shelf of Torres Strait and the large freshwater Lake Carpentaria. Thus we can allow for many differences but continuity in general climatic pattern. It is also worth remembering the essential point that day-to-day weather is changeable, and small boats, then as now, require suitable conditions only some of the time.

The general pattern of contemporary winds and currents is shown in Figures 11–14 (*Indonesia Pilot* vol. III; *Pacific Islands Pilot* vol. I). The southern winter is dominated by the southeasterly trade winds (Fig. 11), which the currents generally follow (Fig.12). In the southern summer, both the winds and currents around New Guinea and the archipelagos both west and east are influenced by the monsoon (Figs. 13 and 14), while the northern hemisphere tropics are dominated by the northeasterly trades (Fig. 13). The general situation in this 'voyaging corridor' is of predictable seasonal reversals of wind and current, a sheltered equatorial position

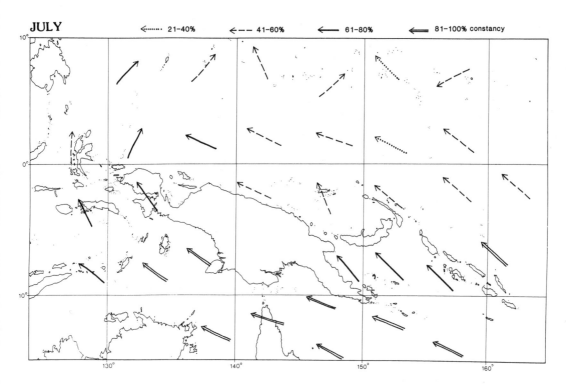

JULY

←········ 21–40%   ←–– 41–60%   ←—— 61–80%   ←══ 81–100% constancy

11. The direction of winds and their constancy in the tropical trade wind season of the southern winter. Seasonal and predictable changes in wind direction allowed simple return voyaging between islands of this region. (Adapted from the Indonesia Pilot *and* Pacific Islands Pilot.)

between bands of cyclones and a large measure of intervisibility, which accommodates all islands but the Pleistocene outliers (Irwin 1989).

Pleistocene boats and navigation

In 1977 Birdsell wrote 'archaeology provides no information as to the types of watercraft which might have been used' (1977:134), and the situation has not changed since. However, he mentioned various possibilities, including logs, bundles of bark and reeds, dugouts, bark canoes and rafts of mangrove and bamboo – the last of which he preferred. He also noted that bamboo occurs naturally in the region, on his Route 1 and as far along Route 2 as Java. Doran (1981), too, concluded from a study of Pacific boat types that the raft would have been used first, even though distributional evidence might suggest the bark canoe could be earlier. Lewis (1977:4-8) also noted that rafts were widespread, easy to build and very functional. Bamboo is ideally suited to rafts as it is strong and buoyant, does not rot and can easily be lashed together, so the case these commentators jointly make is very plausible. However, some other discussion in the literature concerning finer details such as vessel shape amounts to little more than unrealistic conjecture.

More than one kind of craft could have served, because the conditions in the region were not sufficient to exclude all others. Horridge (1987) makes the suggestion that early boats had sails, but distances were not so great that boats without them could not have made the same crossings and have been easily driven by wind on the way. It is inconceivable,

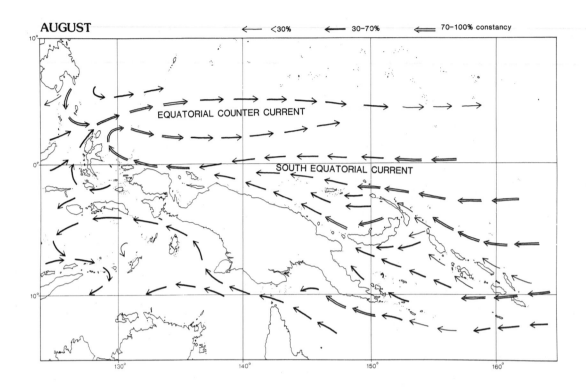

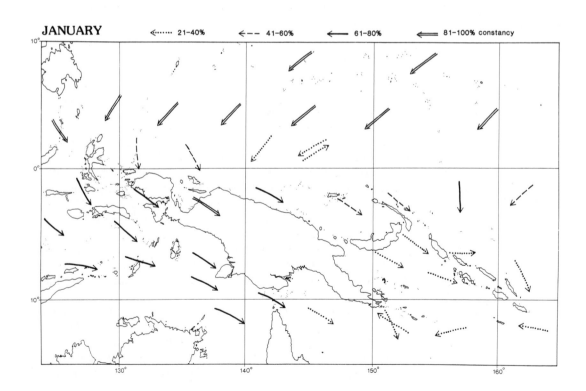

12 (*opposite*). The direction of sea currents and their constancy in the southern winter. (Adapted from the *Indonesia Pilot* and *Pacific Islands Pilot*.)

too, that in 25,000 years of Pleistocene water-crossing boats should not have varied and sometimes improved. Further, arguments based on the modern distributions of boat types as an indication of former distributions ignore the obvious fact that boats are a mode of transport in themselves and not just passively moved like any other cultural trait, and nor is there any chronological control of when ideas about them may have spread.

One detail on which we may be more secure concerns boat size, and White and O'Connell (1979) pointed to the necessity of getting a founder population to a new island all at once. 'The often-promulgated idea that the offspring of a single pregnant woman clinging to a log could ultimately populate a continent . . . can be relegated to the realm of theoretical biology' (White and O'Connell 1979:24). In fact, computer simulations in demography have suggested that founder groups could scarcely have contained less than four or five people to make up a viable unit (McArthur *et al.* 1976), and groups must have been sufficient to reproduce socially as well, which is a more difficult factor to put a number on. Therefore, whatever the boats were, they must have been reasonably substantial, even if still unsophisticated.

13 (*opposite*). The direction of winds and their constancy in the tropical monsoon season of the southern summer. (Adapted from the *Indonesia Pilot* and *Pacific Islands Pilot*.)

14. The direction of sea currents and their constancy in the southern summer. (Adapted from the *Indonesia Pilot* and *Pacific Islands Pilot*.)

Pleistocene passages in the voyaging corridor

Some prehistorians have favoured migration routes that followed shorter water gaps (e.g. Birdsell 1977), but to make fine distinctions between the different distances is to miss the point that they were probably all short enough for the risks to remain much the same. Similarly, the suggestion

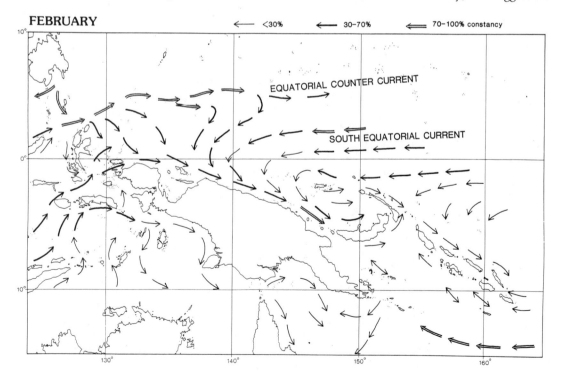

that times of very low sea level may have been more opportune for island-hopping fails to take account of the practicalities involved. A boat that is seaworthy enough to cross 10 nautical miles can probably cross 100 or more, provided it is not of a type that becomes waterlogged and provided the weather remains much the same. Factors other than distance are more telling and, in particular, winds and currents greatly influence the speed and direction of simple craft and can make some relatively long voyages simple while short ones against wind and current are impossible.

Passages of just a few days would have been enough to settle Greater Australia and would have been within the endurance of those who made them. Inspection of the pattern of winds and currents in Figures 11-14 allows assessment of the feasibility of particular links, although one could not say this was necessarily true of the Pleistocene. From Island Southeast Asia to New Guinea one would assume that easterly movement was easiest in the summer monsoon, while the reverse is true in the trade wind season. Contact between Timor and northern Australia has been the subject of a computer simulation by Wild (1985), which assumed similar conditions of climate, and found that most canoes drifting off the south coast of Timor in midsummer (monsoon) reached Australia, but, interestingly, the reverse voyage was difficult at any time of year, and rafts from Greater Australia were blown back again to the Australian coast or into the Indian Ocean (Wild 1985:69). The pattern of currents shown in Figures 12 and 14 suggests that the settlement of both the Bismarck Archipelago and Solomon Islands would be probably in the southern summer, but that Manus was most easily reached from New Ireland in winter, when conditions in the area remain mild.

Voyaging intent and frequency

Keegan and Diamond (1987:66) suggest that Westerners assume they are the only ones capable of purposeful exploration and that others did it by accident while exploiting coastal areas in simple watercraft. In the case of Greater Australia, White and O'Connell (1982:46) have suggested that the long sea trips involved 'implies that the settlement was both accidental and unlikely to have been much supplemented by later voyages'. However, Birdsell (1977:123) took the opposing view that:

> It is highly probable that there was a constant if somewhat straggling trickle of small groups of human beings over all or most of the routes. The size of the watercraft likely to have been used suggests that the groups consisted of small biological families.

Lewis thought the route to Greater Australia could have been crossed accidentally, more than once, but that the intervisibility of islands would also have allowed deliberate settlement (1977:6). Certainly, it is no surprise that, given suitable boats, people should have reached known land near by and, in some areas, with the change in season, crossed back just as easily. Indeed, it is unlikely that if Sahul was reached at all it should happen only once, and also most unlikely that any single voyage penetrated the whole distance from mainland Asia to Sahul. Not all agree, and Thiel (1987) points out that the greatest possible distance from Sundaland to Greater Australia is about 1000 km, a distance that could be travelled 'in about 14 days or, with some knowledge of seafaring, even less. There is no need to suppose generations of island-hopping and perfecting of seafaring ability. The entire journey could have been accomplished in two weeks' (Thiel 1987:239).

One must concede the possibility as a remote one, but, on balance, it seems likely that there were many inter-island crossings and, with growing experience, the number of intentional crossings increased and covered an expanding field. But how and when this happened in pre-Lapita times is not known.

Intentional movement from New Britain to New Ireland may be inferred from the presence of Talasea obsidian in the site of Matenbek some 20,000 years ago (Allen 1989), but the strait between these islands is narrow and has the Duke of York group as a stepping-stone (Fig. 9). It may be a measure of voyaging that no early obsidian has been reported yet from the Solomon Islands, or from across any other substantial water gap, although the archaeological samples are probably too limited to tell.

To attribute the settlement of Greater Australia to the presence of *Homo sapiens* is only to beg the question of how their capacity to cross water was greater than that of earlier humans, although, apparently, this was so. Another suggestion of interest is that environmental changes in the Pleistocene provided an inducement for this. The essence of an argument by Thiel (1987) is that during periods of rising sea-level, land area would have reduced, causing increased population density, especially on islands, and this might have led to people searching for new land. Conversely, when the sea-level dropped and land area increased, together with resources, people had no incentive to leave. This argument is offered in opposition to scholars who have suggested low sea-levels as the best time to cross. The argument has been rejected here already for different reasons. However, with regard to the issue of sea-levels and resources, Bellwood (1986) effectively makes the opposite case, and reports that the sea-level rise at the end of the Pleistocene actually resulted in the approximate doubling of the coastline length of Sundaland (Dunn and Dunn 1977), suggesting such events were actually favourable for the mainly coastal-dwelling population (Bellwood 1986).

Knowledge of the extent to which Pleistocene voyaging was purposeful and deliberate is not accessible archaeologically and to dwell on it might be to overlook the very clear suggestion that the human colonisation of Wallacea, New Guinea, the Bismarck Archipelago and Solomon Islands, was systematic. The available archaeological evidence for the order, elapsed time and nature of early settlement of the islands and groups in the region fits neatly with the factors described above, including angle and distance of island target (Fig. 7), the patterns of intervisibility (Figs 7, 8 and 9) and island size. Further, it is not inconsistent with other factors which are currently less well understood, including geological history and the patterns of Pleistocene climate (Figs 10–14). The coherence of the evidence, although far from complete, now allows us to make general predictions for islands that still lack archaeological control.

At this time, sites that we may reasonably associate with modern humans are no older in Island Southeast Asia than in Greater Australia. Jones (1989) suggests both could have been settled quickly after the first ocean crossings were made. The stone tool industries, consisting of generally amorphous core and flake assemblages, are similar over the whole region and reveal no origins (Bellwood 1989). Regarding age, a number of sites in widely separated parts of the Australian continent have produced estimates of 30,000 years, or more (Allen 1989), and according to Jones (1990) approach the practical limits of the radiocarbon method. Roberts *et al.* (1990) have recently reported a site in northern Australia dated (with a considerable margin of error) to approximately 50,000 B.C. by thermoluminescence. If this is correct, we would expect the evidence to be duplicated elsewhere.

The colonisation of Australia is implicated in a much wider biological debate between the regional continuity model for the the origins of modern humans, based largely on studies of skeletal morphology, and the replacement model invoking intrusive populations, as based on genetic studies of DNA (Mellars and Stringer 1989). Regional continuity between fossil material from Australia and Southeast Asia has been decribed by Thorne and Wolpoff (1981). Within Australia, the case has been complicated by a bihybrid theory of origins suggested by Thorne, which hinges on differences between gracile human remains typified by the site of Lake Mungo and more robust individuals from Kow Swamp, with allegedly different affinities in east Asia and Southeast Asia, respectively (Bellwood 1989). However, Brown (1987) and Habgood (1989) make the case for internal diversification within Australia, rather than separate origins outside, and Allen (1989) comments that we are not in a good position to draw implications for colonisation in the context of such disputes.

Given the evidence, the most likely scenario is that Greater Australia was first settled by modern humans by 40,000 years ago. They were already adapted to a tropical coastal environment, but had the technological flexibility to expand beyond it (Allen 1989; Bowdler 1990). Simple boats and coastal voyaging were part of their repertoire. Evidently, they were also able to survive short inter-island passages, perhaps as long as a few days, which took them out of sight of land. A less likely alternative is that Australia was 'one of those places where the modern sapientization process had a long and complex history' as Jones (1989:773) describes it. Candidates for an earlier crossing by archaic *Homo sapiens* could be found in late Pleistocene Java. If this was the case, we might expect the first sea-crossings to have been fewer and more accidental, but then to have been followed by more systematic colonisation by modern humans, as described.

3

ISSUES IN LAPITA STUDIES AND THE BACKGROUND TO OCEANIC COLONISATION

The first colonists of the remote Pacific Ocean appear abruptly in the archaeological record. The evidence presently supports the view that they were associated with a cultural entity called Lapita, which originated somewhere between Island Southeast Asia, coastal New Guinea and the Bismarck Archipelago, a region formed by a continuous corridor of often intervisible islands. Evidently this had become a 'voyaging nursery' for learning sea-going skills in the sense that the same easy conditions that allowed Pleistocene settlement provided a navigational cradle for Lapita and its peers. There had been more than 25,000 years in which to mess about in boats, although very little of it shows in the archaeological record until it was already well developed. Whoever the first Oceanic settlers were, the essential point is that they had learned how to deep-sea sail and survive, and when they first ventured offshore under predictable circumstances of wind and weather, they left a very substantial safety screen behind to which they could return if need be. The methods implied by this event are becoming clearer, but the motives or impetus are still a matter for conjecture.

There is no obvious navigational factor that recommends one part of the corridor above another as a point of origin. While more difficult voyages were necessary to reach Manus and the Solomon Islands from the Bismarck Archipelago, equally long ones could be found in Island Southeast Asia. Further, communications are something that could hardly have originated in one place, by definition. Rather, we would expect shifting fields of contact to develop and a range of different participants to be involved.

As part of the background to Oceanic colonisation, Green (in press) suggests indirectly inferred improvements to ocean-going outrigger and double sailing canoes and 'additions to the indigenous New Guinea plant roster of root and tree crops sourced to Southeast Asia, plus new items of technology and ornamentation, and not simply pottery'.

15. The location of islands and island groups discussed in the text.

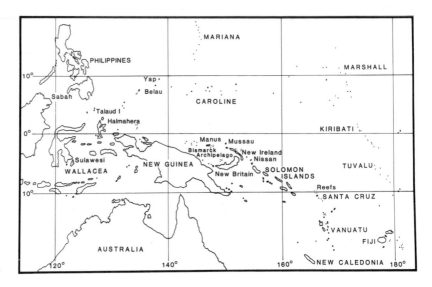

INTERACTION IN THE VOYAGING CORRIDOR

The late prehistory of Island Southeast Asia is marked by a diversity of Neolithic sites with evidence for agriculture, pottery, stone and shell adzes, and their appearance has been linked to the spread of Austronesian languages from the vicinity of Taiwan at much the same time (Bellwood 1985, 1988; Blust 1988). The spread of Neolithic sites occurred after c.3000 B.C. (Spriggs 1989a) and a generally acceptable date for the appearance of Lapita in the Bismarck Archipelago is c.1500 B.C. However, it is also accepted that plant domestication developed independently, and spread in the region of New Guinea and its neighbours, and there is considerable uncertainty as to the contribution of indigenous developments and Southeast Asian introductions to the appearance of Lapita pottery and its cultural associations in the Bismarck Archipelago at this time.

The distribution of broad similarities implies interaction in the wider region and archaeology is providing specific examples of this. Bellwood and Koon (1989) report a collection of 188 obsidian flakes from the site of Bukit Tengkorak in Sabah (north Borneo), and, of 12 analysed specimens, five proved to be from Talasea on New Britain in the Bismarck Archipelago, where Lapita sites are reported in the vicinity of the sources. These flakes date somewhere in the first millennium B.C. but probably prior to 300 B.C., and as such they are too young to relate directly to the origins of Lapita. The other seven specimens are from an unknown source, but they do match one other from the Leang Tuwo shelter in the Talaud Islands, which came from a level of similar age to Bukit Tengkorak (Bellwood and Koon 1989:620). To this evidence can be added the bronze artifact recovered from a site on Lou Island, off the coast of Manus in the Admiralty Islands.

The age is reported as 150 B.C. (Ambrose 1988). Its appearance so far beyond the normal occurrence of bronze in Southeast Asia is seen by Ambrose as 'another witness to the long-term, long-distance communication of the Admiralty islands with the surrounding Melanesian world and suggests a general western Melanesian facility to operate with ease within their archipelagos' (Ambrose 1988:490).

Neither of these instances contribute to our knowledge of the specific origins in the voyaging corridor of the sailing skills of the first people to go beyond it, but there is some indirect evidence on the point. Many Pacific archaeologists accept that the first settlement of eastern Melanesia and Fiji was associated with Lapita; however, the orthodox view of the settlement of western Micronesia is that it was by separate and independent explorers from Island Southeast Asia, who are less clearly identified. So far as we know, the settlers of western Micronesia could have left Island Southeast Asia from anywhere between the Philippines and Moluccas and perhaps even as far south as western New Guinea. The earliest secure dates in western Micronesia are from the Mariana Islands, which go back to c.1000 B.C., whereas those from the other western high island groups, Belau and Yap, currently allow little more than 2000 years of known settlement (Bonhomme and Craib 1987). Yet it is a clear anomaly that the Marianas, which are more than twice the distance from Island Southeast Asia than Belau, and not much less distant from Yap, should be a thousand years older than both. The Mariana Islands dates are not more than some 200 years younger than a conservative estimate for the penetration of the remote Pacific by Lapita. Given the possibility of still earlier dates from Belau and Yap, it is likely that western Micronesia and eastern Melanesia/ Fiji were first colonised within a few centuries of each other. The archaeological signatures of these colonists were different, conspicuously in the details of their pottery, and they may well have differed in biological ancestry and in other respects. However, the circumstances of the voyaging corridor and the presumption of emerging voyaging skills implies continuity between Lapita colonists with other groups farther west who had ocean-going maritime technology in common.

There could be no stronger evidence, circumstantial though it is, for coastal navigation in the region, than the ability to sail far offshore. Between 1500 and 1000 B.C., voyages were made into Remote Oceania from areas both west and east of New Guinea, and communities with the marine technology and motivation to do so were distributed at least that widely. It is interesting, too, that both groups sailed first upwind, the direction from which they could most easily return to the broad nursery that lay behind them.

SOME ISSUES IN THE ORIGINS OF LAPITA

Nowhere in the world has the settlement of so vast an area been identified with such a clear archaeological signature as Lapita, and the situation promises new insights into the nature of human territorial expansion. At this time Lapita is an uncertain and variable archaeological category. It does not begin to approach an ethnic category except in just a few archaeological sites where the data are under reasonable control, but these cases are rare and their connections undefined (Terrell 1989). Melanesia, in ethnographic and late prehistoric times, is characterised by great diversity, and there are few fine-grained spatial correlations to be found in patterns of material culture, society, language and biology. We cannot exclude diversity in Lapita, which appears in the archaeological record c.1500 B.C. and persists in a range of easily recognisable forms for more than a thousand years. One suggestion is that it is made up of what could be seen as the elements of trade, at least in Near Oceania (Terrell 1989; Hunt 1989).

If Lapita appears to be a unique archaeological case, it may be because its geographical distribution is unusually broad. This covers the Bismarck Archipelago and Solomon Islands, which were already long-settled, and it also extends into the remote Pacific to include the Melanesian islands of Santa Cruz, Vanuatu, New Caledonia and Fiji, as well as West Polynesia. Here Lapita more plausibly approaches an ethnic category because it can be shown to be associated with a maritime tradition in a rapid and integrated burst of colonisation, which is likely to have been the first in the region. But there is still no telling how representative a Lapita 'culture' in the remote Pacific was of Lapita in the region it left behind, and it is too soon to say to what extent the deep-sea Lapita colonists were themselves a homogeneous human group.

In recent years there have been two competing models for the location of a Lapita 'homeland', and one of these is said to lie somewhere in Island Southeast Asia (Bellwood 1978, 1985, 1988), perhaps in the region of Halmahera in the Moluccas (Bellwood and Koon 1989); but at the time of writing insufficient field work has been done to show whether the theory is correct. An alternative proposed homeland is the Bismarck Archipelago (Allen 1984), which, like Island Southeast Asia, has been settled since Pleistocene times. However, substantial recent field work in the Bismarcks has not produced evidence for in situ development of Lapita. As a result, many scholars are now following a middle road towards a compromise 'merger' model, which combines elements from both postulated regions (Gosden et al. 1989). But it also seems very possible that future research will show that the modern boundary between Melanesia and Island Southeast Asia is not at all a useful construct to apply to the situation as it was some 4000 years ago.

Allen and White (1989:131) consider that the theory of an Asian origin of the 'Lapita cultural complex', as defined by Green (1979), came primarily from its apparent association with Austronesian languages, and from this followed their association with coastal Melanesians and Polynesians (Bellwood 1978:247). Dyen (1971) challenged the Asian origin of Austronesian; and Green (1979) identified the Bismarck Archipelago as the 'immediate homeland' of Lapita, even though, in the same paper, he said that the ultimate origins were unknown, but 'an eastern area of Island Southeast Asia is certainly a very likely site' (1979:45). White and Allen (1980), Allen (1984) and Allen and White (1989) saw merit in the Bismarcks as an ultimate origin on the grounds of parsimony and the Lapita Homeland Project (Allen and White 1989) was launched to test the proposition.

There had already been suggestions of regional continuity leading to some aspects of the Lapita cultural complex. One example was the results of excavations at Balof Cave on New Ireland (Downie and White 1978), for a time the earliest-known archaeological site in the Bismarck Archipelago. Its lower aceramic horizon suggested wide-ranging resource exploitation and the basal layers produced a date older than 6500 years. From that time obsidian was arriving in very small quantities from Talasea on New Britain, presumably having made a coastal journey with a short crossing to New Ireland. Later in the sequence, obsidian from Lou in the Admiralty Islands appeared in the site, having made an open-sea passage of at least 200 km as well as some coasting. According to Downie and White (1978) Balof suggested a 'gradualistic' model for settlement and that the evidence for sailing and trading, in particular, might be taken to suggest Lapita grew out of existing conditions. Since then obsidian has been dated to 10,000 B.C. at the site of Misisil in west New Britain (Specht *et al.* 1981), and excavations have been undertaken at four New Ireland cave and shelter sites as well as at Balof, and the claim is made that they 'provide a basis for believing that people in the Bismarcks were developing in a direction such that Pacific migrations could have been largely fuelled out of local developments' (Allen and White 1989:140). Obsidian is now known from Matenbek at 17,000–18,000 B.C. on New Ireland and appears farther north at Balof and Panakiwuk around 5000–6000 B.C. (Allen, Gosden and White 1989).

However, it may be an exaggerated claim that the early transport of obsidian foreshadows 'similar but longer-distance exploits by the makers of Lapita pottery' (Allen and White 1989:139). For one thing, Lapita exchange was often much more intensive. For another, movements with Lapita were more extensive, but there is no evidence so far that Talasea obsidian crossed a water gap greater than 25 km to New Britain beforehand. At the time of writing, none is reported from early contexts in mainland New Guinea or the Solomon Islands but it may be in the future. Much more telling is the fact that Lou obsidian, which requires an open-sea passage, does not appear in circulation before Lapita times. It is not remarkable that people at any time should use and move industrial stone, but early movement of obsidian does not necessarily foreshadow Lapita.

Long-term continuity has been sought in subsistence and settlement, and there have been suggestions that Pleistocene sites show movement towards food production, as in the management of vegetation with waisted axes in coastal New Guinea and the Solomons, and in the introduction of wild species of animals to New Ireland, which were subsequently hunted. Following the abandonment of New Ireland caves in the mid-Holocene, the evidence becomes fragmentary, and the introduced pig, dog and fowl are not known to pre-date Lapita in the Bismarck Archipelago. While preceramic horticulture based on the domestication of indigenous plants has been found in the highlands of New Guinea, its expansion beyond there is undocumented.

Gosden *et al.* (1989) have been able to say that there is no link between Lapita and the earlier Pleistocene and Holocene cave sequences. In short, there is no evidence restricted to the Bismarcks that specifies that Lapita should follow, although it remains a possibility. No sites that span the immediate pre-Lapita period and overlap with it have been reported on the large islands of the Bismarcks, but they have on both Manus and Nissan, which are some distance from their larger neighbours. Allen and White (1989:141) infer that Lapita 'may turn out to be simply one phase in an already expanding colonising or exchange system', which had apparently begun in preceramic times, as represented by such sites. This suggestion may be correct, as it relates to 'exchange', but the 'colonising' argument is weakened by the discovery of Pleistocene age occupation on Buka in the northern Solomons, to which Nissan could have served as an available stepping-stone at any time since, and also by late Pleistocene settlement on Manus. Spriggs, who discovered the preceramic occupation on Nissan, is unsure whether it was also pre-Lapita (M. Spriggs, pers. comm. 1990).

It was perhaps, above all, the distinctiveness of Lapita ceramic design that led Golson to 'propose for the S. W. Pacific some early community of culture' (1961:176). However, that does not help much in the matter of origins. All sides agree that pottery was an introduction, even if Lapita did not take on its distinguishing decoration until it reached the Bismarcks, a possibility raised by Spriggs (1989a). Resolution of the question must await more field work on the north and west coasts of New Guinea and in eastern Island Southeast Asia.

In 1983 Anson was able to show for the Bismarck Archipelago, using only meagre samples, that there was nothing rudimentary or developmental about vessel design, and, in archaeological terms, Lapita pottery evidently appeared there full-blown and possibly in a more elaborate form than related wares known farther east in Melanesia, although the latter point is one for debate (Kirch et al. 1987; Specht 1988). Since then a number of new sites with Lapita pottery have been found and known ones reinvestigated (Gosden et al. 1989); only interim results are to hand, but so far the abrupt appearance of this ware still stands. Newly discovered pottery of non-Lapita type has been reported in sites east of the lower Ramu River in northern New Guinea, possibly dating from c.3600 B.C. (Swadling et al. 1989). This could lead to a revision of ideas about pottery introductions, but at present the ware is restricted to one locality and the dating situation is problematical.

With regard to other artifacts, the general situation in the Bismarcks is as follows. Some of the items found with Lapita pottery preceded it there, such as shell adzes and armrings (M. Spriggs, pers. comm. 1990), and therefore it cannot be shown that a whole suite of Lapita artifacts was introduced as one. On the other hand there do appear to be sufficient new items to contest the view that the complex was a local development in the Bismarcks, with little more than the introduction of pottery as suggested by Allen and White (1989:140).

The archaeological debate about the Lapita homeland that has raged through the second half of the 1980s has more than a trace of deja vu. An earlier search for discrete homelands in both West and East Polynesia did not provide a simple answer so much as falsify the question. Instead, prehistorians found much wider and more fluid interaction spheres, and archaeologists in Melanesia and Island Southeast Asia may find that the boundary between them did not exist as such in the period around 4000 years ago.

Linguistic evidence has provided clues to the origins of Lapita, but no identifications. It appears that Austronesian languages spread through Island Southeast Asia and Oceania in the last 5000 or 6000 years, and one view is that diffusion without people over such a vast area is almost unthinkable (Bellwood (1989:23). The location of proto-Austronesian may be in the region of South China/Taiwan and its reconstructed vocabulary implies a Neolithic pottery-using society with pigs and dogs, houses and sailing canoes (Bellwood 1989:24). Austronesian languages evidently spread along the north coast of New Guinea into the Vitiaz Strait/northern New Britain region of the Bismarcks, which is regarded as the homeland for proto-Oceanic (Ross 1988). A working assumption has been that the Lapita homeland and the proto-Oceanic homeland were one and the same (Ross 1987).

In broad terms, the situation seems to be that there is linguistic evidence for the spread of Austronesian languages through Island Southeast Asia to the Bismarck Archipelago, while archaeology indicates a comparable spread of Neolithic features in the same general time range. Some correlation is often assumed, but no details of it are known. These two episodes were followed by the expansion of Lapita sites into the remote Pacific in firmer association with Austronesian languages, but the linguistic homeland in Near Oceania is not identifiable with any precision. In 1981 Pawley suggested that a proto-Oceanic language may have been spoken over a large area, extending from the Bismarck Archipelago to the southeast Solomons (Pawley 1981:278). Ross (1988:387) prefers a more restricted region in northwestern New Britain, where a dialect chain developed and was followed by population movements to the Admiralty and Solomon islands (1988:393), while the settlement of Vanuatu and the rest of Melanesia followed in turn. Ross (1988), speaking of colonists from the homeland area, implied by archaeological evidence of transport of obsidian to Lapita sites in Santa Cruz and New Caledonia, remarked that 'the most which can be said about them linguistically is that they probably spoke Oceanic languages' (Ross 1988:386).

If linguistic evidence is vague about the nature and history of Lapita, current biological evidence is no better. Genetic data suggest 'pre-Polynesians' were derived from a Southeast Asian population that was different from the early settlers of Pleistocene Australia and New Guinea, according to Hill and Serjeantson (1989:286-91). They reject the view of Terrell (1986) and White et al. (1988), that Polynesians evolved from a long-standing population within Melanesia, and, instead, they see elements of similarity between modern Polynesians and Melanesians as evidence of significant interbreeding mainly in northern island Melanesia. Early Austronesian speakers are seen as the source of Polynesian genes, but 'genetic data cannot discern whether the Lapita people were the first Austronesian speakers to arrive in New Guinea' (Hill and Serjeantson 1989:288). Polynesians are found to be homogeneous (Hill and Serjeantson

1989:288; Trent *et al.* 1990), and Micronesians to show evidence of hybridisation between Southeast Asian and Melanesian gene pools (Hill and Serjeantson 1989:91).

These conclusions could be taken to support the Southeast Asian theory of Lapita origins in so far as such Lapita 'people' as reached Fiji and West Polynesia became ancestral to modern Polynesians there. However, one cannot· dismiss the counter-theory, which holds that Polynesians descended from a small founder population derived from one of a number of diverse populations resident in Melanesia (e.g. Terrell 1986). Another option arises from the recent study of cranio-facial form by Brace, Tracer and Hunt (1990), who find in the prehistoric Jomon of Japan the same set of features now demonstrable in Micronesia and Polynesia. They suggest that some resemblances of Polynesians to Melanesian samples are to be explained by admixture during their spread, which is the same mechanism as suggested by geneticists.

Some small samples of human skeletal material found in Lapita sites on Watom in the Bismarck Archipelago, Fiji and West Polynesia suggest a range of different and tentative affinities with Polynesian, Southeast Asian and Melanesian samples (Houghton 1989a, 1989b; Pietrusewsky 1989a, 1989b), but 'Until much larger and more representative samples of Lapita-associated skeletons become available, the biological origins of Polynesians . . . remain[s] obscure' (*Pietrusewsky* 1989b:297). Biological studies offer great promise, but existing samples cannot identify the sources of people who may be associated with Lapita.

ISSUES IN THE NATURE OF LAPITA IN THE REMOTE PACIFIC

Lapita is an uncertain archaeological category with no precise biological or linguistic identification, but once it passed into the remote Pacific, it represents a largely integrated episode of colonisation (Irwin 1980). As Terrell (1989:625) suggests, once the art of making Lapita pottery was carried beyond the Solomons to Fiji, it may be 'safe and historically appropriate to speak, biologically and culturally, of a Lapita people who spoke an Austronesian language'.

The characterisation of Lapita as a cultural complex was mainly based on research in Remote Oceania (Green 1979), where it has been described as a maritime culture of people who fished, kept certain domestic animals, tuberous garden plants and fruit trees, had distinctive sets of pots, stone and shell artifacts and ornaments, occupied sometimes internally differentiated settlements of up to village size and, in places, had exchange systems over considerable distances. It is now known that arboriculture, including nut trees, was part of Lapita economy, although the origins of tree crop domestication are still not known (Kirch 1989). In many ways Lapita was similar to some Oceanic communities that persisted into historic times, but in two ways it was remarkable: firstly, because of its high archaeological visibility; and, secondly, from its first appearance it may have been in a state of explosive expansion.

Gosden *et al.* (1989) have made a preliminary summary of the new Lapita site data from the Bismarck Archipelago and describe some sites as large, stable, and well-organised settlements, which changed their layout through time. As such, they do not sound different from some others farther east. Coherent, internally differentiated open sites with many features in common are represented by the Talepakemalai Site on Mussau (Kirch 1988c), the RF-2 site in the Reef Islands (Green 1979) and on Lakeba in Fiji (Best 1984), as well as possibly in the Arawe Islands and on Watom (Gosden *et al.* 1989), which raises the possibility that related people occupied at least some of the Bismarck sites, as well as those in the remote Pacific. However, many other sites in the Bismarcks do not show the same range of evidence, and Talasea is one example where Lapita pottery may have arrived among a pre-existing population (J. Specht, pers. comm. 1989).

Known Lapita sites are spread from the Bismarck Archipelago to West Polynesia, and their locations are much the same throughout, on small offshore islands or in similar locations on the coasts of large ones. It has been suggested in the past that Lapita sites were constrained in their choice of location in Near Oceania by contemporary aceramic populations, but there is no direct evidence for this; and the similar pattern in Fiji/West Polynesia, where there were none, also tells against it (Irwin 1980; Lepofsky 1988).

The dating of the first spread of Lapita sites will remain an issue for some time as the merits of various radiocarbon dates are argued back and forth (Kirch and Hunt 1988a; Spriggs in press). Dates may go back securely as far as *c.*1600 B.C. for Lapita in the Bismarck Archipelago, and there are a few that could support statistically similar ages in Fiji and in Niuatoputapu in West Polynesia. On the other hand a more cautious interpretation of the same evidence can suggest Lapita was established in West Polynesia by some 3000 years ago (Davidson 1989). Whatever the precise outcome, two conclusions have been clear for some time, one being that the expansion of Lapita was fast by world standards, and the other that it took some elapsed time. 'Insofar as these communities had to reproduce biologically and materially, it was a gradual process that took some time. Yet insofar as archaeological sampling and dating are imprecise, the Lapita expansion appears practically instantaneous' (Irwin 1981:483).

If it took as long as 500 years from the Bismarck Archipelago to West Polynesia, that could represent as few as 20 human generations, and chances are that it was rather faster. Given that human populations in the remote Pacific were lower at this time than ever again, it is unlikely that Lapita expansion was driven by ecological or demographic pressures. Large islands in Vanuatu, New Caledonia and Fiji had the capacity to absorb increasing population numbers, if that was the issue, but they did not perceptibly slow the rate of advance (Irwin 1990).

Although sites spread rapidly, occupation continued in areas settled, which implies that some people became settlers while others continued as colonists, and it is the continuing absence of evidence for a large and early 'homeland' in the Bismarck Archipelago or Southeast Asia, able to supply recruits to a voyaging frontier, that allows us to envisage an expanding number of small populations with the ability to reproduce fast enough to supply their own recruits and equip them as they went (Irwin 1980:325). Once small groups removed themselves from wider contact spheres we would expect to see sharp applications of founder effect. Yet, in so far as communication continued, it might have affected the patterns that followed. Presumably, the deeper colonisation extended into the Pacific, the lower the frequency of additional traits. However, before one can demonstrate any particular origin on the basis of biological, linguistic or archaeological markers, it may be necessary to construct explicit models of advance and interaction. Moreover, interpretation of modern distributions of biological and other traits will need to take account not only of colonisation but of diversification, which followed with ongoing voyaging (Irwin 1990).

Studies of Lapita pottery itself raise other important issues. There is little doubt that its early design constituted an elaborate and unified system, although the meaning and context are far from being understood. There is marked diversity as in the decreasing number of design elements in assemblages from west to east and the identification of design provinces (Green 1979; Anson 1983; Kirch et al. 1987; Kirch 1988a; Specht 1988). Transformation and loss of symbolic information with transmission, in space and time, is exactly what one might expect, but prehistorians have little knowledge of why it follows the pattern it does. A common idea, that the simplification of Lapita in execution and design is a kind of distance decay that reflects the degree of separation of communities, does not take account of colonisation as a two-way process.

There is also the issue of whether the differences between mundane plain wares and elaborately decorated ones are best explained by functional or social differentiation within or between sites, or by some other factor such as their role in gift exchange. Certainly, the ornate vessel types are labour-intensive and the very antithesis of specialised and utilitarian ethnographic trade wares. The data allow many kinds of speculation, and one possibility suggested a number of times is that Lapita design was an emblematic system, which provided a symbolic differentiation for contemporary and competing populations. Finally, there is a range of unanswered historical questions concerning Lapita's relations with different contemporary wares and subsequent ones, both in Island Southeast Asia and in Melanesia, and there are curious parallels over wide areas in the ultimate loss of the Lapita design system, which need investigation.

Another central issue in Lapita research is the role of trade and exchange. At one time it seemed to some scholars to be a primary rationale for Lapita expansion, but afterwards a 'coloniser' model became more accepted (Clark and Terrell 1978; Irwin 1980, 1981; Green 1982; Terrell 1986). However, if colonisation was generally a two-way process, as seems likely, there are further implications for exchange. For instance, some early movement of goods could have been incidental to colonisation; rather than exchange providing the reason for contact. We may distinguish exchanges in 'coloniser-mode' from others in 'settlement-mode', as in south coastal New Guinea (Irwin in press a). Long-distance exchange is usually considered one of the hallmarks of Lapita, and sites in both the Santa Cruz group (Green 1979) and Mussau (Hunt 1989) provide striking examples. However, in other regions evidence for it is slight. It remains to be seen how typical the known examples of ongoing exchange in long-settled areas are of others, and how they were affected by differing circumstances of ecology and geography. It cannot be shown that Lapita sites were ever located primarily from the exigencies of trade (Irwin 1981:484).

There are certain more esoteric questions asked of Lapita, perhaps the most common being the motives for colonisation: many have been suggested and it may be possible to narrow the range of choice once the methods of colonisation are better understood. Another question is whether the system of Lapita ceramic design was implicated in the process of colonisation or simply incidental to it, and associated with this is the question of why there was a widespread decline in its elaboration quite soon afterwards. Other questions are asked about the nature of Lapita society and social organisation, which is already an established field for speculation. In time it may become possible to tease apart the strands of such issues when the archaeological data are under better control.

By way of a summary, the situation is that the first appearance of Lapita pottery was abrupt and its associations are largely unexplained. It is unlikely that Lapita sites imply a single Lapita people, and there were probably more varied cultural associations in the west than in the remote Pacific, although the evidence sometimes has a generally similar appearance in both. The nature of such boundaries as between Island Southeast Asia and Oceania or between western and eastern Lapita is another open question, and one of our archaeological experiences in such matters is that boundaries tend to lose coherence with increasing age. At all events it is most useful in examining various theories to compare their application to the two ends of the Lapita distribution, in so far as even these are known.

Lapita is associated with the first archaeologically visible settlers of the offshore islands of Melanesia and West Polynesia in an episode of colonisation that was systematic and, in human terms, rational. Voyaging involved a kind of technology, which had to be learned, used and passed on as a tradition. It is this, above all, which supports the view of Lapita as a kind of ethnic category in the remote Pacific if not back in the Bismarck Archipelago.

Lapita voyagers carried a different archaeological stamp from the first settlers of western Micronesia, but shared a maritime tradition that we cannot distinguish archaeologically. The coexistence of two groups of offshore explorers implies continuity between them, and perhaps others, within the voyaging corridor that ultimately linked the Bismarck Archipelago, the Solomon Islands and New Guinea to Southeast Asia.

4

AGAINST, ACROSS AND DOWN THE WIND: A CASE FOR THE SYSTEMATIC EXPLORATION OF THE REMOTE PACIFIC

The exploration of the remote Pacific was clearly remarkable, although scholars do not know in much detail how it was done. Consequently, in orthodox opinion early settlers have swung from navigationally competent to incompetent and back again. It is still suggested they made mistakes about their world, but this chapter takes issue with that. A number of propositions arise from the discussion that follows. One is that the coherent pattern of Pacific colonisation implies something about the methods that were used. Another is that return voyaging was always a conventional part of Pacific maritime settlement and had the effect of minimising loss of human life at sea. A third is that navigating in unknown waters was different in key respects than in known ones, but it is only evidence of the latter that has come down to us in ethnography. A fourth suggestion is that useful distinctions can be made between voyaging in the context of exploration, colonisation and post-settlement contact.

While obviously there were impulses to colonise, there is no firm suggestion of compulsion. The archaeological evidence, while patchy, suggests that exploration began rapidly and accelerated through time (Irwin 1990), when human populations were smaller than they ever were again. Nowhere was early Lapita settlement on a scale to stand high losses, which implies that voyaging was unforced demographically. However, there is a division of opinion on this point. Sharp (1963:73) thought most voyagers would die, and pondered the question: 'One can only guess at how many ordeals ended in tragedy during the settlement of Polynesia' (Sharp 1963:108). Finney (1979a:350) thought that many well-equipped voyages must have come to grief in storms or when voyagers died of hunger, thirst or exposure before land was found, and suggested, as a 'conservative' estimate, 10 canoes, each with 25 persons on board, lost every year for 2000 years of Polynesian voyaging. On the other hand, modern navigators in the Caroline Islands are known to be very skilled. Lewis (1972:124) notes that historical accident and loss values are extremely low on Puluwat Atoll and by implication in other areas of navigational competence, whereas in areas of lesser skill, death at sea is higher. This seems the more balanced view.

There is no evidence yet of successful sailing in Remote Oceania before Lapita in Melanesia and the first settlement of western Micronesia, although there was probably a long prior development in and near the nursery corridor. During the development of marine technology we can envisage several important innovations. An early one was the use of sails to increase the downwind speed of rafts or dugouts. The ability to sail across the wind was probably more important because it involved two further changes: a method of stopping the boat from just sailing sideways rather than forwards, and a way of preventing the wind from simply blowing it over onto its side. The solution to the first in Near Oceania was the use of the dugout canoe, which floated deep enough to provide lateral resistance to leeway, and this was increased by addition of the steering oar. Lateral resistance to capsizing was provided either by the use of an outrigger or a second dugout (double canoe); both were efficient in providing leverage in addition to their intrinsic buoyancy or weight. Another important innovation was the ability to change direction in relation to the wind. Greater safety could be found in increased size and also by building up the topsides of canoes to keep out the sea. Larger boats meant bigger crews, the ability to carry cargo and provisions, a bigger catchment for rainwater, more speed and greater range. As boats gradually developed so too could coastal navigation. Finally, knowledge of how to explore at sea, out of sight of land, and to stay alive was a vital threshold. This changing technology should be seen as a developing tradition in an expanding field.

The rest of this chapter sets out a revised theory of oceanic exploration. It describes practical navigation and discusses the higher skills of position-fixing without instruments. It considers what explorers could have known, and the methods they could have used to search and survive. It discusses practicalities of voyaging. It considers the means available for testing the general theory.

TRADITIONAL NAVIGATION

Voyaging canoes

Some of the first Europeans to reach Polynesia saw canoes over 30 m long, while others saw local canoes literally sail rings around their own more ponderous vessels. The consensus of ethnographic and historical information is that canoes were large, fast and safe. According to Lewis (1972), voyaging canoes were often in the 15–22 m range, built of planks tied together and with keels carved from solid logs. They were usually double-hulled in Polynesia and single-hulled with outrigger in Micronesia. Canoes in Kiribati and the Caroline Islands had hulls with asymmetric lines to compensate for the drag of the outrigger and allow the canoe to run straight. In good conditions, speeds of 8 knots were not unusual, and the author has experienced this on the large, double-hulled sailing canoes still used by the Mailu of south coastal Papua New Guinea. Perhaps of greater importance, though, is the fact that such canoes could average 100–150 sea miles in a good 24-hour run. Lewis (1972:274) has said that the carrying capacity of canoes was 'enormous', and their stores, some fermented, able to last 'indefinitely', which implies periods of two or three months, anyway. As for water, Joseph Banks (1962:366) said of Tahitian canoes that they 'carry a tolerable stock in hollow Bamboes'. Clearly, on a voyage of a month, their range was in the order of some thousands of nautical miles, and these were, in fact, the kinds of distances that had to be traversed for the settlement of several island groups to have taken place.

Ethnographic and experimental sailing (Lewis 1972:269) shows that traditional canoes could have made fast and comfortable passages up to about 75° of the true wind direction. In other words they could not sail within the windward arc of approximately 150° within a circle of 360°. Since the prevailing winds of the remote Pacific are from an easterly quarter, and the direction of colonisation lay upwind, we have seen this was an important issue during two centuries of argument and speculation on the origins of people of Oceania.

Sharp (1963:56) suggested that Stone Age canoes tied together with vegetable fibres would be vulnerable to stress, but it is really more likely that some flexibility of movement would have been an advantage as the hulls worked against each other in the seas. One could go so far as to say there are times when a traditional multihull with wooden spars, pandanus sails and coconut fibre rigging would be less at risk than one with modern materials such as alloy mast, stainless steel rigging and terylene sails. Caught in a sudden squall, perhaps at night, the traditional rig would be the more easily damaged, while more resistant materials can lead to modern catamarans capsizing. As for being wrecked, it is probably fair to say that boats smash up on reefs and rocks near land more often than they break up at sea: sea room makes for safety. When winds reach gale force (average speeds in excess of 34 knots), a canoe could not continue to sail but it could expect to ride out a gale safely until conditions moderated. If winds reached storm force (48 knots), a canoe might well break up, but such winds are rare in the tropical Pacific and are usually confined to the cyclone season in the southern summer. The seasonality of cyclones allows some predictability, even if, individually, they may give little warning.

Practical navigation

Traditional navigation survives now in only a few places in the Pacific, but Lewis found that all of the fundamental concepts were formerly widespread (1972:11), although particular methods were more elaborate in some areas than others; examples are the star compasses in the Caroline Islands and steering by swells in the Marshall Islands. Much navigational lore was lost in historic times and perhaps even more in prehistory. In most of East Polynesia, people had lost touch with other island groups, including those their own ancestors came from. Where sophisticated navigation survives today, it is held by highly trained experts and this appears also to have been true at the time of Western contact.

The three main skills of practical navigation were (1) steering a course at sea, (2) maintaining a running fix of one's position by dead-reckoning, and (3) making an island landfall. There are comprehensive reviews of how these were done (e.g. Lewis 1972, Gladwin 1970, Finney 1979a). As for the first, canoes are known to have set off on voyages leaving landmarks behind on fixed bearings related to particular island destinations. At sea, the stars were used as a major source of direction. Apart from the infinitesimal changes of star epochs, which can be discounted for our purposes, they can be seen to rise and set on the same bearing four minutes earlier each night as seen from the one place. Because most stars change their bearing from an observer as they rise, they can be used for steering for perhaps an hour while still close to the horizon and then replaced by other ones rising behind. The stars that rise on one's own latitude keep a constant bearing. Navigators used different known stars for different directions and destinations, and typical star paths might have approximately 10 in a series; different sets were needed at different periods of the year because of the continuous change in rising times. Some star paths were named after a single star, which has confused later commentators into thinking the paths over-simple (Lewis 1972:57). Ethnographic work in the Carolines and experimental work in the Solomons by Lewis (1972:46) shows that different stars can be used on different trips over the same track to allow for changes in current or for extra leeway if sailing close to the wind. One can steer by stars ahead or behind or, when parts of the sky are obscured, by ones in other places, given that their mutual relationships are understood.

Stars whose geographical positions stand over a pole – such as Polaris in the north – never set. They remain visible to anyone in the same hemisphere on a constant northerly bearing. Other constellations of stars with high declination (celestial latitude) can be used for long periods, because they can be seen to change their attitude; for example, the Southern Cross rises inclined on one side, stands vertically when it is south of an observer, and then sets leaning the other way.

This kind of information in very great detail was and is well understood, although perhaps least widely of all by Industrial Age humans, who have substituted tools such as compasses for direct knowledge of the environment. There is a wealth of historical and ethnographic evidence that Pacific peoples' knowledge of the sky was astronomical!

At dawn, one can transfer to the rising sun and use it as a fairly accurate guide early and late in the day, but much less securely between. It also changes its bearing as it rises, like most stars, as well as with its yearly journey north and south of the Equator. One could also steer by the direction of the wind and the waves which it produces locally. Swells are more enduring than waves, because they remain for a time after the wind has shifted or dropped, and they also reflect other wind patterns beyond the immediate area. Both main swells and subsidiary ones travelling in different directions are recognised, and it is clear from various accounts that steering was usually as much a matter of feel as of sight. During experimental voyages, reported instances of disorientation were short-lived and rare.

Dead-reckoning is keeping a running estimate of position as a voyage proceeds, and its elements are direction as given by course controlled for current and leeway, while distance made good is given by speed and elapsed time. Dead-reckoning does not mean fixing one's position in any absolute sense, such as by latitude estimations, although this can be done, but simply knowing where one is in relation to some other known point, such as an origin or destination or some intermediate reference island along the way, or all of these things. On an initial voyage of exploration the origin and previously known islands might be the only reference points and, if no new ones were found, knowing how to find one's way back would be vital.

Andrew Sharp correctly argued that steering by horizon stars could not control for longitudinal displacement, but falsely assumed that current and leeway could not be judged accurately, except over short journeys. Current, he said, cannot be seen (Sharp 1963:35-7), but Finney (1979a:333) notes that the 'equatorial current that sweeps west past most Polynesian islands is a fact of life, knowledge of which was essential to coastal fishermen as well as to interisland voyagers'. Taking back bearings when leaving an island can give an estimate of current and sometimes the shape of waves can show current too, especially when wind and current move against each other. Leeway is the lateral drift made by a canoe under sail which increases as the canoe sails higher into the wind. However, it is something sailors would be familiar with because it relates to the boat rather than to the place. Estimating leeway is usually no more difficult than looking astern to compare the angle of the wake with the fore-and-aft line of the boat. Sharp (1963:51) was also concerned about fog and cloud obscuring the sky, but experienced sailors have observed that the sky is not often completely obscured and, even when it is, other direction indicators, such as swell, usually continue.

The recent ethnographic and experimental approach to navigation has reversed Sharp's (1963:53) view of the 'fallacies inherent in prevailing views of Polynesian navigation', although we may give Sharp much of the credit for stimulating the research. One very telling result is that while errors in dead-reckoning do occur, these tend to cancel each other out over a long voyage rather than to accumulate (Lewis 1972:104; Finney et al. 1986:63), which is opposite to what was thought earlier. On the 1980 voyage of the canoe Hokule'a from Hawaii to Tahiti, a radio beacon was monitored by satellite and the signal relayed to a plotting station so that the actual track could be checked later, against the dead-reckoning. The accuracy of dead-reckoning did change sometimes; longitudinal errors occurred with short spells of increased current and latitudinal errors were made too. However, these were corrected later as the voyage proceeded. Landfalls have now been made after many voyages without instruments over thousands of miles, and the feasibility of indigenous Pacific techiques has been demonstrated. Bad weather does not lead to disorientation, either.

Lewis (1972:36) gives an account of the Solomon Islands' navigator, Tevake, while sailing in the Reef-Santa Cruz group towards Taumako, being driven away by bad weather first to Tikopia, where he could not land, and then on to Vanuatu, from which he later returned. Even in the more extreme cases of gale drift, ethnographic data from the Carolines and the experience of many small-boat yachtsmen suggest that distances are often not great, and, like the direction, fairly easy to estimate.

The ability to detect land from some distance offshore is the third important element of indigenous Pacific navigation, and it applied equally to early exploration and subsequent voyages to known destinations. Island sizes are effectively expanded and gaps between them bridged. The size of many of the resultant island screens absorb a lot of dead-reckoning error and make 'arrival in the block navigationally certain – in so far as certainty exists for small vessels on the open sea – even from a very great distance' (Lewis 1972:154).

A variety of signs, still used, include cloud formations over high islands, while the opalescent colour of atoll lagoons can be seen in the clouds. Swells are reflected and refracted in various patterns, showing the presence and bearing of land, and intricate models of this are known from the Marshall Islands. Swells die down in the lee of land, and, in one notable example, Lewis, sailing the catamaran *Rehu Moana* without instruments towards New Zealand in light easterly winds, lost the westerly swell an estimated 150–200 miles from land (Lewis 1972).

Birds that roost on land but feed at sea show the direction of land as they fly out at dawn and back at dusk. Different species of terns, noddies and boobies have different ranges, which also show distance. Other incidental sea-signs include flotsam, which indicates land upwind or up-current; deep reefs change the colour of the sea and shallow ones affect the waves. It is possible to smell reefs, which can help to avoid running into them at night! Pacific sailors actively search for these signs, which greatly increases the chance of seeing them. One remarkable sign is deep water phosphorescence, which flashes in the water backwards and forwards along the direction of land. This phenomenon can be seen about two metres deep in the the water from about 10 nautical miles offshore, reaching its maximum at 80–100 nautical miles, especially on dark and wet nights (Lewis 1972).

Sea-signs and island screens are used strategically to make landfalls. For example, on a traditional route north from the Carolines to the Marianas, which lie in a line north-south and present a small target from the south, canoes would steer to the windward (east) of the Marianas, allowing for westerly current and leeway. When they had reached the latitude of the target, they turned to a more westerly course, bringing the wind round towards the stern so the canoe could run downwind to cross the north-south island screen obliquely. On the return journey to the Carolines, most of which are small atolls just a few metres above sea-level, it is the breadth of the east-west screen of reefs and islands that makes the landfall secure. Navigators prudently heave-to at night or in bad visibility by day to avoid passing between islands in the screen, and so missing them. Lewis believes a 30-mile expanded sighting radius to be practicable, even for atolls, and that use of these signs was formerly widespread in Oceania (1972:153).

Gladwin (1970:156) suggests that a modern navigator in the Caroline Islands would expect to have a navigational error of not more than 5° when following established courses. It will be shown that many islands in the Pacific present larger targets, and, if this level of skill was general, then a navigator might often actually sight his target and still have the expanded detection radius to accommodate error.

CONCEPTS OF POSITION FIXING

Latitude and longitude are arbitrary Western scales or, as Lewis (1972:5) puts it, 'convenient conventions', which allow navigators to fix their precise position with the help of specialised measuring instruments and an associated system of mathematics. Yet it seems certain that some Pacific peoples had a different but equivalent system of knowledge, which allowed them to explore the Pacific Ocean and to map it mentally. Common to both systems, at the simplest level, are the things one can see in the sky and the islands one knows about in the ocean, although, regarding longitude, the Western system substituted a time relation to one place in the World – Greenwich – some 200 years ago.

If one moves east or west in the world the sky still looks the same, but time changes because the earth is revolving. However, if one moves north or south, the appearance of the whole sky changes. For example, as one goes north, stars in the north appear to rise and set farther south on the horizon than they did, and they climb higher in the sky, while, behind, stars in the south appear to rise and set farther south and climb lower in the sky. Stars that formerly passed directly overhead are replaced by other ones. These facts are obvious and relate systematically to the latitude of the observer. In terms of Western measurement, if one moves north by one degree of latitude (60 nautical miles) the stars in the north will rise one degree higher in angle above the horizon at their maximum (or zenith) and stars in the south will drop by the same amount. If one moves south it is all opposite. The sun obeys similar, more complicated, rules depending on the season and where it lies with respect to the observer.

Almost any star, and the sun for that matter, will climb quickly in the sky until it nears its zenith, when its rise appears to slow – even to a sextant – and it hovers for some four or five minutes before it starts its fall. At this point the star is always either due north or south of the observer, or directly overhead, as it crosses the meridian of longitude of the observer. A star, or the sun, in this 'meridian passage' is a direct indicator of latitude. A 'zenith star', which is one on the observer's latitude, will be directly overhead, and any other star on the meridian but not overhead will have reached its maximum angle above the horizon, and this remains the same from the same latitude, at least for the lifetime of the observer. If anybody knows what the sky looks like from one place, they can tell whether another place lies north or south of it and, within the limits of their measuring system, by how much. For a navigator, to return to an island involves, in general terms, returning to the sky of that island. *In principle, to anyone who knows the sky, however they may conceive or measure it, controlling latitude is as simple as that.*

There is some confusion in the literature on traditional voyaging on this issue. Latitude, in the Western system, is measured on a scale 90° north and south from the equator to each pole. To calculate a latitude in degrees from the sun or a star, one needs to know both the angle of the star above the horizon at its meridian passage (altitude) as well as the celestial latitude (declination) of the sun or star, at that time. The latter is needed to relate one's latitude to the scale based on the equator, which requires calculations and tables and 'the navigator became involved with minus signs and other un-Christian inventions of the Arabs' as Hilder put it (1963:93). In fact, this step is unnecessary. Without any concern for the equator or an arbitrary equator-based scale, it is perfectly possible to ascertain differences in latitude between islands, or between a departure point and the position of a canoe (Heyen 1963:70). One does not need to put a particular number to the difference.

Longitude, or any conceptual equivalent, is a more relative and more difficult matter. In Western terms, it involves a scale of distance (easily convertible to time) east or west of Greenwich. Longitude cannot be told just by looking at the sky, it requires a fine control of time as well. David Lewis (1972:122) concluded that 'Any idea that the human time sense is of such a character that would allow longitude to be even roughly determined seems untenable'. Andrew Sharp (1963) had already recognised the point, laboured it, but ultimately misinterpreted it. He argued correctly that stars cannot show longitude as they pass from east to west and, therefore, if leeway or currents carried a canoe off-course on a north-south track, stars would not show it. At that time the results of experimental voyages were not available to show him that such deviations generally cancel one another out. Sharp (1963:49) went so far as to suggest that Pacific navigators could not control for the sun's seasonal movement north and south, or even orientate themselves by the whole sky. Here, surely, he threw the baby out with the bathwater.

Levison, Ward and Webb (1973:7) observed that 'it does seem to be true that longitude cannot be calculated except in terms of dead-reckoning'. The essential point about longitude and Pacific voyaging is that since navigators could not control longitude, they must have developed a system free of its control. Now the position of an island can be fixed, within limits, by a method that combines elements of both astronomical knowledge and geographical knowledge. Prehistoric explorers entered the unknown ocean of the remote Pacific under a largely familiar sky and afterwards acquired, at first-hand, information on its geography. The position of an island could be first learned, in part, by dead-reckoning from some prior place. A fairly precise estimate of latitude is available in the configuration of the sky. Once a new island is found, the directions to and from prior places can be known by the whole gamut of course-finders, such as horizon stars, etc., while the distance between them is given by the speed and elapsed time of the voyage. If it was true that most voyages of exploration were two-way, then the return would effect a closure and help fix the position of a new discovery. Moreover, the direction and distance could be re-checked every time the track was crossed. So, part of the knowledge of the position of an island can be based on astronomy and the rest from an extension of geographical knowledge by dead-reckoning. Therefore *knowledge of longitude, as such, is not essential to fixing the relative positions of islands.*

Making a mental map of the Pacific combined elements of astronomy and geography, and fixed points could be added to this expanding universe by the ability to steer a set course and calculate a dead-reckoned position. It is suggested that a combination of these elements of indigenous knowledge enabled a prehistoric wave of exploration to flow across the Pacific Ocean, and that as this remarkable event proceeded, increasing navigational skills were both required and acquired (Irwin 1989), as will be discussed below.

Controlled navigation without Western instruments and mathematics is theoretically possible. To what extent, then, was the remote Pacific settled in prehistory by this means? The computer simulation of Levison, Ward and Webb (1973) showed that undirected voyaging was not the answer, which leaves us with the question of precisely how the colonisation of the remote Pacific was carried out; it has already taken more than two centuries of speculation and argument.

The ability of Pacific sailors to steer a course, to dead-reckon and to expand an island target are all securely based. Beyond that we are concerned with esoteric and possibly secret knowledge, which was probably limited to highly trained specialists (Lewis 1972:233), and which may have disappeared from much of the Pacific even before prehistory ended. Tenuous arguments have been made for the use of simple instruments for measuring altitudes of stars and the sun, but Sharp (1963:63) and Akerblom (1968:42) have inspected a number of reports and dismissed them. Such items include a 'sacred calabash', allegedly used on voyages to Hawaii to measure the altitude of Polaris (Rodman 1927), a piece of cane said to have been filled with water for orientation as with the 'sacred calabash', and used to sight on zenith stars in the Carolines (Akerblom 1968:111–12; Lewis 1972:242), and the general possibility has been raised that sticks were held upright and marked for the same kind of purpose (Heyen 1963:70). Certainly such instruments have little support and, as it happens, better evidence suggests they were not necessary anyway.

On the question of using zenith stars for finding latitude without instruments, Lewis reported that nowhere is the technique now used in Oceania. However, he collected numerous primary and secondary ethnographic sources for its possible use in the past as far apart as Tikopia, Kiribati, Tonga, Hawaii and the Society islands (Lewis 1972:235–40). The evidence is frankly tenuous, and while some authorities have been willing to give it credence, others, including Akerblom (1968) and Sharp (1963), generally have not. However, there is better ethnographic evidence for stars being used for latitude estimation by their heights above the horizon, when not in an observer's zenith, and one notable example from the Caroline Islands is the Pole Star (Lewis 1972:243). If this principle was used, it could have been applied to a host of other stars and constellations.

Quite apart from arguments about the meaning of ethnographic information, others have raged over the theoretical possibility of various navigational methods. For example, Gatty (1958:41) and Frankel (1962:43) thought it should be relatively easy to tell when a star was within one degree of the observer's zenith and one way of doing so was to stand up and turn around slowly. Hilder declared this to be 'fanciful nonsense' and that the error could be as much as 10° (Akerblom 1968:38). Such issues could never be resolved while they remained academic, and it is here that experimental voyages have made a marvellous contribution to our knowledge of the possible. For example, when David Lewis sailed the catamaran *Rehu Moana* to New Zealand in 1966, without instruments and attempting to employ indigenous methods, his error in latitude at the time of his landfall was only 26 sea miles (1972:5). His experience of sighting up the mast of *Rehu Moana* was that he could not judge zenith angle to nearer than a degree if a star was much more than 5° from the vertical (Lewis 1972:245). This observation provides a realistic context for an ethnographic uncertainty he describes elsewhere. Two of Lewis's Tikopian informants, then living in different parts of the Solomon Islands, both identified Rigel as Tikopia's zenith star when it actually passes 240 miles to the north even though in A.D. 1000, due to changing declination, it was only 145 miles north. It transpires that the discrepancies of the case amount to little: a distance of 240 miles north over the sea is equivalent to Rigel standing four degrees of angle from the vertical, and 145 miles amounts to little more than two degrees, which falls within Lewis' empirical value of 5° from the vertical within which a star might be useful for estimating latitude.

When *Hokule'a* sailed south from Hawaii to Tahiti in 1976, three people on board accurately predicted, on the previous day, their landfall in the west of the Tuamotus, after a voyage of more than 2000 sea miles (Finney 1979b:340). Two of them, David Lewis and Rodo Williams, were using zenith stars; the third, Mau Piailug, a master navigator from the Carolines, was using a plotting system not yet fully understood by Western scholars. When *Hokule'a* sailed to New Zealand in 1985, her error in latitude was 27 sea miles when the experiment ended, again after a very long voyage. In this instance, as in the case of Lewis' 1966 voyage to New Zealand, the error of the estimates was less than 30 nautical miles on the surface of the sea, which translates to an error in estimating altitude of stars to within half a degree of angle in the sky. In fact, Lewis' general experience was that in 'good weather and with practice, an accuracy of ½° or 30 sea miles could be anticipated – from the deck of a stable catamaran, double canoe, or large outrigger' (Lewis 1972:246), and often his estimate was closer. Now this error, if it can be called that, is of the same order of distance offshore from which some Pacific sailors can *still* conventionally detect the presence of an island by various sea-signs when making a landfall! Estimates of latitude by the stars have been shown to work.

Experimental voyages have enabled attempts to re-learn, or at least approximate, vanished navigational arts (Finney *et al.* 1986). For example, Nainoa Thompson, a Hawaiian navigator, partly self-taught and partly trained by Mau Piailug, has successfully navigated *Hokule'a* many thousands of miles and made many successful landfalls between Hawaii and New Zealand (Finney *et al.* 1986). He learned to calibrate his hand when held at arm's length to measure the angular height of stars above the horizon. There is ethnographic information that the hand was used similarly as an instrument for taking altitudes in the Carolines (Akerblom 1968:113;

Lewis 1972:242), although Mau Piailug does not use it (Finney *et al.* 1986). It is also reported that Arab sailors used a finger's-breadth calibration to obtain their latitude from the height of Polaris above the horizon (Hilder 1963:93).

Thompson also uses pairs of stars that lie approximately north and south of each other and fairly close together because they appear to stand vertically, as the Southern Cross does, as they cross the meridian of the observer, when they can be used for latitude estimation. He also uses the angles between such pairs to provide a ratio that helps to estimate their height above the horizon (Finney *et al.* 1986).

In fact, it is not necessary even to measure the altitude of a star at the meridian passage so long as it is measured at the same relative position in its passage across the sky. One way to do this is to make the observation at the time when some other star, which can be used as a reference, rises above the horizon later in the same night (K. Brockelbank, pers. comm. 1990), or sets while the observed star is still high in the sky. This frees the navigator from needing to determine the moment of the meridian passage and makes for great simplicity.

Such techniques can be applied to many stars throughout the night; they are not restricted to those that are bright enough to be seen through a sextant at dawn and dusk, when their altitude can be measured above the horizon, which was an unnecessary restriction placed on the use of stars by some commentators in the past, as by Hilder (1963:95). Such techniques by no means exhaust possibilities and are at once simple and ingenious. Comparable methods expressing the same and similar principles in different ways are just what we should expect to have been within the power of prehistoric navigators, even if their precise definition is now beyond our reach. Navigators were presented with the whole configuration of the sky, with all of its mutual relationships, and it is worth remembering that the mind is still the only huge computer with both memory and intelligence.

Latitude sailing or windward landfall

Latitude sailing is a technique involving sailing to the latitude of a known island, while still upwind of it, and then sailing down the latitude until a landfall is made. It is suited to traditional Pacific voyaging, where latitude could be controlled by observations at sea, while longitude, or its conceptual equivalent, was a more difficult matter of dead-reckoning. It cannot be shown ethnographically that the technique was known explicitly, and various commentators take up characteristic positions on the issue. Sharp calls the idea of a return voyage sailing 'so far to the east of their home islands on the return journey' as to offset longitudinal error, an 'unrealistic assumption' (Sharp 1963:43–4). Akerblom, also writing before most of the research and experimentation on indigenous navigation, said:

> Theoretically-speaking, it is possible that the Polynesians did navigate by this method, but as there is a complete absence of proof that this was the case it cannot be described, as it sometimes is, as one of their 'exact methods'. [Akerblom 1968:47]

Lewis, who also uses the term 'windward landfall', acknowledges Akerblom's view, but points to the 'ample evidence . . . that standard practice in Oceania was, and is, to make landfall to windward and up-current, on a known side, usually eastward, of an objective', and goes on to give examples known to him (Lewis 1972:243–4). He continues:

> On long voyages spanning several degrees of latitude this procedure is entirely compatible with the use of the zenith star. Dead-reckoning ensures an up-wind approach to the destination, preferably, according to Hipour [a Micronesian navigator], at a distance well under 50 miles. Confirmation by a zenith star that one was then opposite one's island would be an inestimable boon. [Lewis 1972:244]

Lewis takes this as a fair interpretation of statements made to him by a number of experts from Tonga, Tikopia and Micronesia (1972:244). Given that the direction of exploration in the Pacific was generally upwind, the navigational ability to search and return has great implications for survival, if and when it was used.

At the time of writing, there are reports of a dugout canoe, about 5 m long, which is being navigated westwards with the trade winds across the eastern Pacific, with just a plumb bob as a navigational aid. For each leg of the journey the Argentinian sailor, who has memorised the zenith stars of the next destination island, simply lies in the bottom of his boat and sights up the line to the meridian star to check whether he is holding its latitude. He believes he can estimate, by eye, differences of angle to within one degree and apparently has made passages of some thousands of sea miles to prove it (Sadler and Parry 1990). The method is theoretically possible, and a plumb line seems to be a more accurate and practical method than sighting up a mast, as described already by Lewis. We can imagine that most prehistoric canoes carried a simple fishing line and sinker, which could have been used in the same way, to sail back to an island of known latitude.

To summarise this discussion of the higher skills of navigation, a strong case can be made that it is theoretically possible to fix the position of islands in the Pacific Ocean and to find them again without instruments. There is clear evidence that aspects of such skills survive in parts of the Pacific today, and suggestive evidence of others can be found in the data on traditional navigation. Above all, they have been shown to work at sea; some by living Oceanic navigators and others in experimental voyages. Presumably such knowledge was always privileged and, in many island groups, much of it was lost in prehistory and afterwards in history. How far such knowledge was used systematically for Pacific colonisation is a question that can be approached by archaeological inference assisted by computer simulation.

EXPLORATION AND SURVIVAL

Survival is a question of method, but is commonly muddled with motive, which is symptomatic of a tendency to gloss over the weak points in

existing theories of Pacific colonisation with metaphor and romance. There
has been the explicit assumption that, to an early voyager, a watery grave
was the acceptable alternative to a successful landfall, and even scholars
with a pragmatic view of the realities of voyaging have accepted a high
rate of attrition.

What people knew

In the absence of a plausible theory of survival at sea, the mystery of
the success of the first explorers of the remote Pacific has been attributed
to their perception of their world. One must accept, with Lewis (1972:15),
that 'the sea is a highway not a barrier as navigation becomes effective'.
Another common theme is that islanders saw the Pacific as a sea of islands
or a highway (e.g. Davidson 1984:27; Terrell 1986:72), whereas continental
humans see it more as an expanse of empty ocean. Levison, Ward and
Webb (1973:64) suggest that an early voyager might travel 'confident in
the belief that, as usual, islands would rise over the horizon to meet him'
and give, as an ethnographic example, the map of Polynesian islands centred
on Tahiti made for Cook's expedition from the geographical knowledge
of the Raiatean navigator Tupaia. It appears that this map refers to most
of the main island groups of Polynesia with the exception of some at
the margins, including Hawaii, Easter and New Zealand. The islands are
shown as if they might have been seen as a screen; the foreshortened
scale increased land and reduced water, and 55% of the map's circumference
was masked by islands (Levison, Ward and Webb 1973:63). This is a
perceptive suggestion, but it dates from a time when the Pacific had long
been explored and, in fact, inter-island voyaging had already declined
to the extent that Tupaia had visited only a few of the closer islands
among the 74 shown. At the end of prehistory the 'sea of islands' was
one that most Polynesians no longer crossed. Nor did it necessarily seem
like that when they first encountered it. Voyaging after discovery gave
the opportunity to use techniques based on both navigational and
geographical knowledge, but this was not true in the beginning.

The question at issue is whether the Pacific was settled partly because
the first explorers made a happy mistake about what it was really like.
Figure 16 is a map of island sighting radii, adapted from Levison, Ward
and Webb (1973: Fig. 8). One can see that many islands and groups
offered substantial targets to explorers, but equally obvious are regions where
there is a great deal of ocean and no land. Everything that Western scholars
have learned about Pacific Islanders' vast knowledge of the ocean and
its elements suggests a kind of pragmatism, which instantly strikes a chord
with sailors of other cultures. While Pacific explorers may have seen the
sea as a road and not a barrier, we can dismiss the idea that they also
harboured false expectations about the relative amounts of land and sea
and when the next island might be expected to appear above the horizon.

In another argument, that early Pacific colonists were led on by unrealistic
attitudes, Akerblom (1968:93) wrote that because everyone was descended
from a successful seafarer, there were no stories about those 'who failed
to find land and perished at sea'. It was this that provided the self-confidence

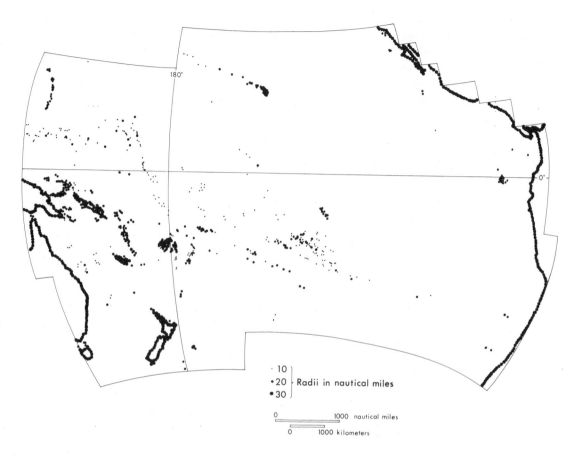

· 10
•20 } Radii in nautical miles
•30

0 _____ 1000 nautical miles

0 ___ 1000 kilometers

16. A map of Pacific islands showing expanded sighting radii. (Adapted from Levison, Ward and Webb 1973, Figure 8.)

needed, and navigation was not such an issue. The argument is perfectly fair, on the assumption that voyages of exploration were one-way, but it will be argued on a number of grounds that voyages of exploration commonly had a return component, and that failure to hear eventually of the fortunes of emigrants could be taken to suggest quite the opposite, that something had gone wrong.

It is worth considering what people could know about a sea passage. In both post-settlement voyages in prehistory and in modern experimental voyages, the crew know three important things – the place of origin, the destination and the likely conditions along the way. On voyages such as this there is little uncertainty and no point of no return. One simply presses on. By contrast, a voyage of exploration has only a point of origin. It might find land or it might not, and there is a point of no return in the sense that if one sails beyond it, one might die. However, it has already been argued that Lapita colonists did not have the resources, human or material, to waste at sea, and they did not have the time either.

In key respects, traditional voyages recorded ethnographically cannot represent the circumstances of first discovery, which is also acknowledged for experimental voyages too, by those who made them (Lewis 1972:4; Finney *et al.* 1986:48). However, what they have shown is that long-distance voyaging is a practical proposition, that canoes are seaworthy and fast and able to make passages on courses up to about 75° from the wind. In terms of endurance they can remain fairly comfortably at sea for a month or more and average 100 sea miles a day. It is no surprise that such voyages are feasible, because even longer ones are required by prehistory, and the modern experimental information that carries greatest implications for original voyages of discovery relates to the feasibility of methods of position-fixing and dead-reckoning.

Survival sailing strategies

In voyages of exploration the options were to search and find, to search and die, or to search and return. From the practical point of view of a sailor, the best strategy is straightforward, and it goes a long way to explaining why the first thrust of Pacific exploration was against the prevailing easterly trade winds. It is safest to go upwind, because one can expect a fast and secure trip back. Voyages across the wind are easier and faster, but rather more dangerous, especially if one gets knocked downwind by unfavourable weather and cannot return. Voyages downwind are most dangerous, because if one goes any distance, one probably cannot get back at all. Voyages outside the tropics meet new and more difficult conditions as well.

Because canoes cannot make passages closer than about 75° from the wind, the strategy circle shown in Figure 17 has an upwind arc of some 150° in which it is safest to search for new land. All that is needed is to wait for a wind that comes from any other point in the other 210° arc of the strategy circle and go upwind on that. It has been understood and recorded since early European times in the Pacific that it is possible to go east on winds other than the prevailing ones, and at certain times of the year their occurrence is predictable. These winds have several different climatic origins, and more detailed information on such patterns as they vary by region and season and fluctuate in the longer term will be considered as the colonisation of the respective parts of the Pacific is discussed. The same argument applies to currents, which commonly, but not always, follow the trend of the winds. The speed of currents would rarely exceed a fraction of the speed of a canoe except in calms and, because they can flow with, against or oblique to a canoe's track, their main relevance, therefore, is to dead-reckoning.

To sail first upwind is one element of survival sailing. It supplies the means to get back, if necessary. A second element, which could be associated, is to sail up-latitude, because latitude sailing provides a means to find one's home downwind. In combination, the two elements provide both the means to sail back and to navigate back.

This suggested strategy needs qualification. Firstly, a case will be made that two-way voyaging was conventional in Pacific settlement, at all times, and the notion of search and return fits naturally into that context rather than being held as a kind of explicit abstract formula. Secondly, it probably developed gradually; return passages in open water were probably part of the repertoire of sailing in Near Oceania before the settlement of Remote Oceania began. As one possibility, trading would have had the expectation

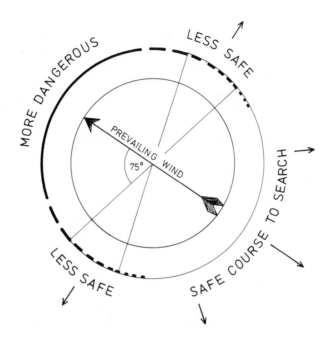

17. A survival sailing strategy. It is obviously safer to search in some directions relative to the prevailing wind, than others, given the ease of returning in the event of not finding a new island. (Reproduced by permission of the editor from Irwin 1989.)

of a return, and the chances are that unplanned returns occurred on outward trips when the weather turned bad; the unexpected conditions that prevent one going forward can most easily carry one back. This kind of experience could have been applied in tentative probes offshore and then, more systematically, in intentional deep-sea exploration. Therefore it seems a fairly safe assumption that, historically, the upwind strategy was probably used first as it applies equally over 500 metres or 500 nautical miles and is a perfectly obvious aspect of small-boat handling. However, latitude sailing requires more esoteric knowledge of the sky, and was probably gradually refined with experience of offshore sailing and added to other methods of dead-reckoning. The geographical circumstances of eastern Melanesia provided an ideal nursery for learning, because the first voyages into Remote Oceania left the widest safety-nets behind and thereafter the general trend was for both target islands and safety-nets to become smaller and farther apart.

According to a general theory of search and return, a typical east-bound voyage would leave with the first signs of a favourable wind and go until the resumption of the trades arrested further progress. At this point the canoe could return or reach across the wind generally north or south, waiting for another favourable wind shift. When the endurance of the outward voyage was running out, the onset of settled trade wind weather would signal the end of the search and provide a fast return. The experience of small-boat sailors in the Pacific suggests that it would be safe to allow approximately a week of return for every two or three weeks out.

A mode of exploration by search and return has important implications for establishing the position of the islands discovered. Outward voyages with a preferred upwind direction would tend to be rather erratic as they climbed out against the wind shifts and took fair winds as they came.

Keeping control of the dead-reckoned position would be more difficult on the longer outward track, but the return would normally be more direct and systematic. It has been described how, without instruments, a navigator could find the latitude of his origin island and turn his canoe downwind to find it. The experimental error in estimating latitude from the stars translates to a line stretching north and south from the canoe usually less than 30 sea miles on each side, as it runs towards the west, and these distances almost exactly match the range from which one can reliably detect the presence of land from offshore! The prudent sailor would probably stop at night when he was nearing the target, a common technique in ethnographic times, to avoid overrunning it in the dark or in bad visibility in daylight.

There is a second point to be made about latitude sailing, which is that it is possible to make mistakes in dead-reckoning and even lose track of one's position, and still get back. This was more than just a safeguard in prehistory. It meant that upwind exploration could virtually escape from navigational limits. Given the immensity of the Pacific Ocean, we now have an insight into how it might have been explored. The ultimate limit of early voyages into the east was set by the human body and spirit almost without navigational constraint.

So we have a paradox. The hard way was also the easy way. What has always seemed most marvellous about the settlement of the Pacific is that it went against the prevailing winds and it now transpires that, for people interested in staying alive, it was taking that very direction that made it possible. Unsuccessful voyages of exploration were usually two-way, and successful ones commonly were as well, securing a navigational closure (among other things). Outward voyages were the more erratic and returns the more systematic, and the position of a new discovery became secure when the return was complete. It is rather like the old joke of going there and back to see how far it is!

The order of settlement implied by the general strategy presented here conforms to what we know of Pacific prehistory. The trajectory of earliest settlement is upwind. Melanesia was crossed and settlement pushed on to central East Polynesia. Then it moved across the wind, and Hawaii is one example. Last of all, it was across and downwind to New Zealand, which alone of the Polynesian islands lay beyond the tropics, a threshold that apparently delayed settlement by more than a thousand years. On the available radiocarbon dates, the Chatham Islands, which lie downwind even from New Zealand, were utterly last, as one would predict.

For the sake of safety, sailing across the wind requires a knowledge of islands to leeward of the starting island, in case that could not be reached. Sailing downwind usually requires returning by a different route to a different island.

The model presented here allows learning and requires it. The exploration of the remote Pacific was accompanied by expanding geographical knowledge and increasing sophistication of navigational skills, especially as it probed the far reaches of Polynesia.

A number of authorities have made observations that fit this theory of relatively directed and safe colonisation. Levison, Ward and Webb, reporting on their computer simulation, said that we must accept the idea of navigated voyages of 'search and colonisation' for some parts of East Polynesia (1973:51). With regard to sailing upwind, David Lewis recorded that 'not a few' canoes are known to have storm-drifted from the Carolines to the Philippines and then made their way back 'against the prevailing wind' (1972:286). These downwind voyages were inadvertent, and it was fortunate that a safety screen lay downwind and the case conforms to the sailing strategy proposed here, in so far as the upwind returns were intended and show such voyages to be possible. Lewis went on to note that contemporary Caroline navigational practice is quite 'the reverse of recklessness, caution and conservatism being stressed' (1972:289), which is precisely the suggestion here. Akerblom (1968:93) wrote that 'setting out on a voyage into the unknown does not call only for compelling motives, it also requires confidence in one's own ability to come back alive'. Terrell (1986:74) observed that pioneers did not have to explore so far that reasonable hope of a return was lost.

Heyen (1963:68) wrote that 'No experienced seaman would deliberately sail down wind, into the unknown, with little chance of beating back'. On the question of reaching across the wind, he said that it would be possible to make long boards to the north or south with the knowledge that, on the return leg, the canoe would be windward of the point of departure. He also noted (1963:73) that on arriving at the required latitude it would be possible to run down it to the destination, which is what is also suggested here for returns. In 1979 Finney wrote that:

> Exploring to windward would also have made good sailing sense. If a craft is sailed far downwind, there is always the problem of the return, either by tacking against the wind or by waiting for a wind shift. This would not have been an enviable prospect for an exploring party low on food and water, and perhaps with a battered canoe. In contrast, if a craft is sailed to windward, it is relatively easy to return home by sailing swiftly downwind. The Polynesian drive to the east was a logical as well as a successful settlement strategy. [Finney 1979a:347]

This passage conforms to the argument here, but elsewhere Finney has noted that exploring was risky enough anyway, but to trust to episodic westerlies as the means of travelling east 'was to compound uncertainty with grave risk' (1985:21). He suggested that to argue that Pacific explorers followed this as a strategy 'is to assume that the Lapitans, and their Polynesian successors, consciously sought to expand to the east, and that they actively tried to find and settle islands in seas never before navigated' (1985:21). This, of course, is the position taken here and elsewhere (Irwin 1980), and most recently by Keegan and Diamond (1987).

Andrew Sharp's rather jaundiced view of the same tropical seasonal westerly winds to which Finney was referring, was that:

> Because they are unpredictable, often intermittent, and frequently violent, however, they would have been unreliable for systematic long voyaging from west to east. These same characteristics made the summer westerlies highly suitable for initiating a slow succession of one way voyages of settlement from west to east. [Sharp 1963:61]

There has been a clear turn-around from Sharp's vehement opposition to the idea of purposeful and skilful navigation although Finney, who has had a significant role in it, has cautioned that (1985:21):

> Nonetheless, it would be a mistake to presume too much planning and
> purposefulness . . . a scenario that solely stresses systematic voyages of
> exploration and colonizing presumes far too much order and predictability
> in what must have been a most uneven and hazardous expansion.

This comment cannot be lightly dismissed, but, to put it into context,
Finney may have been allowing for a human loss rate that has become
more arguable in terms of archaeological evidence. And, moreover, he was
introducing the idea that the anomalous and enduring westerlies of some
prehistoric episode of El Niño could have carried a founder population
from West Polynesia deeply and directly into East Polynesia. This would
conform to the early dates from the distant Marquesas and provide a more
mechanistic vehicle than the more rational strategy argued here. (The role
of El Niño in the settlement of East Polynesia is problematic and will
be returned to later). However, since publication of his 1985 El Niño article,
Finney has described a voyage of the *Hokule'a* from West to East Polynesia
using sub-tropical winter westerlies, which has increased his assessment
of the feasibility of strategic sailing to the east (Finney 1988, Finney
et al. 1989).

SOME VIEWS ON VOYAGING REALITIES

A number of points have been made already, supporting the view of two-
way or return voyaging. One concerns the developing communications
inferred for the Pleistocene voyaging corridor. A second refers to offshore
explorers preferring to return, in the event of not finding new land, to
dying at sea. A third concerns the increased ability to fix the position
of a newly discovered island following a systematically navigated return.
Another general point is that the cessation of exploration in the Pacific
after its colonisation was complete suggests feedback of information in
a system (Irwin 1980).

When areas of empty ocean were explored, the probabilities suggest
there were many voyages of non-discovery, and it makes sense that these
were usually return ones. Given the effort and extra resources needed to
prepare a well-equipped colonising expedition, carrying plants and animals,
men and women, it could have been deemed simpler for explorers to
travel rather than colonists, in the first instance, when the prospects of
discovery were low. This consideration invokes a common theme in
Polynesian voyaging traditions, of early travellers and explorers returning
home with sailing directions to new land.

There are other reasons for making a distinction between exploration
and colonisation. One is that the arithmetic of human reproduction says
that a founder population cannot send off another in less than a generation
or more, while the navigational arts of deep-sea sailing are founded in
knowledge and extensive practical experience, which, to survive, had to
be used by every passing generation. Four or five longish voyages in a
lifetime of shorter ones do not seem an excessive number in modern
experience, and only a minority could be expected to show up in the
archaeological record as a new colony. Colonisation was probably preceded

by a frontier of exploration. Further, many voyages that were made could have been to established settlements.

Nor did new islands have to be settled as they were found, and this possibility may account for several anomalies and apparent delays or pauses in colonisation. It might also acccount for evidence suggesting the fleeting use of islands some time before settlement is archaeologically assured. For example, Kirch and Yen (1982:312–14) estimate the settlement of Tikopia at c.900 B.C., but report a radiocarbon date of mid-second millennium B.C. age. The explanation they prefer is that there was sporadic human activity on the island before permanent settlement, which conforms to the argument here.

Traditional sailors in the Pacific today show that making a passage is not difficult, as described for Micronesia, and as I have seen many times myself in coastal and island communities in Papua and the Massim regions of New Guinea. After a few days' preparation, one can slip away, perhaps after waiting for good weather, or perhaps not, because it is more important to have settled weather for a landfall than a departure. In prehistory, five days could very easily mean 500 sea miles covered. While European explorers of the Pacific thought and organised in terms of months and years, prehistoric explorers probably operated in weeks and months, and could have done so for various immediate and pragmatic purposes. They already understood their environment and could operate with less elaborate preparations; many islands, perhaps mostly unoccupied, would be known to them. In the early days we can envisage that only a small number of voyages were elaborately equipped for colonisation and those that were could have sailed directly towards known destinations. Moreover, establishing a new colony could have taken several trips over some time. It has been suggested that, at this time, people were not simply searching for new land because they sailed much farther than they needed to find it (Irwin 1980). Later on, as colonisation probed the margins of Polynesia, demographic stress may have been more of a motivation, but there are many responses to it that involve solutions simpler than emigration.

Archaeologists have laboured the point that these colonists were agriculturalists, not strandloopers, but they probably did not garden everywhere they went. On a sea passage they would presumably have carried stored food, but there was a relative abundance of unexploited wild food for the crews of occasional canoes on the empty islands that they knew of already, and on those that they found, including turtles, fish, shellfish and endemic birds. Today, some of these resources still provide a reason (usually not the only one) for fairly frequent trips to satellite and empty islands in New Guinea, Micronesia and elsewhere. They were a resource for oceanic exploration as well as a kind of shock-absorber for founder populations in what Kirch (1988a:252) refers to as a 'kind of colonization-agriculture transfer stage'. These things, which Keegan and Diamond (1987) have referred to as a 'reward' of colonisation, were probably as much a tool of it.

Unfortunately, the tools of archaeology are too blunt to capture Pacific colonisation with precise detail and realism, and consequently most models of interpretation are hopelessly coarse-grained. So much so, in fact, that some modern writers have been willing to believe that early colonists did not know what they were doing perhaps because we do not.

TESTING THE GENERAL MODEL

It is suggested here that the Pacific was settled by return voyaging and that developing skills of exploration allowed the highest chance of survival rather than the fastest rate of advance. It credits prehistoric navigators with the competence to manage their oceanic environment, and it removes excessive elements of mystery and romance. The direction of advance has always been a puzzle, but now we have a suggestion that it was influenced by a preferred direction of return. This model predicts that the harder it is to return from a part of the ocean the later the islands there will tend be settled. Places more or less equally easy to return from could be settled in the order of ease with which they could be reached. The case is complicated by crosswind voyages veering off the main upwind line of advance while that was still in train, but generally it can be shown that these propositions conform to the order of the radiocarbon dates, which also show, clearly, that the order in which places were settled was not the order of ease of reaching them.

The first level of testing for this theory is to examine it for correspondence with detailed archaeological evidence. Secondly, a computer simulation has been run in which different simulated outcomes are compared with one another and with the pattern of the radiocarbon dates. The results of simulation refine the model and provide insights regarding the kinds of navigational methods required for colonising different parts of the Pacific, especially as geographical circumstances became more demanding.

AUTOCATALYSIS

One other theory can be considered without delay. Keegan and Diamond (1987) have offered a general interpretation of the colonisation of islands by humans, and their term 'autocatalysis' refers to the argument that 'the discovery of some islands led to the expectation of more islands to be discovered' (1987:67). They suggest that:

> it was the configuration of islands in the Pacific that rewarded Pacific peoples, more than the peoples of other oceans, for developing maritime skills. Other oceans offer fewer accessible targets . . . and voyagers could not have returned with tales of new lands to justify the risk of voyaging. [Keegan and Diamond 1987:68]

They also note that island distribution, not sheer proximity, determined the direction of settlement. Going from west to east a virtually continuous series of island chains encouraged migrants to sail farther and farther out into the ocean by rewarding them with island after island on which to settle, while in contrast the open ocean between New World shores and Polynesia provided no such opportunity and incentive for those who lived along the Pacific coast of the Americas (Keegan and Diamond 1987).

This argument is a valuable comparison of the Pacific with other cases and provides many useful insights. One very strong point is its acceptance that colonisation proceeded by return voyages and the feedback of information. This is not an established view in Pacific archaeology even though there are reasons for thinking so other than those given; however, the authors do present an alternative version of their autocatalysis theory which does not require return voyaging.

But there are some problems with the theory. While the suggestion that the configuration of Pacific islands explains the general west to east direction of stepping-stone settlement, and fits the sphere of Pleistocene settlement, which reached as far as the Solomon Islands, Keegan and Diamond make little of the distinction between this region, where water gaps are short and the islands large and intervisible, and Remote Oceania, where islands are so far apart that the comparison with other oceans is scarcely tenable. To argue that the west to east settlement of Polynesia can be explained by the fact that this is the general way the island chains go has, in itself, little more basis than the view of Thor Heyerdahl that it was settled the opposite way because that is the way the prevailing winds blow. The differences in island distribution constitute a real threshold, which requires more detailed explanation.

More importantly, the theory contributes nothing to the question of how great distances were actually crossed, except to say that people were rewarded for doing so and for improving their technology in order to do so. It is not very specific, in cultural terms, about these 'rewards'; nor does it explain the 25,000-year gap between the settlement of Near and Remote Oceania when the 'rewards' were apparently inoperative. Finally, the theory leans towards accepting the views of some Pacific scholars that there was enough latitude in the numbers of colonists for many to die at sea, and also that the settlement of Remote Oceania was punctuated by discontinuities, which now seem less likely (Irwin 1981; Kirch 1986).

The theory of autocatalysis is too general to explain much about Pacific colonisation, although the weight it adds to the idea of feedback or return voyaging will probably turn out to be fundamental.

5

THE COLONISATION OF EASTERN MELANESIA, WEST POLYNESIA AND CENTRAL EAST POLYNESIA

THE OFFSHORE ISLANDS OF MELANESIA AND FIJI

At present there is no clear evidence in Island Melanesia east of the main Solomon Islands for any settlement before Lapita. Enigmatic tumuli of New Caledonia and the Ile des Pins, which have given radiocarbon dates many thousands of years earlier (Shutler and Shutler 1975:66–7), have now been attributed to an extinct bird *Sylviornis neocaledoniae* (Green 1988). They may be incubation mounds for the eggs of this giant megapode rather than the work of humans, although whether we have heard the last word on this subject is another matter. Even so, we still cannot exclude the possibility that other voyaging colonists earlier than Lapita were in the area. The possibility was noted by Green (1978) and as recently as 1989 a number of archaeologists have observed:

> If we are looking for areas which were colonized rapidly and for the first time within the Lapita period then at present we would have to designate Fiji and West Polynesia as the only certain candidates (the period of initial colonization of Vanuatu and New Caledonia must now be further researched following evidence of people reaching the Solomons chain by almost 30,000 b.p.). [Gosden *et al.* 1989:577]

In some respects, the case is parallel to the situation in East Polynesia, for which both short and long chronologies are proposed (Irwin 1981; Kirch 1986), and where the latest evidence appears to be closing the gap between east and west, rather than favouring one over the other. The essential difference, however, is that there was an obvious source in West Polynesia for the first colonists of East Polynesia – the descendants of Lapita itself. But the case of Island Melanesia is more neutral, because there is no such concrete archaeological identification of a potential ancestor for pre-Lapita colonists. The debate revolves around issues in colonisation and sampling, and especially the high archaeological visibility of pottery and the relative difficulty of finding aceramic settlement.

If there was such a population in the offshore islands of eastern Melanesia, we could presume it had a sailing ability approaching Lapita's to have successfully crossed from Near to Remote Oceania. Indirect support for the possibility of other such groups existing can be found in the settlement of Western Micronesia, in much the same time range as Lapita, by colonists with a different identity. However, the analysis of island accessibility shown in Figure 7 found a clear navigational threshold between the Solomon Islands and the islands farther east, and must greatly reduce the chance of Pleistocene or early Holocene settlement in Santa Cruz, Vanuatu and New Caledonia. Also, it is the last of these, New Caledonia, which has seemed to offer the best archaeological chance of preceramic settlement, that lies farthest from a source of migrants.

Another indirect reason for suspecting a hypothetical pre-Lapita population would not be very far ahead is the radiocarbon date of 3470± 210 years ago for the collagen fraction of bones of *Sylviornis neocaledoniae* (megapode) in New Caledonia (Green 1988). A general pattern emerging from the isolated islands of Oceania is the extinction of flightless and other endemic birds soon after the first arrival of humans. We can expect more evidence of the history of interaction between natural populations and humans to come to light in the remote islands of Melanesia. However, at the time of writing it seems ironic that the very New Caledonian bird that once allowed prehistorians to concede, rather against their better judgement, that humans could have arrived long before Lapita, now supports the opposite argument: that it was not long before, if at all. My own view is that Lapita sites are the earliest, but the question stays open and will be considered again in the computer simulations.

Practicalities of sailing across Eastern Melanesia

The dominant weather pattern of the southern winter is southeasterly trade winds. Figure 18 shows the stretch of ocean from the Bismarck Archipelago to Fiji, with information on wind direction and strength for the southern summer taken from the *Routeing Chart of the South Pacific Ocean* (1967) based on observations for the month of February. In the wind roses, the arrows fly with the wind, their length shows the proportion of winds from each direction and the thickness of the tails shows mean wind force. Winds of Force 8 and above are gales and worse, while most of those less than that would have been navigable. Although the dominant weather pattern in the region is southeasterly trades, the influence of the summer monsoon can be seen in frequent and predictable northwesterly winds around Papua New Guinea and for some distance down the coast of northern Queensland, and offshore. However, westerlies become increasingly intermittent going east. Presumably sailors would have already understood and used these seasonal wind reversals over short distances of open water in the Bismarck Archipelago and Solomon Islands and, beyond there, summertime eastward ocean crossings offer the most plausible scenario.

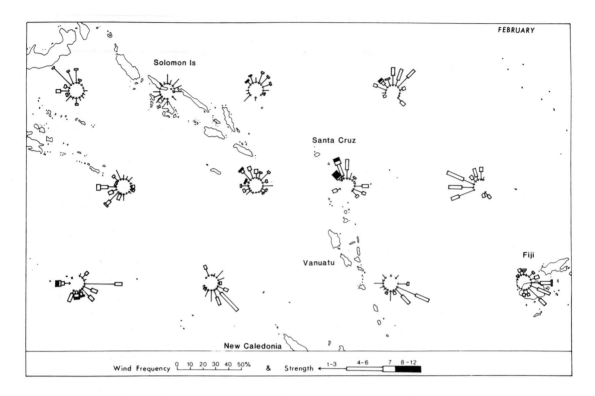

FEBRUARY

Solomon Is

Santa Cruz

Vanuatu

Fiji

New Caledonia

Wind Frequency 0 10 20 30 40 50%   &   Strength ← 1-3   4-6   7 8-12

18. Wind patterns for Island Melanesia for February. In the wind roses, arrows fly with the wind, their length shows the proportions of winds by direction and the thickness of the tails shows mean wind force. The summer monsoon made eastward voyages feasible. (Adapted from the Admiralty *Routeing Chart* of the South Pacific Ocean, for February; reproduced by permission of the editor from Irwin 1989.)

Voyaging in summer would have meant running the gauntlet of the southern hurricane season from November to April. Figure 19 shows the tracks of cyclones between 1974–79, which are representative of the area now, and were quite possibly similar 3000 years ago. They scarcely touch the Solomon Islands, and sailors might not have known of their severity until the settlement of Remote Oceania was already under way. It follows that any innocents abroad might not have avoided a summer crossing for this reason. However, the chances of any individual voyage being struck by a cyclone are small today and were probably the same then.

Figure 20 shows angles of target and relative distance for various passages. The Santa Cruz sector lies closest at 200 sea miles, and, while being generally upwind, it is also up-latitude, which would make for the simplest return if people knew about latitude stars this early, which is doubtful. Vanuatu is a large target too, some 350 sea miles upwind in the southeast, while New Caledonia at 550 sea miles from the Solomon Islands presents a more difficult initial target. However, the closeness and large size of Melanesian groups implies rapid penetration once the first contact was made, which is what the distribution of Lapita sites suggests.

The shortest straight-line distances to Fiji are approximately 500 sea miles from central Vanuatu, a little over 550 from the Loyalty Islands, which lie east of New Caledonia, and 770 from Santa Cruz. Given that few such passages could follow a straight line, especially towards an unknown destination, there is not a great deal to choose between them. It is also true that the Fiji group presents a similar angle of attack to all three of these possible origins, but lies directly up-latitude only from central Vanuatu.

19. Summer crossings mean risking the southern cyclone season. However, the chances of any canoe being run down by a cyclone would not have been great. (Adapted from the *Pacific Islands Pilot*.)

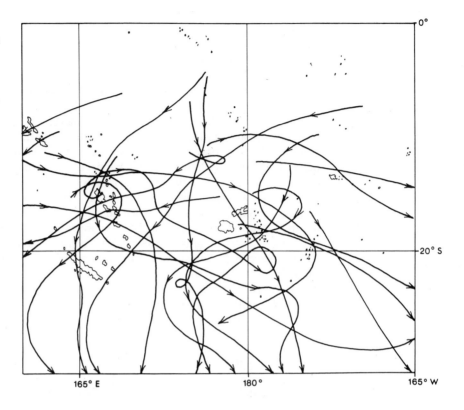

20. Angles of expanded island target and relative distances for various passages in Melanesia. Santa Cruz and Vanuatu may have been easier initial targets than New Caledonia, but all three groups were accessible to one another. Together they made up a broad safety screen for canoes exploring to the east towards Fiji. (Reproduced by permission of the editor from Irwin 1989.)

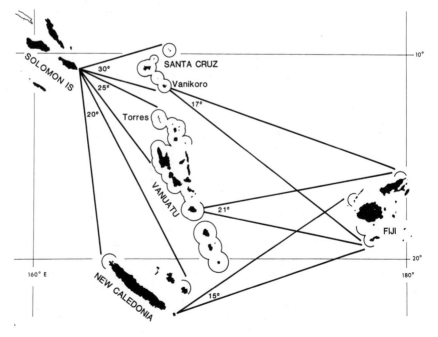

In terms of the February wind map (Fig. 18), there seems to be a higher chance of westerlies and northerlies across the northern part of the region than farther south, and if one can argue such a particular case in terms of a general sailing strategy, Vanuatu and possibly to a lesser extent the Santa Cruz group would offer a more optimal origin than New Caledonia for the first discovery of Fiji, in summer, but not necessarily in winter. Winter, it should be remembered, is not severe at these latitudes and this is when sub-tropical westerlies affect the southern tropics.

When the first forays were made to the east of Melanesia, a huge safety-net was left behind. Prehistorians have been too distracted by the distance of this water gap, and the presumption of easterly movement across it, to notice an arc of islands covering more than 50°, which, without major breaks, stretched across the return route. It has been suggested that an ocean voyage of the order of 500 sea miles was too great for two-way voyaging, which accounts for the cultural severance of Western and Eastern Lapita between Melanesia and Fiji (Green 1979:47), but, as it happens, there is little concrete evidence of more contact between the western province with New Caledonia than with Fiji: the two flakes of Talasea obsidian found at Naigani, Fiji, match the known imports of Bismarck material in New Caledonia. Also, while there was evidently some movement of Lapita pottery between New Caledonia and Vanuatu, the volume has not been shown to be large. As for the pattern of decrease in the number of Lapita motifs from west to east, this could be as much a function of transmission as of distance alone. There is evidence for occasional later contacts both ways across the gap to Fiji and, in Polynesian Outlier times, West Polynesian influences stretched the whole length of Island Melanesia into Micronesia. The first exploratory crossings from Island Melanesia to Fiji should not be seen as necessarily cutting Lapita in two in the colonisation period.

The island groups of Vanuatu and New Caledonia are large enough to have absorbed many settlers and to have slowed the advance of Lapita, but they did not do so appreciably, which counts against the possibility that colonisation was driven primarily by population growth and the need to expand. The evidence of radiocarbon dates makes it easier to apply that argument to Fiji/West Polynesia, but its failure in Melanesia might make us wary of doing so.

Speed across the western Pacific is best estimated, now, by the time of arrival in Fiji, and Figure 21 shows that the island groups of Fiji and West Polynesia presented each other with such large, close targets to imply that all were reached within a century or two. The greatest direct distance between any two groups is approximately 400 sea miles from Fiji to Samoa, but all of them could be linked by a series of indirect passages less than half that. There are problems in dating the first arrival; the early calibrated range of 1684–1416 B.C. (1 SD) for Sample GAK-1218 from Natunuku (Kirch and Hunt 1988a:21) in Viti Levu is considered suspect (Spriggs in press); there is some chance that a sample of *Tridacna* shell, I-10,632 from Site NT-90 on Niuatoputapu, which gave a calibrated range of 1410–1230 B.C. (Kirch 1988a:140), was shell older than the occupation. On the other hand Naigani, a Fijian site thought on the grounds of pottery style to be early (Best 1981), has four dates (NZ-5615 to NZ-5618), which

21. The islands of Fiji and West Polynesia are quite close together. It is no surprise that the radiocarbon evidence suggests all were settled within a few centuries of each other, by 1000 B.C., or before.

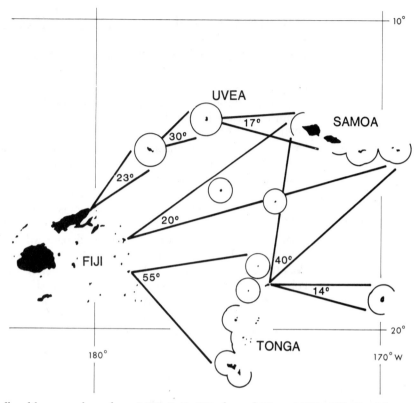

all calibrate to less than 1000 B.C. (Kirch and Hunt 1988a:21). Davidson (1989) concludes that it is clear that Early Eastern Lapita was established throughout Western Polynesia between 1000 and 700 B.C., but how much earlier than this it might have been remains to be seen.

Recent research in Fijian and West Polynesian Lapita raises several of the same issues as in the Bismarck Archipelago. In both regions there are open sites and some in caves or shelters; in both there are some with clear internal patterning. Settlement patterns appear to be no different, and intensive field work has revealed areas with relatively high site density in both regions; most recently in Beqa (Crosby 1988), an island offshore from southern Viti Levu, as well as the Southern Lau and the groups of Tonga. Sites may be hidden by substantial landscape changes on the large island of Viti Levu, where the Lapita-period shoreline lies at the back of large river deltas. The similarity with Western Lapita extends to the possibility of sub-provinces of pottery design in the east. The history of inter-site contact and exchange is unclear in both areas. Considerable imports are demonstrated for Reef/Santa Cruz and Mussau sites, but this will not set the pattern for all others. For Fiji and West Polynesia, Hunt (1987) and Kirch (1988a) take the view that there was early widespread contact followed by increasing isolation, but Davidson (1978, 1989) considers there is still not the evidence to show such a change. A general point to take from these comparisons is that the pattern of archaeological evidence often looks much the same right across Lapita's distribution, but interpretations diverge, between west and east, more than the data.

ARCHAEOLOGICAL AND LINGUISTIC ISSUES IN POLYNESIAN COLONISATION

Polynesia lies at the heart of the subject of this book, and its people were possibly the most widely scattered on earth. The three sides of the Polynesian Triangle measured as great circle distances clockwise from Hawaii are 3880, 3980 and 3670 nautical miles long and, in kilometres, nearly twice as far. Most of its many hundreds of islands are of modest size or smaller, so it is no wonder that Polynesians have usually enjoyed a high reputation as navigators. Their cultural unity was recognised early by Europeans, and so was the question of their historical origins and dispersal.

Only a decade ago, modern archaeologists, linguists and others had outlined a plausible answer from various data points in the region. However, some alternative views are now under debate, while the evidence itself remains insufficient to settle them. Among these are three related questions: Was there a 'Long Pause' in West Polynesia before the settlement of East Polynesia? Were there 'homelands' in both West and East Polynesia, any more secure than the elusive Lapita 'homeland' in the far west? What was the order and time of the first settlement of the island groups of central East Polynesia and its margins? Because earlier works have not

22. One of several similar versions of the 'orthodox model' of Polynesian settlement, but the current view has now substantially changed. (Reprinted by permission of the publishers from Jennings 1979, Figure 1.1.)

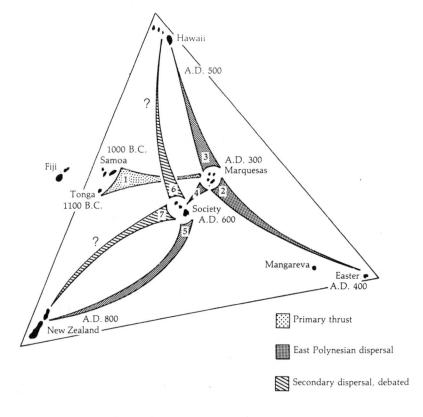

focused on voyaging issues in relation to archaeological evidence, this study adds to the debate. However, the theory of voyaging and colonisation does not stand or fall on this account.

The orthodox view, which prevailed towards the end of the 1970s, included the following elements (Bellwood 1978; Davidson 1979; Finney 1979a; Green 1979).

1. Lapita colonists reached Fiji and West Polynesia without appreciable delay and were widely settled in the larger groups and some of the smaller islands by the end of the second millennium B.C.

2. Within a West Polynesian homeland the distinctive characteristics of Polynesian language and culture developed in some isolation over a period of 1000–1500 years, when there was no further colonisation to the east.

3. About A.D. 300 the Marquesas were probably the first East Polynesian group to be settled, and thereafter became a 'dispersal centre' for colonists to Hawaii, Easter Island and the Society Islands, the last of which became in its turn a secondary dispersal centre for later movements to Hawaii and New Zealand. Numerous such schemes have been proposed, which differ in detail, but were generally similar to the one shown in Figure 22, reproduced from Jennings (1979: Fig. I.1). All have been based upon the interplay of patchy artifact distributions, radiocarbon dates and historical linguistics.

The case of the long pause

One reason to doubt this pause was that a similar model set within West Polynesia itself, between Tonga and Samoa (Groube 1971), had failed shortly before. It had been thought that successive steps of settlement from west to east ran parallel to the pattern of linguistic sub-grouping, as if the latter was an expression of history, rather than classification, even though Biggs (1972) had objected on theoretical grounds to this kind of argument. The first West Polynesian pause closed when Lapita pottery was dredged from the sea at Mulifanua in Western Samoa in 1973. A second reason for doubt was that a discontinuous model of colonisation was inconsistent with the evidence for Lapita. Why should colonists who had spread rapidly through the western Pacific, apparently without compulsion or stopping before, suddenly do so in West Polynesia, and why, 1500 years later, should their descendants begin to explore upwind again? Further, what happened to voyaging technology in the meantime? Certainly Lapita's conspicuous ceramic trail led no farther east, so the seemingly abrupt stop was possible, but the pause was really needed more for prehistorians' retrospective theories about the process of diversification (considered below), which are unrelated to the motives and methods of those first oceanic explorers. They could not realise, for instance, that they should stop and transform themselves into Polynesians before going farther.

My objection to the pause was as much a dispute about models of interpretation as about the facts of prehistory, and some alternatives to the pause were proposed (Irwin 1980, 1981). Firstly, it was suggested that colonisation could have continued, but pottery-making, which provides high archaeological visibility, could have stopped, something that has been known to happen when manufacturing technology is mismatched with unfamiliar raw materials. One cannot expect to find good clay on atolls, and Claridge (1984) has since documented the worsening quality of raw materials for ceramics on crossing the Andesite Line to the basaltic high islands of the Pacific Plate. Some six finds of prehistoric pottery are now known in East Polynesia, two in the Southern Cook Islands on Ma'uke and Atiu, and four in the Marquesas, although there are less than 20 sherds in all and uncertainties about archaeological context. Some, at least, of the sherds were imported from Fiji and West Polynesia, but others in the Marquesas are said to be of local origin (Kirch 1986; Kirch et al. 1988; Walter and Dickinson 1989).

> Polynesian Plainware has now been documented at four localities on three islands in the Marquesas, and at all of these at least some sherds are of local manufacture . . . Thus, Green's argument . . . that these finds are all in secondary context, and must point to as yet undiscovered primary ceramic-bearing assemblages in the Marquesas, deserves serious consideration. [Kirch et al. 1988:105]

It seems plausible that the earliest settlements in the east should be marked by the final stages of local pottery-making, as this craft died from some combination of technological maladaptiveness and other functional and social changes. As for imported wares, they could occur in the east for as long as they were made in Fiji and West Polynesia. What is rather surprising is the scarcity of pottery in East Polynesia.

A second factor invoked for absence of early sites was sampling error. Field work in much of East Polynesia has been patchy, and archaeological sites can lie buried by erosional deposits or submerged under water, such as Mulifanua. Spriggs (1984) elaborated the general argument about the burial of sites by accelerated alluvial/colluvial deposition following human settlement, and Kirch and Hunt add a new dimension to the problem by suggesting that throughout

> virtually the entire region where Lapita sites have been recorded (from the Bismarcks through Vanuatu to Fiji and Tonga), they are associated with landforms undergoing active tectonic uplift . . . Upon crossing the Tonga Trench and entering the oceanic realm of active tectonic subsidence, Lapita disappears. [Kirch and Hunt 1988a:17]

They suggest archaeologists 'must seriously entertain the possibility that Lapita dispersal did extend eastwards of Samoa to the Cooks or beyond' and, if so, given their dominant low-lying setting can be expected to be wholly submerged (Kirch and Hunt 1988a:17). On the other hand, J. T. Clark (1989), in a general review of Pacific sea-level change, concluded that circumstances are locally variable, and the data may not support such a broad model.

One other kind of sampling error that has arisen lately is that archaeologists have simply not looked in all of the places where sites could be found. Recently, Lapita sites have been found on Sohano Island in the Northern Solomons (S. Wickler, pers. comm. 1988), and on Nissan

(M. Spriggs, pers. comm. 1988), on fringing coral reefs, where prehistoric settlements were probably built over the water on piles, just like ones known in parts of Melanesia today.

As originally stated, the continuous model for East Polynesian settlement was not unduly ambitious. 'Discovery of just one eastern site dating as early as 500 B.C. does not seem an outlandish possibility and would favour the continuous model as much as the discontinuous one' (Irwin 1981:489).

On 'homelands', interaction spheres and the pause

The West Polynesian pause was a timetrap set by latter-day theorists of culture change for the ancestors of the Polynesians, but has not held them very well. The argument, especially as it related to language, went rather like this: because all Polynesians share certain traits in common, these (1) must have developed in isolation – to account for their distinctiveness, (2) must have developed prior to their dispersal throughout Polynesia – to account for characteristics being shared, and (3) must have developed over a time-period of the order of 1000 years or more – because of the substantial nature of the changes. In essence, when Lapita people reached West Polynesia they went into a cultural chrysalis to emerge after 1000 years as Polynesians only then able to go east. However, the three elements of this metamorphosis of Melanesian immigrants into Polynesian emigrants can be contested.

Firstly, archaeology raised problems for the isolation theory. The ceramic histories of Fiji, the Lau group, Tonga, Samoa, Uvea and Futuna are generally similar, which argues for continued contact between them. The sequence began with an elaborate set of finely decorated vessel forms and associated plainwares. Decoration quickly diminished and finally disappeared together with associated vessel forms (Green 1979). Afterwards, the limited range of surviving plainware became coarser and then extinct by the early centuries A.D., except in Fiji, where the pottery sequence continued. Different island groups exhibit broadly similar devolutionary sequences, although there are some differences – as in duration. Davidson (1978:386) pointed out that during the first 1000–1500 years of settlement, some form of regular contact was maintained throughout the region, by which ideas about pottery and other aspects of culture were shared. She still subscribes to the idea of contact, but now doubts the widespread similarity of pottery (1989), although others do not (Best 1989; Kirch 1988a).

> One theory able to accommodate the evidence is that language and some elements of material culture diverged within the context of continuing communication. There are many ethnographic instances of regular contact between different culture groups – the specialized traders of Melanesia are good examples: some speak the languages of neighbours, while others use trade languages. Isolation in Western Polynesian prehistory was of a selective kind and occurred among interacting populations. [Irwin 1980:327]

Green (1981) made a comparable point, as it related to language, saying it need no longer be assumed that the settlement of an island led to the break-up of language.

> Rather it means that a linguistically unified Pre Polynesian language community was distributed over much if not all of the West Polynesian area, and perhaps even extended outside it, well before the break-up of Polynesian began. The development of a distinct Polynesian branch of Central Pacific did not take place in isolation on a single island group of West Polynesia. [Green 1981:147]

The breakdown of the isolation theory jeopardised the associated theory that Polynesians could not have dispersed prior to the development of the traits they share in common. The pertinent question is: if the case can accommodate wider dispersal in West Polynesia, can it also accommodate any parts of central East Polynesia? The suggestion has been made that it might (Irwin 1981:489–90). One option is that a dialect chain stretched as far as the nearer islands of East Polynesia for a time. Or, alternatively, multiple migration and settlement, along the general lines envisaged by Biggs (1972:149), carried new elements of language to settlements already in East Polynesia. However, the key point to note is that this issue is essentially a *geographic* one, and the assertions and counter-assertions of archaeologists and linguists about the size of an interaction system will need the support of some suitable analysis before any carry much conviction.

The third element of the pause listed above was that the language changes involved would have taken a significant time: 1000 years or more was a popular guess, but it appears to be reducing lately as the radiocarbon dates close in. Most of the research to date has focused on the diversification among Polynesian languages rather than on differences between Proto-Polynesian and its predecessor, Central Pacific, and if this separation was faster than supposed, then the need for the standstill in West Polynesia substantially reduces (M. Ross, pers. comm. 1988).

Moreover, it is unlikely that there are any comparable historical models that could help to calibrate the expected rate of change for this case. In the colonising period we are dealing with a dynamic situation of a handful of small communities scattered through a number of archipelagos some hundreds of miles apart. Groups separated, but remained in touch with one another, according to changing patterns of contact, as settlement expanded. It may be that the dispersal of Polynesians will eventually tell us more about the potential speed of language change than inappropriate models of change will tell us about Polynesian colonisation.

The orthodox model of Polynesian settlement also proposed some marking time by the first colonists in central East Polynesia (usually the Marquesas), for much the same reasons, prior to the final dispersal to the margins (e.g. Emory 1959:34). However, following the ongoing revision of West Polynesian prehistory, there is now a more ready acceptance that there was a wide contact area in East Polynesia, where a number of early, shared changes in language and material culture took place (Irwin 1980; Davidson 1981, 1984; Kirch 1986; Finney *et al.* 1989), but there is still more resistance to suggestions of significant contact between West and East Polynesia after settlement (Davidson 1984).

The order and chronology of settlement in East Polynesia

Kirch (1986) has reviewed the archaeological evidence in East Polynesia and his conclusion is that what Sinoto (1970) described as 'Archaic East Polynesian Culture' and Bellwood (1978) called 'Early East Polynesian Culture' was not truly 'archaic' at all, but an intermediate phase in the development of central East Polynesian culture. The Marquesas currently have the oldest known archaeological sites, but Kirch (1986) suggests that the earliest settlement phase there has yet to be identified (Kirch 1986:36). He sees archaic assemblages, which date between A.D. 700 and 1100, as a central East Polynesian development after the settlement of Easter Island and Hawaii, but which appears to be associated with the later settlement of New Zealand. Walter (1990:15) sees archaic assemblages as also having many affinities outside East Polynesia and variable associations within.

To consider the archaeological settlement evidence briefly, group by group, the work of Suggs (1960) secured a central role for the Marquesas in East Polynesian prehistory. While other archaeologists were critical of aspects of his interpretation and, in particular, the second century B.C. settlement date, which now seems more reasonable again, the Marquesas were established as a potential dispersal centre for other parts of East Polynesia (Sinoto 1966) and the idea found linguistic support as well (Green 1966, Pawley 1966). Sinoto (1966) revised and up-dated Suggs' sequence largely on the basis of excavations at the Hane Dune Site (MUH1) on Ua Huka, but no dates were reported from the lowest levels and the evidence always allowed it to conform to the early date originally reported by Suggs (1961) from the NHaa1 site on Nuku Hiva (Irwin 1981; Kirch 1986). The more recent radiocarbon date of A.D. 150 reported by Ottino (1985a) from a cave on Ua Poa may add some support, too. Given the sampling problems, Kirch (1986:25) suggested the Marquesas could have been settled by the mid-first millennium B.C., but equally it could prove to be younger.

The Society Islands were occupied by at least the ninth century A.D. by communities sharing a material culture very similar to upper levels of the Hane site (Kirch 1986:29). However, this island group has geomorphological sampling problems involving tectonic submergence, coastal aggradation and the deposition of alluvium on coastal plains and into former lagoons (Kirch 1986:30). The Society Islands were an earlier candidate for an East Polynesian dispersal centre (Buck 1938; Emory 1959) and could easily have been part of a wider homeland region, a concept accepted today although actually anticipated by Suggs (1960). This suggestion also fits with Bellwood's argument against the Marquesas being the East Polynesian homeland (1970:94).

It has been argued that Hawaii was settled as early as A.D. 300-400 (Kirch 1985) and 'sampling considerations again dictate that we leave open the possibility of yet earlier deposits' (Kirch 1986:31). In terms of voyaging (see below) and material culture, the Marquesas make a plausible source of Hawaiian settlement, but this, of course, is in the absence of early sites elsewhere in central East Polynesia.

Easter Island, similarly, may have been settled before the so-called 'archaic' appeared in central East Polynesia, but archaeological evidence that bears directly on its settlement period is lacking. There is a very questionable radiocarbon date of approximately fourth century A.D. (McCoy 1979:145), as well as items of early material culture, but the earliest secure radiocarbon dates are some centuries later. Linguistics could support a very early settlement of Easter Island, too, and Green (1985) describes evidence of the break-up of Proto-Eastern Polynesian into Rapanui and Central Eastern Polynesian and notes that this could have happened by the fourth or fifth century A.D. or, alternatively, it may have been settled rather later, but because of extreme isolation it 'was never re-settled to the extent that the linguistic indices of difference were obliterated or distorted' (Biggs 1972:150).

The Cook Islands, in the orthodox model, were settled from the Society group according to the suggestion of Buck (1938). Chikamori (1987:110) has reported a radiocarbon date of 2310 ± 65 years ago (which may require correction for the marine reservoir effect) from Pukapuka in the Northern Cook Islands, which consist of some half-dozen very scattered atolls. By contrast, the earliest archaeological evidence from the more substantial Southern Cook Islands is confined to the period A.D. 800–1200, although it is thought that they may have been settled long beforehand (Walter 1988). Walter and Dickinson (1989) report a single potsherd recovered from deposits of fourteenth century A.D. age on Ma'uke and attribute it to a Tongan source on the basis of temper. Another, similar sherd was found on the surface of the same site, suggesting to the authors that pottery-making, conventionally thought to have ended in Tonga in the first few centuries A.D. (Davidson 1979:94), could have lasted several centuries longer. But the age disparity would be more simply explained if the Ma'uke sherd were in secondary deposition there. Another sherd was found on Atiu, but has yet to be described (Walter and Dickinson 1989).

Preliminary palynological research on Atiu suggests there may have been some forest clearance associated with the planting of coconuts earlier than a radiocarbon date of 1150 B.C. (Flenley 1989:8). Further results are awaited with interest and will need to be reconciled with results of palynological work on Mangaia (P. Kirch, pers. comm. 1989).

The Southern Cook Islands may have been part of the earliest sphere of settlement in East Polynesia. There has also long been the ethnological and linguistic suggestion that they were the source of New Zealand Maori. However, in a recent summary of the biological affinities of Southern Cook Islanders, Katayama concludes there is little to support an especially close affinity between New Zealand Maori and Southern Cook Islanders as suggested. In so far as Mangaians are representative of the Southern Cook Islands, they are more similar to West Polynesians than to Maori. For their part, New Zealanders more often lie closer in the data to other East Polynesians. Katayama suggests (1988) that the Southern Cook Islands were possibly settled

> much earlier than is usually considered, or more specifically at the time of initial Polynesian dispersal to East Polynesia from Tonga and/or Samoa. An alternative is that there were unexpectedly quite frequent contacts between the Cook Islands and West Polynesia in later prehistoric times. The former

may be called a 'stepping stone hypothesis' of the formation of the Cook Islands populations.

In fact, the alternatives proposed by Katayama by no means exclude each other, as early settlement from West Polynesia and later contact are both likely. These results of human biological studies appear to be at odds with the patterns of linguistic similarity, which show the strongest links of New Zealand Maori with the Southern Cook Islands. However, the position could change with recovery of more adequate prehistoric collections of skeletal material in the latter.

With regard to the settlement of New Zealand, there is little in the available radiocarbon evidence to suggest a time of settlement before 1000 years ago (Caughley 1988; Davidson 1984). However, a recent article by Sutton (1987a) suggests New Zealand was settled between A.D. 0 and 500, but it is not clear that the reasons that may have made other parts of East Polynesia earlier necessarily apply to New Zealand. As for origins, a source in central East Polynesia is indicated, although linguistic and biological clues do not always point in the same direction. New Zealand will be considered in more detail in a later discussion.

The early sequences of several island groups not considered above are unknown, including the Tuamotu and Austral groups, Mangareva and Rapa.

Summary of changing archaeological models for Polynesia

Until recently the orthodox view has been that after the settlement of Fiji and West Polynesia there was a long pause before the settlement of East Polynesia began. Its length may be eroded at the bottom end by more cautious interpretation of Lapita dates, while a small number of radiocarbon dates allow the settlement of the east to be back-dated tentatively to approximately 100 B.C. There is more acceptance of the possibility that still earlier sites will be discovered in certain island groups in central East Polynesia. Just how early these sites might be is a moot point. Voyaging considerations suggest a date some centuries earlier than the Marquesas, but a few centuries after West Polynesia. The earliest possibility is as old as classic Lapita itself (Kirch and Hunt 1988a:17), but this author does not favour quite such an early date.

At the same time as the revision of chronology, there has been a more general movement away from the idea of discrete 'homelands' or 'primary dispersal centres' in West or central East Polynesia. More recent efforts to find one in the Bismarck Archipelago have been no more successful. Further, within East Polynesia, more uncertainty is allowed as to the sequence of settlement. The Marquesas have the oldest evidence now, but earlier sites can be expected in the Cook, Society, Austral and Tuamotu islands, where one or two may even be associated with the dying stages of pottery-making. Complications may arise in so far as islands were not settled as they were discovered, and this may apply, in particular, to smaller, more distant islands with difficult canoe landings.

With regard to the margins of East Polynesia, it still seems established that they were settled from central East Polynesia – Hawaii possibly as early as A.D. 400 and, while the archaeological evidence for Easter Island is insecure, a plausible case can be made for it being much the same age. As for New Zealand, far downwind to the west and well south of the tropics, there is almost nothing in the archaeology to suggest settlement before A.D. 1000, and, as far as earlier settlement is concerned, it may be the exception that proves the rule.

GEOGRAPHICAL AND VOYAGING ISSUES IN POLYNESIAN COLONISATION

Archaeological models no longer constrain theories of voyaging as much as they did, but the same data exist to test against a wider range of possibilities. There is no longer as much need for the first voyages into East Polynesia to wait for so long or travel so far. Now that we are less bound by cultural delays in settlement in Polynesia it makes sense to see whether there were natural factors to influence the order and time of settlement. In fact it is really necessary to control one to identify the other.

Time and area

As a general rule, the two factors must be related. Several writers have made the point that there are parts of Polynesia where greater distances could have affected the time it took to cross them. However, more important than distance was the area of ocean that had to be searched to give a reasonable chance for an island within it to be discovered. Figure 23 is a simple model of the effect of area on time in the colonisation of the remote Pacific. It shows arcs 1000 sea miles apart centred on the main archaeological line of colonisation, which is also aligned against the prevailing wind according to the search and return strategy proposed here. The point of origin is the start of Remote Oceania, and the end is 5000 sea miles away, at Easter Island; the arcs are set widely enough to capture the other two points of the Polynesian Triangle – Hawaii and New Zealand. The trend of early radiocarbon dates follows the direction upwind, before deviating across it to Micronesia and Hawaii and, finally, to New Zealand. It is clear that the area within each successive arc increases greatly from west to east; therefore, even if the linear rate of exploration remained constant, more time would be needed to search the expanding space, if the number of voyages was constant.

Figure 23 supports a number of observations:

1. The first arc containing the smallest area reaches Fiji and, from there, the islands of Western Polynesia are so close as to make their rapid discovery almost automatic. This is also what the pattern of radiocarbon dates from early Lapita sites has to say, and the differences between archaeologists' estimates are contained within 500 years.

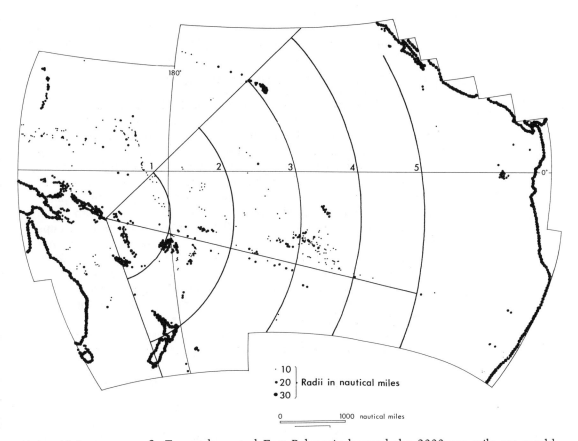

23. A model showing an expanding area of ocean aligned to the main path of colonisation. Even if the rate of exploration remained constant, more time would be needed to search the increasing space. This factor may account for apparent pauses. It is also clear that many islands were not settled in the order of closeness or accessibility. For instance, New Zealand is closer to the source of Lapita colonisation than central East Polynesia, but was settled more than 1000 years later; Hawaii is 2000 miles closer than Easter Island, but both were settled at much the same time. (Reproduced by permission of the editor from Irwin 1989.)

2. To reach central East Polynesia beyond the 2000 sea mile arc would require some elapsed time to search the expanding space. The arguments about chronology now require a millennium to contain them! The suggestion of a preferred upwind direction of search is supported by central East Polynesia being settled long before New Zealand, which lies much closer in the second arc.

3. The margins of Polynesia would need more time to be settled than central East Polynesia. Hawaii and Easter Island provide another example of the influence of direction: in terms of linguistics and archaeology, they could have been settled within a few hundred years of each other, and it is interesting that Easter Island lies most distant upwind, while Hawaii, 2000 sea miles closer to the source of colonists in Near Oceania, lies across the wind.

4. New Zealand is anomalous in being close and late, but it is nearly 900 sea miles farther from the Equator than Hawaii. Explorers had to manage more testing weather conditions in the higher latitudes outside the tropics and find new ways home in the event of not finding land.

5. Details aside, the conclusion is that variations in settlement dates are to be expected, but these occur in continuous time, not simply in culturally interrupted time, as in the orthodox model (Irwin 1981). Fiji/West Polynesia could be expected to be settled early, central East Polynesia rather later, and its margins relatively later again if the rate of colonisation

remained the same. It is possible to make finer distinctions than this by considering other factors.

Area, dates and colonisation rates

Figure 24 is a transformation of the map of the Pacific made to search for coherence in the pattern of available radiocarbon dates for early settlement, which could throw light on issues raised (Irwin 1990). The figure is a log/log version of a Mercator projection map. Its point of origin is at 160° E. Longitude and 10° S. Latitude near Guadalcanal in the southeast of the main Solomons chain, which is appropriate archaeologically, because that is close to where Lapita voyagers passed from Near into Remote Oceania. Space becomes foreshortened logarithmically both north and south of the origin and also from west to east of it. The positions of islands and groups are plotted on the transformed grid, and contours shown are time lines at regular 500-year intervals, which express one view of the radiocarbon ages for their settlement. The direction of colonisation is generally from west to east, so a line to the west of an island suggests that it has a settlement date after that time, whereas one to the east of it implies it was settled earlier. Because the pattern of reported dates is uneven, solid lines are used to refer to actual data points while dashed lines interpolate between them as well as offering a qualified prediction of results to come.

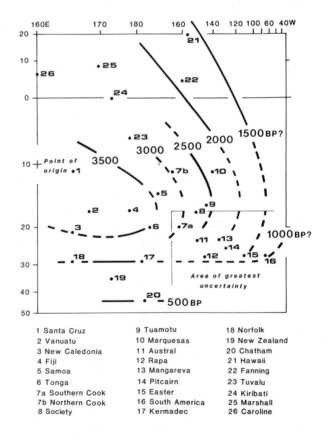

24. A log/log transformation of a Mercator projection map of the Pacific with its point of origin in the eastern Solomon Islands near to where Lapita passed from Near Oceania into the remote Pacific. Island positions are plotted on the transformed grid, and time lines are based on an early interpretation of available radiocarbon estimations, which produces much greater coherence than when they are plotted on a standard Mercator map. A major implication is that the rate of ocean exploration, which began fast, continued to accelerate. This is something of a surprise, because it has generally been considered to have slowed. (Adapted from Irwin 1990, Figure 2.)

1 Santa Cruz	9 Tuamotu	18 Norfolk
2 Vanuatu	10 Marquesas	19 New Zealand
3 New Caledonia	11 Austral	20 Chatham
4 Fiji	12 Rapa	21 Hawaii
5 Samoa	13 Mangareva	22 Fanning
6 Tonga	14 Pitcairn	23 Tuvalu
7a Southern Cook	15 Easter	24 Kiribati
7b Northern Cook	16 South America	25 Marshall
8 Society	17 Kermadec	26 Caroline

Inspection of Figure 24 supports the following conclusions:
1. When the islands of the remote Pacific are plotted logarithmically, the intervals between the date lines become approximately equal. The implication is that the colonisation of the area was accelerating at a rate approaching exponential. This is a surprising conclusion, because it is generally held that the rate slowed through time, and especially when late exploratory voyages were made towards distant islands at the margins of Polynesia.
2. The primary direction of advancing colonisation clearly shows the alignment towards the southeast trade winds of the southern tropics supporting the suggestion that the general trajectory of Pacific colonisation was first upwind, then across and down the wind. This implies pragmatic strategies of exploration, which allowed not the fastest rate of advance, but certainly the highest chance of survival. Obviously, it is safest to search in the direction from which one can most easily return in the event of not finding new land.
3. In the south, the time lines compress together near the southern limit of the tropics again, confirming that higher latitude and late settlement were correlated. There is no secure archaeological evidence for it on any island earlier than approximately 1000 years ago.

To consider the results in more detail, the time lines are intended as generalisations. Those shown in Figure 24 follow the earliest of the current interpretations of the radiocarbon evidence for Lapita (e.g. Kirch and Hunt 1988a) and central East Polynesia (Irwin 1989), rather than the more cautious approach that I have followed in this text. However, the interpretation of the dates in marginal Polynesia shown in Figure 24 is fairly conservative. Similarly, an estimate of A.D. 500–1000 is shown for Polynesian contact with South America, which could be regarded as conservative, as it does not require the sweet potato to be carried from there in time for the first settlement of Hawaii, as well it might have. However, it is on hand to be taken to New Zealand a thousand years ago.

One safe way of dealing with chronological uncertainties is to extrapolate back from the margins of Polynesia, where New Zealand and Hawaii are both tolerably well-dated. From Hawaii, we can assume reasonably that the Marquesas, Society Islands, Cook Islands and Samoa become older in succession, within the period between A.D. 500 and 1000 B.C. Thus, while Figure 24 includes areas of greater or lesser archaeological uncertainty, whose details of dating may prove difficult to resolve, a general Pacific-wide pattern is revealed. It would be possible to adjust the position of the time lines in Figure 24 to accommodate various shades of opinion. However, the essential point is that all possibilities fit with much greater coherence on the logarithmic projection map, arbitrary though it is, than on the Mercator projection. Therefore the general conclusions about the rate and direction of advance, and the 'high-latitude' pause, still hold.

When the model of the West Polynesian pause was first challenged, it was on the basis of what preceded it, that is to say, the speed of Lapita advance. But now that argument is reinforced by what followed. If it should transpire that there was some pause between tropical West and East Polynesia, the implication is that the progress of colonisation would have had to have increased even more sharply afterwards to catch up with the accelerating advance into the east.

Having previously described the spread of Lapita as almost instantaneous on a world scale (Irwin 1980), it is disconcerting to find that the settlement of the rest of the remote Pacific was apparently even faster. However, this claim has to be put into proper context. Firstly, intervals of 500 years, as shown in Figure 24, represent something in the order of 20 human generations, and that number can accommodate many voyages, especially if there were numerous and increasing, contemporary points of origin. Secondly, the increasing rate of exploration relates to the amount of ocean that was searched and not to the number of new settlements founded, for the number of islands still to be discovered in the Pacific was reducing with further progress into the east as the area of empty ocean was increasing.

While this analysis has obtained a coherent general pattern of colonisation, it has not been able to consider the detail of settlement of individual island groups.

The relative accessibility of island groups

Several models of East Polynesian settlement turn on the ease or otherwise of reaching certain island groups. In 1972 Biggs wrote that

> the known facts of geography and meteorology, and the more plausible speculations about Polynesian navigational capabilities . . . argue strongly for a situation in which islands which were closest would be settled first in the upwind struggle to the east. [Biggs 1972:148]

Lewis, too, thought the Marquesas, at that time favoured as a dispersal centre in East Polynesia, a long and unlikely direct voyage with no chance of drift (Lewis 1972:300). His view was supported by Levison, Ward and Webb (1973:60), who simulated navigated voyages east from Samoa. Of these, 31% reached the Cook Islands and 12% the Southern Line Islands; only 7% reached the Marquesas, 6% the Tuamotu Islands and 8% the Society Islands.

However, in 1979 Finney put the opposite case: that major groups in East Polynesia, the Society Islands and Marquesas would be reached first, and that other groups in central East Polynesia, such as the Australs, Cooks, Gambier and Tuamotus were too insignificant to be hit and used as stepping-stones on the way (1979a:343–4).

> Although the armchair voyager might consult his map and choose routes that hopped from one isolated atoll to another in order to reach these East Polynesian groups without having to make such long voyages, I doubt that the first colonists could have followed such a strategy without prior knowledge of the possible stepping-stone islands. [Finney 1979a:344]

At that time, when the pause theory was still accepted, the inter-island zone of Fiji/West Polynesia seemed a good place to learn extra sailing skills before the long voyage east, and it also allowed time for the double canoe to be further adapted to carry greater loads over greater distances (Finney 1979a:344). In fact, the very difficulty of reaching East Polynesia was taken by some prehistorians as one reason for the pause.

25. The accessibility of island targets from eastern Melanesia to the Southern Cook Islands in East Polynesia. While island groups generally become more difficult targets from west to east, there is no navigational threshold sufficient to explain a long pause in West Polynesia. It should be remembered that discovery and settlement did not necessarily occur at the same time, and that the latter was affected by further variables as discussed in chapter 9.

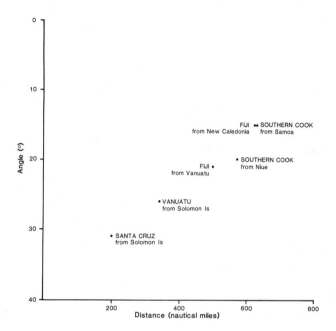

On the basis of more recent experimental voyaging, Finney is persuaded of the feasibility of reaching some of the closer islands first (Finney *et al.* 1989). However, the original case has been re-stated by Keegan and Diamond (1987) in their review of island colonisation.

> Unless the 1000-yr 'Long Pause' on Fiji, Samoa and Tonga proves to be an artifact of available radiocarbon dates, we suggest that it may indicate a period of stasis in long-distance voyaging due to the lack of readily accessible targets. When a lucky voyage finally did reach the Societies or Marquesas and returned with the news of these verdant islands with now-extinct, easily hunted flightless birds, the effect must have been electrifying. It would have ended the Long Pause and stimulated new explorations. [Keegan and Diamond 1987:68]

It is rather surprising to find this view in a biogeographical analysis, because that usually emphasises the role of stepping-stone islands, which mitigate the effects of distance as the authors say themselves (Keegan and Diamond 1987:60). Such islands do intervene in this case between West Polynesia and the Society Islands and Marquesas.

The issue is examined in Figure 25, which plots angle and distance of island targets on a number of voyages through eastern Melanesia to Fiji, and from Samoa on to the Southern Cook Islands, but no navigational thresholds are apparent. Sailing east from West Polynesia did not present a vastly more difficult proposition for explorers than some of the voyages made already in Island Melanesia. It can be seen that the shortest voyage from the west to Fiji was 500 sea miles from central Vanuatu and the target angle was 21°. The Southern Cook Islands are a minimum distance of 630 sea miles from Samoa and offer a 15° angle, which, incidentally, is almost exactly the same as a voyage from New Caledonia to Fiji. The distance to the Southern Cook Islands is shorter from Tonga via Niue.

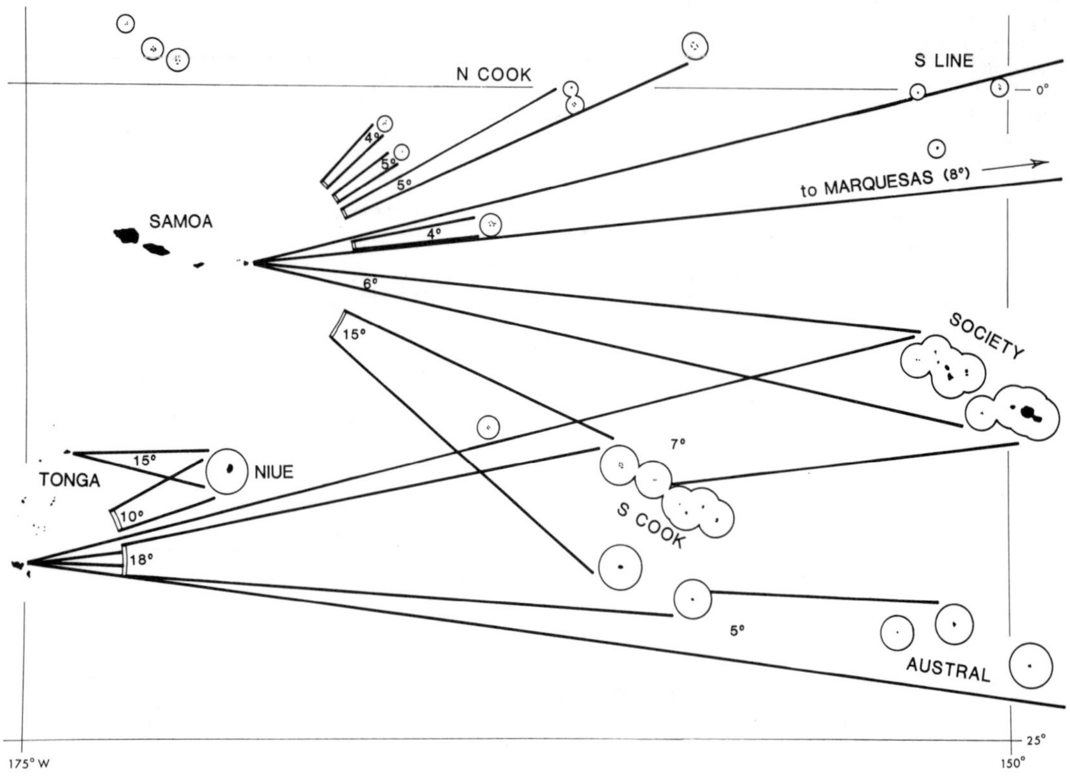

26. Several proposed models of East Polynesian settlement turn on the ease of reaching certain island groups. The figure shows target angles from West Polynesia. In broad terms, the Southern Cook Islands offer a target twice the size and at half the distance of high island groups farther east in Polynesia. (Reproduced by permission of the editor from Irwin 1989.)

Several of the Fiji Islands are large, high and more easily seen than the Southern Cooks, except Rarotonga, but nevertheless, the Southern Cooks do present a broad, expanded target to voyagers experienced in detecting land from offshore – a widespread skill in ethnographic times. The presence of Lapita sites on some of the smaller and more remote islands in Fiji and West Polynesia, such as in the southern Lau and Futuna, suggests skills of this kind existed already. In short, while the first voyages to reach East Polynesia may have required some time, there is no support for a substantial pause in this data.

Figure 26 is a map of island angles and distance from West Polynesia to central East Polynesia. The Northern Cook Islands are low coral islands and atolls, which, while relatively close to West Polynesia, each offer small target sectors in a wide but discontinuous arc. Moreover, there is an additional problem about when such islands became available for settlement; geologically, even the atolls on the Pacific Plate are coral crowns on volcanic seamounts. Existing atolls were submerged by rising post-Pleistocene seas and were still under water when the sea reached its modern level at approximately 4000 B.C. Even excluding a possibly higher sea-level stand after then, it would have taken growing coral some time to catch up with the surface again, and still longer before sand and coral detritus formed islets on the reef available to be colonised first by plants and birds and then by humans.

Chronology is uncertain, but there are implications for the island chains available to Lapita and other explorers. Best (1988) found evidence that one of the atolls of the Tokelau group was habitable some time after 300 B.C. and before A.D. 400. However, this estimate rests on just two dates, while it is known that the process of land building and alteration to atolls is complex (Leach and Ward 1981), and one can expect different ages in different parts of the same island. The situation is further complicated by the dynamics of the Pacific Plate and the possibility that islands on it were sinking (Kirch and Hunt 1988a).

Returning to the discussion of Figure 26, the Southern Cook Islands are less problematical geologically and more visible, with Rarotonga being a high volcanic island and the rest raised coral and volcanic, or raised coral. Mangaia, Atiu and Aitutaki are all over 100 m above sea-level, while Ma'uke and Mitiaro, which are both raised coral with volcanic interiors, are respectively 46 m and 28 m high. The raised coral islands of Tukutea and Manuae are no more than 24 m and 18 m to their treetops (*Pacific Islands Pilot*, vol. III, 1982). While many of the islands of the Southern Cooks are individually fairly small and several not very high, as an expanded screen they present a wider target arc from West Polynesia than do the generally higher volcanic groups of the Society Islands and Marquesas. From Manu'a in the Samoan group, the Southern Cooks cover an arc of 15° at a distance of 630 to 820 sea miles. From Tongatapu they lie within an unbroken sighting arc of 18° between 870 and 1000 sea miles distant; however, the distance from Niue is only 570 sea miles. For comparison, from Samoa the Society Islands lie between 1000 and 1200 sea miles away, within a 6.5° arc, and from Tonga they present a similar-sized target, partly obscured by the Southern Cooks, at minimum distances of between 1350 and 1500 sea miles. From Samoa the Marquesas are a small target, partly blocked by the Southern Line Islands, and the distance is 1700 sea miles. From Tonga to the Marquesas is still farther, and to the closest of the Austral Islands, again partly obscured by the Southern Cooks, the distance is 1250 sea miles. In round figures, from West Polynesia the Southern Cooks are roughly twice the target and half the distance as the Society Islands and Marquesas, and, with the pattern of overlapping target arcs, must be rated as having a reasonable chance of intercepting exploratory probes to the east. The Marquesas, in spite of their early archaeological remains, are particularly remote.

Figure 27 shows target angles in central East Polynesia. The Society Islands lie 400 sea miles in a 28° arc from the Southern Cooks. The closest of the Australs is only 300 sea miles southeast, and upwind, and this group could have been settled as early as the Society Islands. From the Society Islands the Tuamotus are spread over a huge 110° of arc, and the closest are only between 100 and 200 sea miles away. The Society Islands and Tuamotus together constitute a massive continuous target arc in central East Polynesia, which, once known, could be approached from all quarters, and this has significance for the history of later contacts in East Polynesia. The Marquesas are found at a shortest distance of 400 sea miles from the Tuamotus and are a much closer and larger target from there than from the Society Islands. Hawaii, Easter Island and New Zealand will be discussed in a later chapter.

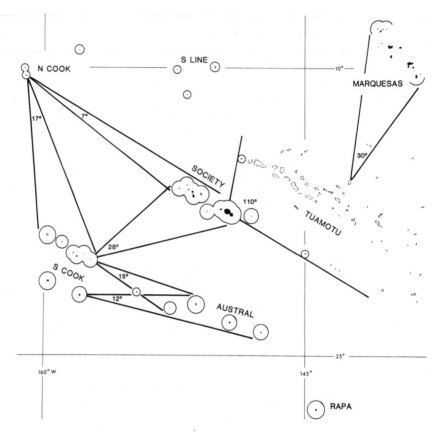

27. Target angles in central East Polynesia. According to these, a likely sequence of settlement was from the Southern Cook Islands to the Society Islands, to the Tuamotu Islands and then on to the Marquesas.

Time and adaptation

If voyaging did not stop beyond West Polynesia, settlement might have slowed on crossing the Andesite Line, which marks a broad division between continental resources and the more restricted ones of islands of the Pacific Plate; it particularly affected rock types and prompted technological innovations. However, the remedy for impoverished or unequally distributed resources is exchange, which is often held as typical of Lapita. One example of Lapita settlements that continued to receive imported commodities were those of the Reef/Santa Cruz group, and Green (1979) has documented links within that region, with the main Solomon Islands chain and the Bismarck Archipelago. One supposes the first settlers of the Southern Cooks could have received some outside reinforcement in much the same way, but there are no failed or abandoned late Lapita sites known in East Polynesia to testify to the problems of diminished resources there.

Models of colonisation

Terrell (1986) neatly accommodates scepticism about the West Polynesian 'standstill' with the absence of early sites in East Polynesia by proposing

28. One possible reason for the absence of early sites in East Polynesia that does not require a West Polynesian voyaging pause is that canoes may have continued to sail east, but met with accident of 'natural sampling'. (Adapted from Terrell 1986, figure 27.)

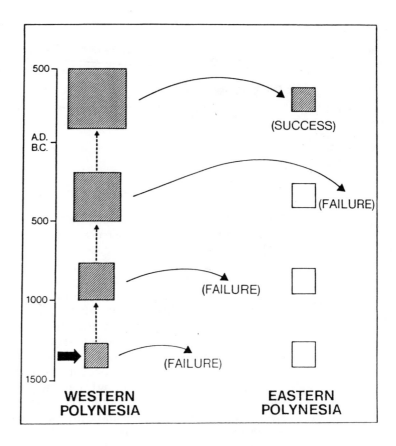

(as one possible solution) that canoes may have continued to sail east, but, by chance, none made a landfall. They met with accidents of 'natural sampling', and many lives were lost at sea (Terrell 1986:86). Figure 28 is taken from Terrell (1986: Fig. 27) and shows entry to West Polynesia after 1500 B.C., continuity of settlement there and expanding population. Unlike the pause model, there is no break in impetus to voyage, whatever the motives were, but all attempts end in failure. However, early in the first millennium A.D., after cultural changes had occurred in West Polynesia, a successful landfall is made in the east.

In fact, Figure 28 shows only one of many outcomes envisaged by Terrell, who compared four different colonisation models, including that of 'chance discovery' (1986:84–5). He examined their variables explicitly, which included intentions, motives, voyaging frequency, sailing direction, skilfulness and rate of success. He considered the kinds of archaeological evidence that could distinguish between the models. To this useful discussion we can add further considerations. These include the importance of directed return voyaging to the survival of potential colonists. Another is the study of island accessibility, which does not find a geographical threshold to account for voyages remaining unsuccessful for so long in this part of the Pacific, if attempts to sail on were still made.

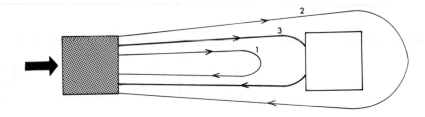

29. A 'continuous' settlement model for East Polynesia shows exploration as an ongoing process that requires some elapsed time. It follows a basic upwind, up-latitude method of search and return as it probes the expanding area of ocean in East Polynesia.

A continuous settlement model

No compelling explanation has been found for the persisting, but shortened, archaeological pause in the settlement of Polynesia and so Figure 29 shows exploration as a continuous process, which requires some elapsed time, following a basic upwind, up-latitude process of search and return. The first voyage shown is an undershoot; the second overshoots or, more probably, take a wrong direction; a third voyage makes a hit.

Figure 30 is a schematic view of the whole of Polynesia. Once again the Lapita founder population arrives in West Polynesia approximately 1000 B.C. or earlier. East Polynesia is split into nearer and farther groups because the voyage to the Southern Cook Islands, in particular, seems more likely than longer direct ones to major groups farther east (Biggs 1972). There is no systematic delay before voyaging starts, but people require some time to multiply and go forth. The figure shows that many attempts are needed before both nearer and farther central East Polynesia are settled, but there is learning in the model as exploration adds geographical knowledge to navigational knowledge. Back-communication is maintained after settlement, which allows reinforcement of new communities and the

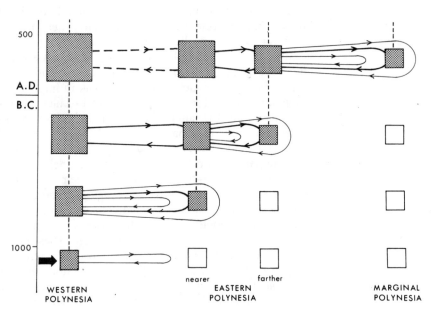

30. A schematic view of the continuous settlement of East Polynesia showing a very general estimate of chronology. (Adapted from Irwin 1989, Figure 9.)

movement of materials and ideas. As the margins of Polynesia are explored, links between West and East fall away and steeper gradients of isolation and cultural diversification develop where the water gaps are most telling. With regard to chronology, Figure 30 is not specific, but reflects my belief that the first part of central East Polynesia was discovered and possibly settled by 500 B.C., and probably before, and the Marquesas, which are the least accessible part of it, by around A.D. 0. In the early centuries of the first millennium A.D., settlement begins to reach the margins of Polynesia, starting with Hawaii c. A.D. 400 and probably Easter Island; New Zealand is settled by A.D. 1000 (from 'nearer' Eastern Polynesia, as shown in Figure 30), but the Chatham Islands not until later. This scenario accepts that differences in accessibility of islands would influence the order of settlement, but it can be expected that random events would intervene as well, although not to the extent that wider coherence was lost. Voyaging and chronological considerations are combined here, but this is not essential.

SAILING UPWIND TO EAST POLYNESIA AND SOUTH AMERICA

Since Europeans took an interest in Polynesian origins there has been difficulty in reconciling a journey of ancestors from west to east against winds that prevailed from east to west, and various arguments have tried to mitigate the force of those winds. Bridgeman (1983) has suggested that climatic change may have influenced migrations; that in the Little Climatic Optimum (A.D. 750–1250) persistent trade winds, clear skies and limited storminess favoured long-distance voyaging, while in the Little Ice Age (A.D. 1400–1850), more variable trades and increased storminess did not. In fact, most of the Pacific was already settled before both episodes, and it is difficult to see how persistent trades in the LCO could be of much help anyway. Generally, such arguments have not dealt closely with the archaeological chronology of colonisation or with voyaging practicalities.

The main feature of weather is that it is changeable, and sailing methods cope with exactly that. If there were prehistoric climatic changes of the kinds proposed in the colonisation period, they would have affected the location and frequency of various normal weather patterns, such as high and low pressure systems, ridges and troughs, while the basic global patterns of air pressure and movement persisted. In other words, a certain ocean passage might become easier more often, or difficult more often, but it would take fairly major climatic change to override a sailing technology that had developed to accommodate variability and short-term unpredictability in the weather. To cover the possibility of latitudinal shifts in wind systems in prehistory, Levison, Ward and Webb carried out a series of 'wind shift' experiments in their computer simulation of Pacific settlement, in which weather data were moved 5° north and then 5° south of their normal position, but their conclusions were substantially unchanged (Levison, Ward and Webb 1973:27).

It should be remembered, too, that a range of different weather patterns were encountered progressively by Pacific colonisation in its spread, including the trade wind systems of both hemispheres, the doldrums between, cyclones, the monsoon of the western tropics, sub-tropical variables and westerlies, as well as the movement of high and low pressure systems within them, and the variable seasonal shifts in their latitude. It is not a forceful argument that colonisation would have been greatly assisted or constrained by climatic variations in time, when the evidence says it was able to cope with plenty of it in space.

East Polynesia and El Niño

Recently, a much more serious case has been made in relation to the major global climatic anomaly referred to as El Niño–Southern Oscillation, or ENSO. If one accepts what Keegan and Diamond (1987:68) call the 'mysterious pause' in West Polynesia as well as the possibility of the direct settlement of the Marquesas because of the relatively early dates there, while also acknowledging that they lie outside the limit of normal westerly winds, then the stage is set for either a 'lucky voyage', as Keegan and Diamond put it (1987:68), or quite a different kind of explanation. In an important paper published in 1985, Finney proposed that the anomalous westerlies of El Niño could provide one. While he no longer confines himself to the case as stated (Finney et al. 1989), it is still an important issue, which requires consideration.

This major episodic perturbation of the climate of the South Pacific Ocean is the subject of considerable scientific attention, and, among other things, surface air pressures change, the trade winds slacken, sea-levels and currents change, and warm equatorial water extends down the South American coast. El Niño events have occurred several times this century, but at irregular intervals with different orders of severity. A major one happened in 1982-83, with little apparent warning, but considerable consequences for a sizable fraction of the world's population (Barnett et al. 1988). It brought a major shift to westerly winds, and, in the period from December 1982 until April 1983, there were sustained favourable winds for voyages between Samoa and the Marquesas. Finney considered that after eastward voyages began again from West Polynesia: 'Waiting for the west wind might have grounded voyagers for months at a time, but that strategy was preferable to trying to tack dead into the trades' (1985:15). However, he notes that 'it is difficult to imagine . . . how such a strategy could account for the evidence of the early and apparently direct settlement of the Marquesas' (1985:16) because of the normal lack of westerly winds to reach them. One option is to reject the idea of direct settlement; the other is to regard El Niño as an alternative possibility, which he did at that time. The model is represented in Figure 31, which shows entry to West Polynesia soon after 1500 B.C. from Melanesia; no voyages go east for more than a thousand years and then there is a direct carriage of a founder population to the east by El Niño.

El Niño may indeed have been a factor in the settlement of East Polynesia, but there are difficulties with it as the primary mechanism.

31. El Niño has been suggested as the means by which the Polynesians crossed from West to East Polynesia, after a delay, but there are some difficulties with this theory. Indeed, it would have taken such a remarkable and mechanical method to account for the apparent anomaly of first settlement in the remote Marquesas, which currently have relatively early settlement dates, but only in the absence of evidence from elsewhere in central East Polynesia.

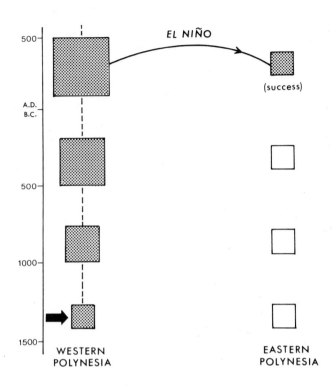

1. It is important to explain why, if there was such a suitable vehicle for travelling east, there should have been any substantial delay in the settlement of East Polynesia, let alone the thousand years favoured by some scholars. If seasonal monsoonal westerlies carried small populations of Lapita people as far as West Polynesia, why should not the more striking anomalous westerlies of El Niño have carried them on?

2. The theory leaves out the people concerned. Even now the ability to predict El Niño events is arguable (Ramage 1986), and a complex matter requiring large-scale data and sophisticated statistical modelling, and involving errors, including the time of onset of an event (Barnett *et al.* 1988). For prehistoric voyagers, without instruments and only local weather to see, there would have been nothing to distinguish El Niño from any other break in the trade winds, until it had already blown for an unusually long time, and a case can be made that explorers would not sail beyond their first landfall because they could not rely on *any* westerly persisting. Even if an island were small, it might still be preferable to use it as a staging post rather than press onward in the expectation of an impending return of the trade winds.

3. Also, what would happen in the quite likely event of a voyage travelling on an El Niño westerly failing to make a landfall? In this event the logic of the survival strategy would then be reversed: El Niño could mean a dangerous downwind voyage from which there might be no return.

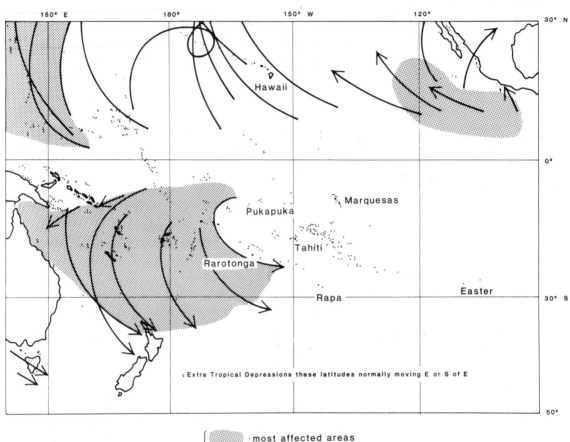

Tropical storm activity { most affected areas / some selected tracks }

32. Sailing east in Polynesia became progressively harder, but safer. In summer, cyclones decrease with distance east, but so do westerly winds of monsoonal origin. (Adapted from the *Pacific Islands Pilot*.)

Sailing to East Polynesia – summer winds

Sailing east into Polynesia was accompanied by the reducing influence of the summer monsoon and fewer breaks in the trade winds. Compared with the route traversed so far, a summer crossing would have been progressively safer, due to the decline in frequency of cyclones as shown in Figure 32, which is taken from the *Pacific Islands Pilot*, vol. III (1982:52), although some cyclones do form east of the most affected areas, in a zone of cyclonic wind shear on the north side of the South Pacific Convergence Zone (SPCZ) shown in Figure 3 (Thompson 1986a:9). The general situation is that while the summer route became safer it became progressively harder.

The information shown in Figure 33 is taken from the *Routeing Chart of the South Pacific Ocean for February* (1967), a month that offers as good a chance as any for sailing east in summer. Between Fiji and the Society Islands, looking at winds that blow from north through west to south that can be used for reaching or running, one can see that an eastward crossing is feasible, but difficult. Certainly there are recorded instances of sailing

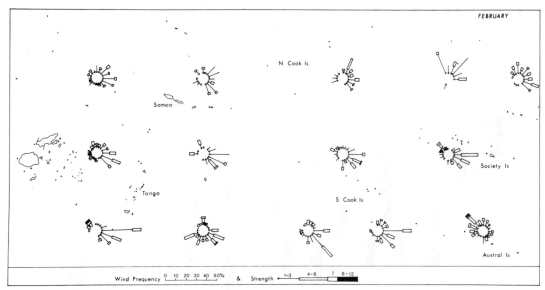

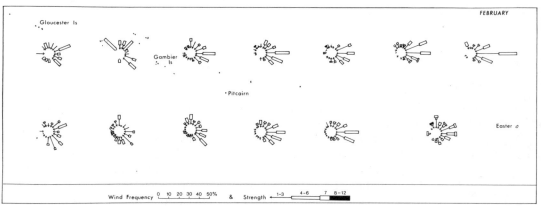

33. February winds between Fiji and the Society Islands. Sailing east in the tropics in summer is possible, but not easy. (Adapted from the Admiralty *Routeing Chart* of the South Pacific Ocean, for February. Reproduced by permission of the editor from Irwin 1989, Figure 10.)

34. Fair winds for sailing east towards Easter Island in summer are rare indeed. (Adapted from the Admiralty *Routeing Chart* of the South Pacific Ocean, for February.)

ships making the passage easily, and this is to be expected now and again. However, east of the Northern Cooks and northeast of the Society Islands towards the Marquesas, the incidence of westerlies is so rare that the prospect of a tolerably direct trip from the west is remote, unless this, indeed, is where El Niño played its part. Most probably, an indirect route was taken through the Tuamotus to the south. In the wind roses of Figure 34, which covers the stretch of ocean from the Mangareva (Gambier) Islands south of the Tuamotu chain to Easter Island, fair winds are rare indeed and the best one might hope for is northerly winds to allow a reaching track east. As Sharp said (1963:106), a voyage from west to east direct to Easter Island would be difficult to sustain with unpredictable summer westerlies for such a great distance. Contrary to some archaeological models of settlement, Easter Island virtually cannot be settled from the Marquesas direct, as shown in Figure 22 (from Jennings 1979: Fig.1.1) and the reverse would be easier. In fact the settlement of both through intermediary islands is most likely.

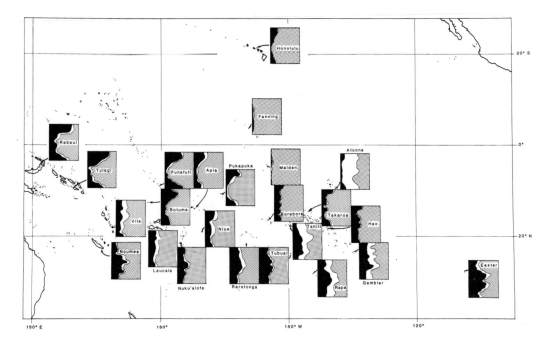

Sailing to East Polynesia – winter winds

35. Winds recorded at meteorological stations on islands as shown. Each wind diagram is in horizontal divisions by month, with January at the top. The light-shaded area includes easterly winds and the dark area winds from other quarters (as shown in greater detail in Figure 36). In the northwestern region of the map, monsoonal westerlies allow sailing east in summer. In the southern reaches of the tropics from New Caledonia to Easter Island, there is a marked pattern of winter 'westerlies'. (From information in the Pacific Islands Pilot; reproduced by permission of the editor from Irwin 1989, Figure 11.)

Winter in the southern tropics is barely wintry, but it is the trade wind season, and conventional wisdom has it that this is not the time to sail east. However, in winter, the southern limit of the trade winds shifts north, and weather patterns outside the tropics have more influence on the south of tropical Polynesia, sometimes interrupt the trade winds and bring winds from other quarters. These anomalous winds have a different origin from the westerlies of the summer monsoon; they affect islands in the south of both Melanesia and Polynesia and offer opportunities for sailing east, on the southern fringes of the tropics, in more mild conditions than those found in higher latitudes farther south.

Records of wind observations made at sea, as in Figures 33 and 34, are of uneven quality and are sparse away from sealanes. They are complemented by data from land stations on many Pacific islands where weather records have been kept, sometimes over many years. Winds on islands are subject to local effects unlike those at sea, but, nevertheless, broad patterns can be discerned for the South Pacific Ocean. Figure 35 summarises wind direction for 24 island stations from Rabaul, PNG, to Easter Island, extracted from the Pacific Islands Pilot (vol.I 1970, vol.II 1969, vol.III 1982). Figure 36 is an enlarged version for Noumea, New Caledonia, and shows more explicitly how these should be interpreted. Each wind diagram is in horizontal divisions by month (January at the top) and three classes of wind are shown. In the centre is an unshaded area of calms. On the right is a light-shaded area, which sums the percentages of winds from northeast, east and southeast. The darker-shaded area on the left sums the percentages of winds from all other directions from north through west to south. The distinction is really between easterlies, calms and

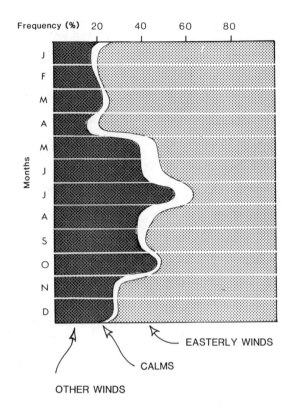

36. Wind patterns at Noumea, New Caledonia. The diagram is in divisions by month. The light-shaded area sums percentages of all winds from an easterly quarter. The dark area includes other winds from north, through west, to south. When an 'other' wind is blowing, it is possible to make progress to the east. During an easterly, a canoe can do little better than sail north or south.

'westerlies'. When a 'westerly' wind is blowing, a canoe can sail east. When there is an easterly, the best tight-reaching course takes it south or north rather than east.

Figure 35 actually shows wind patterns for the whole year. The summer monsoon is marked in the western Pacific especially in the Bismarck Archipelago and Solomon Islands, and, without doubt, summer was a good time to cross northern Melanesia. Summer westerlies are less common farther south in Melanesia, at Vila, Vanuatu and Laucala, Fiji, but they do extend across Rotuma, Tuvalu, Samoa and as far as Pukapuka in the Northern Cooks, with decreasing frequency, and they occur intermittently in Tahiti. East of the Northern Cooks, for more than 1000 sea miles in the north of central East Polynesia, the trade winds blow all year round and vary in direction only between northeast and southeast. However, in a band that extends right across the south from New Caledonia to Tonga, Rarotonga, the Austral Islands, Rapa, Gambier and Easter, there is a distinct pattern of winter 'westerlies'. In higher latitudes they are as common as easterlies. Notwithstanding the local effects of land station records, there is a means of sailing east during the trade wind season. Easter Island becomes a better prospect then, but the Marquesas remain just as difficult to approach from the west, and an approach from the south is still more feasible.

The origin of these winter winds can be seen in Figure 37, which has been adapted from Hessell (1981: Appendix 3B) and shows typical weather patterns in the South Pacific Ocean, where, below the tropics, there is a regular procession of rotating high and low pressure systems from west

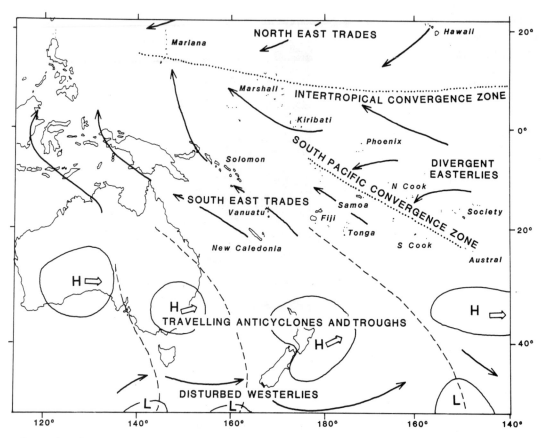

37. Subtropical weather systems are rotational and affect the southern tropics as they travel from west to east. In the southern hemisphere the circulation is anticlockwise around high pressure systems (anticyclones) and clockwise around lows. Troughs that extend north from low pressure systems bring predictable wind shifts as they pass through the southern tropics. Usually the wind will veer into the north and then back through west to south until the trade wind is re-established from the southeast. (Adapted from Hessell 1981, Appendix 3B.)

to east. Troughs associated with depressions at higher latitudes sometimes affect the southern region of the trade winds in winter from about 20° south of the Equator (*Pacific Pilot* vol. II 1969:16). Thompson (1986a:14) describes it without this latitudinal constraint:

> In any season, cold fronts move into the trade-wind region of the tropics. When cold fronts enter the trades they usually become slow-moving, lying across the region in a general west-north-west to east-south-east direction (Hutchings, 1961). Cold fronts may become quasi-stationary for several days, or even move southwards again as warm fronts, especially if a marked upper-air trough is approaching from the west. Most frontal systems eventually merge with the SPCZ [South Pacific Convergence Zone].

The point of interest is that in winter the SPCZ lies generally farther to the north than it does in summer, as shown in Figure 38, which is taken from Thompson (1986b: Figure 2), corresponding to the time when westerlies become more prominent (Thompson 1986b:22).

The possibility that these winds were implicated in colonisation was mentioned obliquely by Cook (Beaglehole 1967) and, in modern times, explicitly by Ferdon (1963). Recently they have assumed even more importance (Finney 1988; Finney *et al.* 1989; Irwin 1987, 1989).

Typically, with the approach of a front, the wind will veer to the north, and then, over the course of a few days, it will back through west and south and then settle in the southeast again. In the tropics this may be

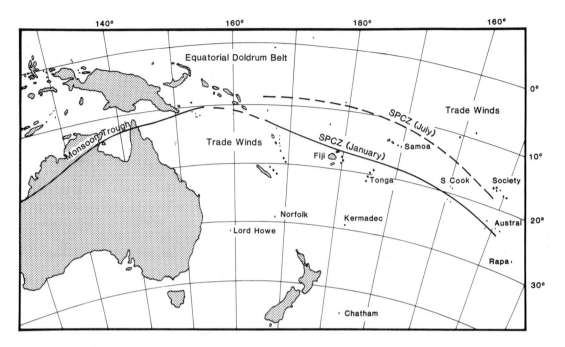

38. In the southern winter the SPCZ follows the sun on its journey north. At this time the effect of subtropical low pressure systems reaches deeper into the southern tropics and provides opportunities to sail east. The settlement of some islands, including the Pitcairn Group and Easter Island, seems barely feasible without the use of such conditions. (Adapted from Thompson 1986b, Figure 2.)

accompanied by cloud, rain, fresher winds and squalls (*Pacific Pilot* vol. II 1969:16), but conditions are not nearly as bad as they are farther south, closer to the centre of the associated low. When a front comes through, there are clear signs of its approach, the pattern of wind shifts is predictable and can be used strategically for passage-making. This is well-known weather in the South Pacific, and one would assume prehistoric voyagers used it just as small-boat sailors conventionally do today. The feasibility of sailing east in winter in a replica canoe has been shown by a voyage of the *Hokule'a* from Samoa to central East Polynesia (Finney *et al.* 1989). Wishing to avoid a passage in the cyclone season, the Hawaiian navigator, Nainoa Thompson, studied winter weather records and put the possibility to the test on passages from Samoa to the Southern Cooks and then to Tahiti, experiencing frontal systems on both sections.

The latitude of the southern tropics varies year by year and so does the extent to which southerly weather systems intrude into them. If one were considering the chance of picking up winter 'westerlies' over a given track, as, for example, between Tonga and Rarotonga, there would be considerable variation year by year, and this would create an artifical view of the probabilities. However, if the question was asked in a less specific way, and a sailor was prepared to 'feel' his way south, then these conditions could be found more predictably.

However, this is a very different matter to sailing clearly south of the tropics into the zone of prevailing westerlies, which has been proposed by several authors as a possible way explorers made easting without having to confront trade winds. But, as Sharp observed (1963:120), this 'involves a sophisticated knowledge of meteorology which would be difficult to account for'. One difficulty is knowing how far east to sail before returning to the trade wind belt. Unlike modern sailors who can measure longitude with instruments, prehistoric sailors could hardly have maintained a dead-reckoned track in the zone in which they sailed as well as a hypothetical one in another separate zone to the north. In addition, sailing in higher southern latitudes involves more bad weather, and there is no evidence for such voyages in early times.

Models for central East Polynesian settlement

A number of feasible early outward passages arise from this discussion:

1. A voyage from Samoa to the Southern Cooks could have occurred in the area of declining influence of the summer monsoon or with the help of the winter westerlies. There may be little to choose in terms of navigation between Samoa and Tonga as western starting points, but the Southern Cooks are a very likely first eastern landfall.
2. In central East Polynesia, the Australs and Mangareva are well placed for winter westerlies, but the island targets are dispersed. A voyage from the Cooks to the Society Islands sometimes reaching across the trade winds, followed by stepping-stone progress through the Tuamotus, may be more likely.
3. A southern route to the Marquesas via the Tuamotus appears to be the only serious choice (discounting El Niño), but this group is almost remote enough to belong with marginal East Polynesia rather than central.
4. Pitcairn lies at 25° S. and Easter Island (like Rapa) at 27° S., a latitude showing the strongest pattern of winter westerlies, and there seems no alternative to a southern route. Voyages towards Easter may have begun before crosswind ones towards Hawaii, but it is not easy to predict which was settled first, given that Hawaii presents a much larger target.

Discussion of the settlement of Hawaii, New Zealand and their neighbours, follows in the next chapter.

A general summary model for the colonisation of Remote Oceania, excluding Micronesia and the higher latitude islands, is shown in Figure 39, which was drawn according to two rules (Irwin 1989). The first is that people went most often in the safest direction and, in the figure, 60° arcs of exploration are aligned against the prevailing winds. The second rule is that there is learning in the model. As colonisation proceeded in space and time, the voyaging range increases from 500 sea miles in the west by 100 sea miles with each further stage. Shorter ranges in the west are accommodated by shorter inter-island distances there, while longer ranges are required for increasingly longer passages in the east; explorers had the opportunity and the need to develop their skills.

It can be seen that if people went the safe way, and paid attention to geography, they could colonise most of the Pacific islands, using an upwind strategy of search and return. However, this does not reach Hawaii or Micronesia across the wind or New Zealand outside the tropics, which require different strategies. But it does reach America.

Starting points for the voyages in the model are arbitrary but not unrealistic. In Melanesia and West Polynesia they are all known Lapita sites except for one in the central Solomons, which is a prediction. In the Northern Cooks, as described, Pukapuka has a date of the order of

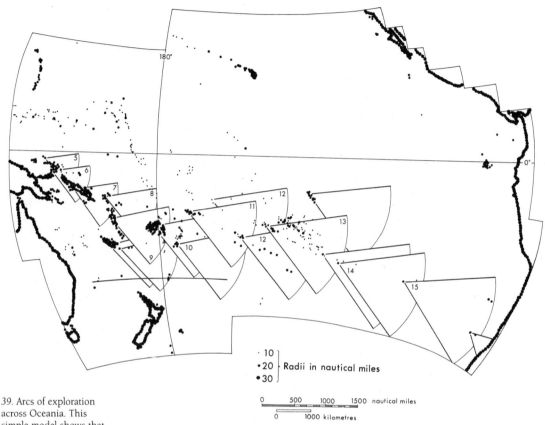

39. Arcs of exploration across Oceania. This simple model shows that searching in an upwind direction will settle most tropical islands of Melanesia and Polynesia and ultimately reach South America. The numbers in each arc refer to distance in nautical miles. The sequence of voyages allows learning in the model, while the extra ocean distances require it. However, Hawaii and New Zealand remain undiscovered by this method, and so, too, do intermediary islands, including Norfolk and the Kermadec Islands, to the north of New Zealand, and the Line Islands, south of Hawaii. (Reproduced by permission of the editor from Irwin 1989, Figure 12.)

A.D. 0 while the Southern Cooks, which were probably earlier, have only preliminary palynological research to hint at this. In the Society Islands, Raiatea has been chosen as a starting point because of its traditional credentials (Buck 1938), while the Marquesas have demonstrated early material. Mangareva, Pitcairn, Easter and the Juan Fernandez group are shown as suitable jumping-off points to the far east.

South America

A crucial point about navigation is that, if one searches upwind, to get home requires latitude sailing above all, and it is theoretically possible to lose track of one's dead-reckoned position and still get back. Therefore, upwind exploration had virtually no navigational limits; nor, within the tropical Pacific, did the double canoe. Its capacity to carry provisions was great, although water supplies may have been the most telling factor. Certainly the range of these canoes was demonstrated by the settlement of the three points of the Polynesian Triangle.

Contact with South America has been a puzzle in Pacific prehistory for a long time. Archaeological evidence seems to require that the sweet potato be carried from South America to East Polynesia in time to be transmitted to the margins before contact with them ceased, and probably even before then. Buck's (1938) view was that Polynesians fetched the sweet potato themselves, but Heyerdahl (1952) took the opposite view. Sharp (1963:128) thought that occasional one-way voyages came from America to Polynesia, and on one occasion brought 'cumar' (kumara). Finney (1979a, 1985) leaves the question open, seeing both one-way American raft trips and the two-way Polynesian canoe as possibilities. My own view is that the true context in which to see South America's role in Pacific prehistory is in relation to one or more large and fast Polynesian double-hulled sailing canoes, with great endurance and a crew essentially free to range east with little navigational constraint, but with geographic knowledge of what lay behind them. Or, less probably, there could have been an involuntary voyage by a canoe trapped, rather than assisted, by an episode of El Niño. Least likely is an accidental raft trip from America. The relative lack of genetic diversity of this plant in Polynesia (Yen 1974) may be taken as an index of the low frequency of contact with America.

Evidence of contact with both South America and Australia is indirect and slight. But a case can be made that not only did Oceanic people explore and settle the remote Pacific, they found the continental limits of their island world. America was hard to reach, whereas Australia was so easy it is inconceivable that this did not happen many times, accidentally or otherwise, and Pacific artifacts have been found on its northeastern coast, although their archeological context is unknown. South America could have been reached as the climax and perhaps the simultaneous anticlimax of the upwind thrust to the east.

In terms of the practicalities of such a voyage, Easter Island lies at the west of an area of high pressure that extends much of the way to the South American coast (Fig. 4). Winds in this system become variable, but there is a tendency for anticlockwise rotation to produce easterly winds across the top and westerlies across the bottom, allowing progress in both directions. Over the final few hundred miles from the American coast, at the latitude of Easter Island, the high produces prevailing southerly winds, which would involve a final cross-wind section in the passage to South America. In terms of a timetable for contact with America, the case is too particular to make any claim. However, I should not be surprised if it was some time after the settlement of Easter Island, because of the greater distance, and also after some experience of cross-wind passage-making and, therefore, perhaps at about the same time as the first discovery of Hawaii, or not long after.

The various conclusions of this discussion are examined by a computer simulation to be described in chapter 8.

6

THE COLONISATION OF HAWAII, NEW ZEALAND AND THEIR NEIGHBOURS

Long voyages were made at some risk, but evidently not successfully until there was sufficient experience, knowledge and skill. The logic of survival suggests that successful voyages across and down the wind were made after upwind ones and the radiocarbon dates apparently confirm this. Voyages beyond the tropics, especially those downwind in high latitudes, were made last of all. Islands both hard to reach and return from can be expected to have been settled late and to show the influence of remoteness in their subsequent histories.

SOME NAVIGATIONAL ISSUES IN LONG-DISTANCE EXPLORATION

It is important to be clear about the factors that made for delay. As Lewis explains (1972:223):

> Navigational accuracy is not a function of the length of voyage (if anything the longer passages providing the greater opportunity for random sea effects and judgement errors to cancel out). Thus if a 15° arc of accuracy, for example, can be attained over 300 miles, it is just as navigationally feasible over 1000. The special problems of the longer journey concern such factors as food supply, manpower, motivation, and the strength of the vessel – not navigation.

Lewis (1972:158) says of modern Micronesian voyaging that the longer voyages are regarded as tests of endurance rather than especially difficult navigational exercises, a point also made by Gladwin (1970:61). In fact,

Lewis says that the length of a voyage is regarded as less important than the size of the target-island screen. Making a landfall was the vital thing in exploration, even if this was only back at the point of departure. Thus, ease of return affected the order of long-distance settlement, and the elapsed time taken to settle various parts of the Pacific involved other variables, including accessibility of targets, the area of ocean to be searched, latitude and weather patterns, and development of suitable sailing strategies. The archaeological evidence implies these were all systematically related.

Sailing by reaching and running

The simplest case of a return voyage across a steady wind between two points requires averaging a direction of 90° or less to the wind over both legs. Since traditional canoes could make good a course of about 75° this does not appear to be a problem, but allowing for adverse wind shifts and currents, being becalmed in a current or caught in bad weather, in practice it is not so easy to maintain a course that requires keeping the wind on the beam or ahead of it. It is a fair inference that voyages across the wind became more sure when expanding geographical knowledge allowed a return to land downwind of the point of origin. In theory and practice, cross-wind voyages around a triangular course are easier than out and back between two points, because they need less on-the-wind work. As an extension of this reasoning, downwind voyages into the unknown involve the rather desperate risk of being unable to return over the same track in the event of not finding land, or else an intention to return by a different route through a more favourable weather system, or to a different place, or both. In other words, downwind exploration could be as much a matter of round-trips as direct return-trips, and to be successful would require a sophisticated knowledge of both navigation and geography. There has been a long and rather fruitless debate between one-way and two-way voyages, but it now seems that we have to allow for various kinds of 'three-way' voyages.

Return voyaging

In 1963 Andrew Sharp observed that:

> The idea of systematic exploration involves the presumption that explorers were prepared to go twice as far as any island they happened to find, and to do so many times without success, for an explorer cannot hope to find new land more than very occasionally, if at all. [Sharp 1963:17-18]

Sharp saw this issue very clearly, especially as it relates to more distant and difficult destinations, but because of his negative view of prehistoric navigation, he thought a theory of one-way voyages of simultaneous exploration and colonisation was more economic and realistic (1963:74). The tide of information and opinion has moved against many of Sharp's views, but his point that systematic exploration requires returns still deserves respect. We can expect many return voyages of non-discovery when people were probing the margins of Polynesia. The more difficult it became to find the remaining land, and the more empty ocean there was to traverse, the more they would become conventional.

Moreover, we should remember that return voyages could be made just as easily in the event of finding land or not. There are several reasons for thinking this happened. One relates to finding the position of new-found land. Interruptions to the trade winds useful for exploration are commonly accompanied by deteriorating weather and worse conditions for celestial navigation and dead-reckoning. South of the tropics the passage of cold fronts would make things even harder. On the other hand, return voyages in or near the tropics, instead of leaving during unsettled weather, could head off in steady conditions to intercept and run along the latitude of their starting island. Discoveries can certainly be made by one-way voyages, but their positions are known better when the track is covered again. To be fair to Sharp, when he said he did not believe that people returned, already 'having noted their courses on outward voyages to distant islands which they did not know existed' (1963:74) without instruments, he had half a point. The other half, which he did not see, was that the return could make the discovery more firmly than the outward voyage could.

This raises the question of the general structure of the two-way voyage. To Sharp (1963) and others, it contained these elements: (1) discovering a new island, (2) fixing its position, (3) returning home, (4) sailing again to the new island to demonstrate (mainly to modern prehistorians) the ability to find it again. In other words, the structure was A to B to A and then back to B again. However, a more likely sequence is actually: (1) discovering a new island, (2) establishing some estimate of its position, (3) returning home and securing the position of the new land. This structure is A to B to A, and any further outward leg was simply a matter of choice, not necessity. The structure of the 'three-way' voyage is from A-B-C-A, the essential point being it is normally not feasible to return directly from B to A. There are many variations: for example, in a voyage of exploration if C was already known, B need not be, but turning towards C was essential for survival. The final stage from C to A would be optional. Indirect voyages around known tracks were probably necessary as well.

Multiple settlement and tradition

One of the most compelling reasons for the view that the colonisation of islands involved multiple settlement (adding to others described already) is statistical (Law 1988). Briefly, he took the case of Hawaii, Easter Island and New Zealand and assessed the probability of all receiving a first voyage before any received a second or third voyage and showed that multiple settlement of one or two islands before all were reached was the likely solution, all other things being equal. However, given the varying difficulty of reaching different islands, we can be fairly confident of the multiple settlement of many, and a body of archaeological and linguistic evidence already points to examples.

These issues bring us close to oral traditions of Polynesian settlement, which have often been misused or maligned during more than a century of European scholarship. To quote Sharp (1963:15) once more:

> Over the past eighty years most people have imagined that the farther islands of Polynesia were discovered by prehistoric navigators who sailed back to their home islands and organized colonizing expeditions to their discoveries.

Although these 'people' often did describe return voyages in unrealistic terms and with unnecessary cultural associations, they are navigationally plausible. As mentioned already, if we are right to suppose that mounting a colonising expedition to the far reaches of Polynesia was a costly venture for a community, especially in the knowledge that the chance of finding land was slight, it might be simpler for explorers not colonists, to go first. In fact, most colonising voyages could have been to already-explored destinations. The point is conjectural and cannot be pushed too hard, but it strikes a chord with some oral traditions, and it would be of interest to see what insights a careful reanalysis of them might bring.

On the question of voyaging frequency, Davidson (1984:27) has said it is 'unlikely that long-distance voyages were ever common' but deep-sea sailing had to be done by each generation for it to pass on. Also, in the margins of Polynesia, there had to be enough exploration of largely empty ocean to find what habitable islands there were. The establishment of new colonies would have slowed earlier than the amount of voyaging as the number of undiscovered islands reduced.

NORTH TO HAWAII

A triangular Marquesas–Hawaii–Tahiti track is one long proposed in the literature. Rodman's theory (1927) called for determining latitude by measuring the altitude of Polaris with a 'sacred calabash', which held water to provide an artificial horizon and had a sighting aperture to check the angle of the star, but other aspects of his theory were more plausible. Makemson (1941) suggested the use of the star Aldebaran as a zenith star for Hawaii, but it has taken modern experiments to show precisely how zenith and other stars can actually be used for telling latitude. Akerblom (1968) followed Sharp (1963) in seeing voyages to Hawaii as one-way, with no control of longitude 'and probably none of latitude, either', but accepted that the prevailing winds were relatively favourable for voyages in both directions and that the islands formed blocks that could compensate for some error in longitude (Akerblom 1968:81). Levison, Ward and Webb (1973:53) concluded, from simulation, that people intended to go to Hawaii, and Lewis (1972:302) agreed, saying: 'it is in precisely this cross-wind direction that an explorer would choose to sail, so as to penetrate far into the unknown while, at the same time, being sure of a fair beam wind to speed his return.' Both Hawaii and the Societies/Tuamotus present substantial targets; Lewis thought the Tahiti–Hawaii leg not very difficult navigationally and that it might take three to four weeks to sail. As for a voyage from the Marquesas, Lewis thought that would have to be one-way, as they lie so far upwind, unless the return was made to Tahiti.

There is a world of difference between predicting and doing as shown by the building of the Polynesian replica canoe *Hokule'a*, and the assembling of the distinguished navigators who sailed her over the Hawaii–Tahiti track in 1976 (Finney 1977, 1979b, Finney *et al.* 1986), which she later re-crossed. Since then she has voyaged to New Zealand (Babayan *et al.* 1987), north to West Polynesia, and from there across to East Polynesia (Finney *et al.* 1989). These voyages were not intended to duplicate conditions of first discovery, but showed their feasibility and, together with experiments by Lewis (1972), Siers (1977) and others, shifted the issue of voyaging in Pacific canoes from the realm of theory to experience. They also provided remarkable insights into methods of navigation that could have been used by the first explorers and, in particular, measuring latitude, dead-reckoning, and the strategic use of predictable weather, which are crucial for understanding how explorers could have found islands and made their way home.

Hawaii, which straddles the Tropic of Cancer, presented diverse landforms and a 'graded set of opportunities for agricultural Polynesians' (Kirch 1985:32). There is some archaeological evidence for settlement as early as the fourth to the fifth centuries A.D. and by then there may have been such different sites as the rich Pu'u 'Ali'i (H1) fishing camp in an arid leeward region of South Point, Hawaii, with no permanent streams and low agricultural potential, but adjacent to deep-sea fishing grounds; and the Bellows Site (O18) in a fertile and well-watered area of windward O'ahu, with its evidence of dwellings, a pavement and an absence of typologically distinct Archaic artifact forms. Kirch (1986) suggests the Marquesas as a plausible source, but that sampling considerations could permit suitable early sites elsewhere in central East Polynesia.

The earliest known sites in Hawaii suggest it was settled with imported food crops, and the pig, dog and fowl; but the very earliest sites are probably still unknown. In fact it is possible that the first Polynesian discoverers of Hawaii did not carry these items on board, for reasons discussed already, but the first colonisers did so. However, it is not very likely that these two events, if they were different, could or will be distinguished archaeologically.

SOUTH TO NEW ZEALAND

Reaching New Zealand involved a more complex voyage across the trade winds, through a belt of variables to the latitude of prevailing westerlies. These weather systems shift south in summer, north again in winter, and in summer variables reach New Zealand. The settlement of New Zealand is often spoken of in the same breath as other islands of Polynesia, but, navigationally, it was very different. In the matter of age, this gives a good argument for New Zealand to be late, quite apart from the internal evidence, which currently says the same thing.

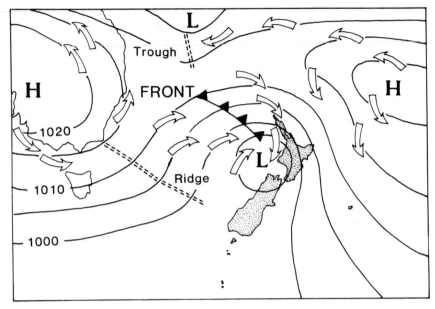

40. A typical weather pattern showing the easterly passage of high and low pressure systems through the latitudinal zones of variables and westerlies. New conditions were met on voyages to New Zealand, south of the tropics. There are a number of ways to reach New Zealand through these weather systems. (Reproduced by permission of the editor from Irwin 1989, Figure 13.)

Figure 40 shows detail of the belt of variables and westerlies south of the tropics where there is a regular passage of high and low pressure systems, from west to east, with ridges extending from highs, and troughs from lows and meridional fronts. The figure shows also that these wind systems are rotational – the lows clockwise and the highs anticlockwise (anticyclonic) – in the southern hemisphere.

With regard to sea-routes to New Zealand, there are a number of ways of sailing south. One method predicted by Heyen (1963:74) is to sail close to the rhumbline course using easterly tail winds blowing across the top of summer high pressure systems as shown in Figure 40. It is fairly well known among sailors in this part of the world that the best time to do this is in early summer, especially November, before the start of the cyclone season. *Hokule'a*, by good management and good luck, sailed to New Zealand in this way in November 1985 (Babayan *et al.* 1987). Yet at almost the same time the canoe *Hawaiki Nui* struck more difficult conditions on her voyage south from the Cook Islands. In November–December 1965, David Lewis made an experimental voyage to New Zealand, navigating the catamaran *Rehu Moana* without instruments, and he recorded 64 wind shifts in a month-long voyage to New Zealand through variables (Lewis 1972:3–5, 93). On a return passage from Australia in my yacht *Rhumbline* in November–December 1986, we experienced fairly steady easterly or northeasterly winds for 11 days in a row, which originated from a high pressure system to the east of us. While these were headwinds for us, they would have made for good sailing from Polynesia. The early summer high pressure system route to New Zealand is a good one, but it works best with foreknowledge, which the first explorers would not have had.

Another way of getting south is by the northerlies on the leading edge of an advancing front and behind a high, where the two systems rotate against one another and the pressure gradient can cause strong winds. This happens regularly throughout the year, sometimes as often as once a week, and seems quite a likely explanation from my own experience. We can imagine that, sooner or later, a canoe crossed the trades, into the variables and arrived at a suitable position at the right time to pick up freshening northerlies approximately 200 sea miles ahead of a typical front and then flew south before them, initially from choice and then perhaps even gale-driven for a day or a night as the front closed in. After the front passed through, the canoe would be well placed to make a landfall in clearing weather. The most likely place would be on the east coast of Northland. Alternatively, because there is a strong northeasterly component in the gales that cross the northern North Island, a canoe caught just north of New Zealand could be blown west of North Cape and, in the moderating westerlies behind the gale, make its landfall on the northwest coast. Landings south of East Cape or Cape Egmont would almost certainly be secondary ones from farther north, even though their impact might be the same.

To sail so far south where the weather is often bad seems very deliberate, but there are various sailing directions to New Zealand in the settlement traditions, including ones that specify the easiest period from the end of November to February (Best 1923:28–9; Smith 1921:216). However, these may have been affected by a century of sailing by European ships. While Sharp (1963:116) reports flotsam from the Pacific on Ninety Mile Beach in the far north, he found no reports of historic drifts either to or from New Zealand, which is a measure of its isolation in prehistory. Why the first canoes came this way is a matter of conjecture, but it is quite possible, as Lewis says (1972:171–2), that migrating birds had been noticed, again as mentioned in traditions. The long-tailed cuckoo comes from tropical Polynesia to New Zealand in September, and shearwaters fly south in October. The golden plover goes from Tahiti northward. People could infer that land lay in a particular direction, although at an unknown distance.

In the wider context of Polynesia, Hawaii provides a maximum age for New Zealand because Hawaii is the easier voyage. To reach it from central East Polynesia meant sailing north out of the southeast trades, through the doldrums and then on across the northeast trades, whereas to reach New Zealand involved a more complex voyage south of the trades to the variables and westerlies. The big island of Hawaii straddles 20° N. Latitude, whereas Easter Island and Rapa, at contact the southernmost settled islands at the fringes of the tropics, are 27° S. – or more than 400 nautical miles farther from the equator than Hawaii is. The northern tip of New Zealand at approximately 34° S. is still another 400 sea miles south of the closest inhabited land. If Hawaii was settled around A.D. 300–400, New Zealand, so much farther from the equator, might well have been substantially later.

High latitude appears to correlate with late settlement, and the Chatham Islands provide a minimum age for New Zealand, lying 550 sea miles below the latitude of North Cape in a dangerous downwind direction from New Zealand, the closest land and most likely source. So far, there are no archaeologically controlled dates for the Chatham Islands older than

A.D. 1500. Navigational and geographical factors suggest that the first settlement of New Zealand should fall somewhere in the interval between the settlement of Hawaii and the Chatham Islands. Orthodox opinion places that event rather neatly, in terms of this argument, some 1000 years ago.

The issue of back-dating the settlement of East Polynesia (Irwin 1981; Kirch 1986) has been invoked for New Zealand recently by Sutton (1987a), who postulates a date of A.D. 0–500, but while the gap in the evidence between West and East Polynesia has closed a little, the same is not demonstrated for New Zealand, and the arguments that suggested East Polynesia should be earlier than previously thought do not in turn necessarily make New Zealand earlier.

Sutton (1987b:24-5) raises the question of whether New Zealand was settled prior to the development of the Marquesan 'Archaic' as defined by Kirch (1986), but suggests that a pre-Archaic artifact horizon comparable to that attributed to Hawaii would not be found in New Zealand if its origins were more complex and involved a greater number of island groups. In other words, artifacts could not settle the question. However, much of Sutton's argument for early settlement rests not on archaeological evidence, but on his (1987a) reinterpretion of palynological and geomorphological evidence; but it has not found support from specialists in those fields. In a review of the case, Enright and Osborne conclude: 'We do not dispute that Polynesian arrival in New Zealand may substantially predate the oldest known archaeological sites. However, we cannot accept a much earlier date for settlement based on the palynological and geomorphological evidence provided by Sutton (1987)' (Enright and Osborne 1988:144).

One piece of palynological evidence that has been taken to support a date for human impact on the environment in the Bay of Islands by A.D. 600, comes from a study by Chester (1986) of two pollen cores from the Waitangi Forest. However, this date was established only by extrapolation from sedimentation rates in the core below a volcanic ash identified as Kaharoa Ash, while the date that was taken for this ash was 930 ± 70 years ago, derived from an early and incorrect radiocarbon date (NZ10) from a different site. 'Most workers now use an age . . . of 650-670 B.P. based on a number of more recent radiocarbon determinations' (Enright and Osborne 1988:141).

Rather less secure than the age of New Zealand's settlement is the origin of its founder population in Polynesia. The Society Islands have been considered a possible source because of the material recovered from the Vaito'otia-Fa'ahia site on Huahine and the Maupiti burial site, which has striking similarities (and some differences) to New Zealand sites such as Wairau Bar. The late first millennium A.D. dates from the Society Islands sites fit as well. However, Davidson points out other possible sources, which are archaeologically less well known (1984:94-6). Walter (1988) reports that recent excavations in the Southern Cook Islands support their role as a possible source of New Zealand settlement. During the A.D. 800-1200 period, there were a number of village-sized communities in the group; some were engaged in offshore comunication and trade and he notes their proximity to New Zealand.

Comparative ethnology and language have always invoked close links between the Southern Cooks and New Zealand (Walter 1988), and there may be a biological link with respect to DNA (Hill and Serjeantson 1989). However, a recent review of other biological affinities of New Zealand Maori does not point in the same direction. From an examination of several traits, Katayama (1988) concludes that there is little to support an especially close biological relationship between Maori and Southern Cook Islanders as has been suggested in the past by various authors. In so far as Mangaians are representative of the Southern Cooks, they are more similar, at present, to West Polynesians than to Maori, who, for their part, more often lie closer to other East Polynesians in the data. So, while a specific origin for New Zealand Maori culture is problematic, a general East Polynesian one is indicated by the evidence. This is in spite of the fact that New Zealand lies closer geographically to islands in Melanesia, Fiji and West Polynesia, than to the nearest part of East Polynesia. It is also much closer to the source of Lapita than any other part of East Polynesia. Were it not for cultural and navigational considerations, this would be a real anomaly.

Early New Zealand settlement

Colonists brought plants and animals from the tropics to a relatively huge, temperate archipelago, mainly covered in forest and with abundant animal populations quite without experience of human predation. On land there were many species of *moa* – flightless birds ranging from perhaps 20 to 250 kg – and other birds that went extinct, while sea mammals, particularly seals, were abundant on the coast, as were fish and shellfish. Especially in the south, East Polynesians arrived in 'a land for hunting, fishing and gathering, more or less in that order' (Anderson 1982:49). Gardening cannot have been so difficult that it was not successfully started by at least one group of immigrants in their very first season, perhaps in a suitable microclimate in the North Island. More species of domesticates arrived than survived in New Zealand, because the absences are those that could not have lasted, especially the coconut, breadfruit and banana, while, among the animals, the absence of the pig and fowl is scarcely surprising in a land that had plenty of fish and amazing wildfowl.

Caughley (1988) contrasts a popular model of fairly rapid coastal settlement, exploration and interaction proposed by Green (1975:609), Bellwood (1978:386) and Davidson (1984:223), with a model closer to one suggested by Trotter and McCulloch (1984) of a 'patterned spread' or 'rolling wave' (Caughley 1988:252, 259) of colonisation that spread both north and south from the northeastern South Island, coinciding with a brief peak in local exploitation of *moa* and accelerating as it was driven by rising human population. The argument has various problems (Anderson and McGovern-Wilson 1990), one being that it has nothing to say for the North Island, which lies much nearer the source of colonists from Polynesia.

New Zealand is such a large archipelago it would have been hit again and again, almost as if for the first time, as maritime settlers shifted on the coast, and this model has appeal for the North Island, where the evidence is too sketchy to exclude it. The associated archaeological sites should be found near to where a canoe could be beached in shelter and with good access to a range of resources.

Given the general case that has been made for return voyaging and multiple settlement, we can conceive of one or more colonising groups operating in the early years of settlement and very possibly supplemented by a few others in the first few centuries. At some quite early stage, their activities would become archaeologically visible, and sites showing the movement of distinctive industrial stone could signal their presence much as pottery does more conspicuously in other parts of Oceania. At present, archaeological evidence does not sustain the idea of a long pre-visibility tail to the prehistoric population curve and, in particular, the striking evidence of bird extinctions is itself an implicit argument against a 'pre-Archaic' New Zealand.

It is a nonsense to regard New Zealand as being settled by one event, and there is the possibility of a few last 'Hawaikis' on the New Zealand coast to which people returned in an early period of exploration and settlement. This could include places able to keep alive the climatically fragile introduced tropical food plants that were lost or not taken on forays elsewhere, and particularly to the cooler south. Many possibilities come to mind and these include the larger northern offshore islands. Great Mercury, for instance, has a mild climate (Edson 1973), an all-weather harbour offshore from the exposed beaches of Kuaotunu, a major focus of early settlement and an important stone source. There is abundant secondarily processed Tahanga basalt to suggest Great Mercury's role in the interaction system of an early time.

If the conventional settlement model turns out to be wrong, New Zealand could have been settled as early as Lapita. However, it appears that those seaborne explorers had reasons of their own not to search in this direction.

A return voyage to East Polynesia

A voyage to East Polynesia from New Zealand might have been a rather more difficult proposition than the outward one (Lewis 1972:305-6). Variables and westerlies could carry a canoe north some way, but then to make easting on a long voyage against the trade winds would be as hard as it usually was to sail that way. One consequence is that voyages from New Zealand could be expected to reach islands to the north, especially the Kermadec Islands and even Norfolk Island which, while small, are high and close to New Zealand, while north of them again lie islands of Melanesia or West Polynesia. Heyen (1963) suggested that canoes going from New Zealand to Tahiti could sail east at the latitude of the westerlies and then turn north. However, as discussed, this would raise the difficult problem of knowing when to turn.

The cultural divergence of New Zealand from its East Polynesian relatives makes sense, given its distance and the quite difficult return.

THE KERMADEC, NORFOLK, CHATHAM AND LINE ISLANDS

With the exception of the Chatham Islands, these islands were among the 'mystery' islands of Polynesia, having been reached in prehistory, but abandoned by historic times (Bellwood 1978). They contribute to the case made for Hawaii and New Zealand's settlement because they stand to intercept traffic on its way in and out. Norfolk is 400 nautical miles northwest of New Zealand approximately half-way to New Caledonia, the nearest major island and also the closest part of Melanesia. The Kermadec Islands are centred some 500 nautical miles to the northeast, half-way to Tonga, the nearest part of tropical Polynesia. The Chatham Islands lie some 350 sea miles southeast of the southern North Island of New Zealand, but at the latitude of the central South Island. The Line Islands are spread, in clusters, between central East Polynesia and Hawaii and several have evidence of interest.

Navigational predictions

The Kermadec Islands and Norfolk Island

Norfolk Island is closer to New Caledonia than any part of Island Melanesia is to Fiji. The Kermadec Islands are closer to Tonga than Tonga is to East Polynesia. Both Norfolk and the Kermadecs, while fairly small targets, are high and often easily seen from the sea. If the colonisation of the Pacific was undirected, they were within easy range of Lapita or early post-Lapita settlement.

However, in terms of my general voyaging argument, these islands would not have been settled until crosswind voyages were made from East Polynesia into sub-tropical latitudes. Norfolk Island and the Kermadec Islands are still well north of New Zealand, but, because they present much smaller targets, would not necessarily have been settled first, and could have been reached almost as easily on a navigated voyage from New Zealand as from anywhere else. Of all the islands to the north, the Kermadecs and Norfolk are the ones easiest to reach from New Zealand; for instance, the Kermadecs are less than half-way to the Southern Cooks, the closest part of East Polynesia, and it has been noted already that canoes returning north from New Zealand could have found it difficult to sail east in settled trade wind weather and could easily have found themselves west enough to find these islands. One would expect then, that the Kermadecs and Norfolk should have been settled at much the same time as New Zealand, or not long after, and that they could show signs of multiple contacts, from New Zealand and from elsewhere in East Polynesia. We might expect the Kermadecs, too, from their more easterly position to have been the more likely stepping-stone to or from Polynesia, if one existed, than Norfolk, which lies more isolated in the west. Further, because we know that New

Zealand was effectively cut off from the rest of Polynesia by European times, and that both Norfolk and the Kermadecs had no human inhabitants then, one would expect archaeological evidence of contact with these small islands to be earlier rather than later in their prehistories, in the increasing isolation of this part of the Pacific.

A model for the Chatham Islands

The Chatham Islands are a different case. At more than 43°S. they mark open-ocean voyages at the highest-known latitude sailed by Polynesians, made in the westerly wind belt and exposed to regular bad weather of frontal low pressure systems. It is not difficult to suffer from exposure while ocean sailing in much gentler latitudes than this, and it does not require particularly bad weather to make conditions very wet, cold and unpleasant. Even allowing the possibility of past variations in weather systems, it is difficult to conceive of conditions being much different. In terms of my argument, this voyage should have been the last successful voyage of discovery in Polynesia. It was more difficult than reaching South America and very much more difficult than getting to Australia.

Because few sailors could, or willingly would, push into westerly headwinds at high latitudes (although Captain Bligh tried to unsuccessfully on his way to the mutiny on the *Bounty*), New Zealand is the only obvious origin for Chatham Islanders. The probabilities are that a number of voyages left New Zealand for one or more to have hit land. On the other hand, from a sailing point of view, it is unlikely that many navigated voyages ever returned to New Zealand from the Chathams, unless it was by a reach across the southwesterlies to the North Island. In fact the tropics may have been more accessible than New Zealand, and any canoe that missed the Chatham Islands and sailed very far past them would have to head north to survive.

The Line Islands

The Central and Northern Line groups, in particular, are to Hawaiian settlement what Norfolk and the Kermadecs are to New Zealand. In terms of expected settlement dates, Hawaii is a large target, which stands at a great distance, whereas the Lines are small low targets at various shorter distances. So, again, there is really little to choose between the two in time. The Lines lie generally to leeward of the optimal track to and from Hawaii. One or more of them could have been encountered on a search directed west of the track needed to reach Hawaii or, quite possibly, they could have been found when a canoe on its way to or from Hawaii was unable to hold to the optimal windwind track.

'Mystery islands'

The final element in this predictive case, is to consider what might happen to the settlers of these various small, isolated intermediary islands, and similar ones elsewhere, when the frequency of voyaging fell away, as it evidently did, in much of the remote Pacific (Irwin 1980), reducing the chance of outside contact and reinforcement. The Line Islands are scattered and isolated, often small, flat coral islands or atolls, which did not offer much to settlers. Moving south from the Equator, the high islands of Rapa and Easter Island at 27° S. were occupied at contact, but smaller Pitcairn at 25° S. was not. Norfolk and the Kermadecs were evidently unable to remain settled at 29° S. New Zealand was easily large enough to sustain its population at a still higher latitude, especially in the agricultural north, but the Chathams were in a more difficult adaptive situation. While large by the standards of many inhabited tropical islands, and with abundant marine resources, they lay too far south for agriculture. The mystery islands are included in a study of accessibility in chapter 9.

Archaeological evidence

The Kermadec Islands and Norfolk Island

The archaeological evidence from the Kermadecs and Norfolk, although sparse and patchy, does not contradict the voyaging argument and could not be expected to appear to conform so well by chance. A summary of the evidence from the Kermadecs is provided by Anderson (1980). Raoul, the largest island, is the only one on which he would expect prehistoric occupation; it is forested and generally 'precipitous and ravined' (Anderson 1980:131). The Low Flat site, at a beach facing north, is quite extensive, and in one area has two levels dated to approximately A.D. 920 and A.D. 1330 respectively. There is evidence for the dog and the Polynesian rat (*Rattus exulans*), but not the pig or fowl, which is the same pattern as for New Zealand. Anderson concludes that Raoul was occupied by people from central East Polynesia at the end of the first millennium A.D., that it is hard to tell whether occupation was continuous after that, but the radiocarbon dates and styles of adze types and a bone pendant all sugggest two periods of occupation with the later one also originating from central East Polynesia or from New Zealand. Anderson notes the canoe *Aotea*, of New Zealand fame, arrived at the Kermadecs in legend, and also the correspondence of the dates with 'major events in prevailing versions of Maori settlement legends', which invite speculation:

> but all that can be safely asserted is that the archaeological evidence comfortably provides a cultural stepping stone between early east Polynesia and New Zealand, without prejudice as to which way, or how often, it might have been used. [Anderson 1980:140]

This conclusion fits voyaging expectations neatly. Of the same evidence, Davidson (1984:24) remarks that the Low Flat site may be too young to be associated with the initial colonisation of New Zealand. If she means that Low Flat was not a staging post in the first voyage to New Zealand, she is probably right. However, there is little to suggest that New Zealand settlement is very much older and, if exploration was conventionally two-way over some elapsed time, the Kermadecs fit comfortably into that picture.

Specht (1984) reviewed the miscellaneous information on Norfolk Island prehistory, although, as yet, there has been no excavation of *in situ* archaeological deposits. One group of adzes found at Slaughter Bay suggests an East Polynesian origin. Another group of Duff Type 2B (Duff 1956), a common New Zealand form, but not one generally associated with early prehistory, was found in other parts of Norfolk, and made of a kind of stone, which could be, but may not be, from the South Island of New Zealand. Groves of bananas found growing by Captain King in 1788 were evidently not planted by Captain Cook, who rediscovered Norfolk in 1774 some time after Polynesians abandoned it. Specht's conclusion is that a likely initial East Polynesian source of settlers could have been the Cook Islands, Society Islands or New Zealand in the period A.D. 1000–1400, and New Zealand a second possible source after *c.* A.D. 1400. These dates are obviously rough estimates, but find some support in evidence of the age of the imported Polynesian rat (Meredith *et al.* 1985), which is widely regarded as a commensal of humans and was distributed throughout the Pacific by voyaging canoes. In Unit C4 of a test excavation at Cemetery Beach, four radiocarbon dates cluster around A.D. 1050–1150, overlying bones of *Rattus exulans* and providing a minimum age for them, while, in the upper part of the same unit, evidence of extensive burning is possibly the result of forest clearance by humans. With respect to origins, Specht (1984) refers to some of Levison, Ward and Webb's previously unpublished data, which showed 65 landings on Norfolk from more than 8000 simulated drift voyages, 22 coming from New Zealand, 41 from the Kermadec Islands and two from Rapa. This information sits well enough with the archaeological conclusions, and confirms what has been said about conditions for voyaging in the general area, but the likelihood that the actual voyages were by drift is low, which is a conclusion Levison, Ward and Webb (1973) subscribe to themselves.

It is interesting to note the parallel structure of the tentative prehistories of the Kermadecs and Norfolk, which include initial settlement perhaps a thousand years ago, and in the same general time range as New Zealand, multiple settlement from East Polynesia over some centuries in which New Zealand plays some part and, finally, abandonment or extinction at some time in the last 400–500 years.

The Chatham Islands

The situation for the Chatham Islands is more contentious. Sutton argues that one-way drift voyages were the most likely form of first settlement (1980:70; 1982:167). While possible, it is inconsistent with the arguments regarding order of settlement, etc., presented here. He estimates the time of initial settlement between A.D. 1000–1200 (1980:87) or A.D. 800–1000 (1982:167) and suggests there were no further arrivals after A.D. 1400 (1982:167). However, both he (1980:74) and Davidson (1984:24) note that no excavated sites of this early period exist. McFadgen, on the other hand, from a study of coastal geomorphology, believes the Chathams were still unoccupied 500 years ago (pers. comm. 1988) and first settled after then. The voyaging situation favours some elapsed time between the first settlement of New Zealand and the Chatham Islands and, whatever the position, as yet there are no published radiocarbon dates from controlled archaeological excavations older than the sixteenth century A.D.

Biggs' suggestion that the Moriori language was most similar to South Island or eastern North Island dialects of Maori is confirmed by Clark (1988). Chatham artifact collections from sites at Owenga, Kaingaroa and Pitt Island are said to duplicate ornament forms found at Wairau Bar in

New Zealand, which is dated to approximately A.D. 1300 on collagen (Caughley 1988) as well as adze forms shared with early New Zealand (Sutton 1980:74). This material supports a New Zealand origin, but does not supply a precise timetable for its arrival, because such items are not closely dated in New Zealand. The Chathams material inventory includes items that are not regarded as particularly early. The only human-introduced animal was the Polynesian rat, and, unlike New Zealand, dog bone has not been found. However, like New Zealand, the pig and fowl are unknown. The pattern of evidence is consistent with the suggestion that the Chathams were settled after New Zealand, and probably from New Zealand on one or more occasions; my estimate is after approximately A.D.1300. A hunting and gathering technology developed in the Chatham Islands based especially on abundant marine resources, but without the capacity for intensification (Sutton 1980:83, 87) in this marginal habitat for isolated Polynesians. There is no archaeological evidence in New Zealand for a return voyage from the Chathams, and Davidson reports that Maori and Moriori apparently did not know of one another's existence at the time of European contact (Davidson 1984:24).

New Zealand obsidian in the Kermadecs and Chathams

A recent paper by Leach *et al.* (1986) examines in detail the origins of prehistoric obsidian artifacts from the Kermadec and Chatham islands. In spite of difficulties of analysis and interpretation, the authors attribute the probable sources as follows: six of 11 Kermadec samples to Mayor Island (New Zealand) and the rest to Raoul Island (Kermadecs); 77 of a total of 81 Chatham samples to Mayor Island (New Zealand), one to the central North Island of New Zealand, another to Awana (New Zealand) while the remaining two are designated as 'cf. Rapanui' which means that they are most similar to an Easter Island source, although not necessarily from it (Leach *et al.* 1986). Thus the New Zealand connection with the prehistories of the Kermadecs and Chathams is confirmed, and the suggestion is also made that this was prior to A.D. 1400, although for the Chathams that point would be contested by McFadgen.

The authors then proceed to discuss the nature of that contact and leave as an open question whether contact between these islands was by one-way accident or two-way navigation (Leach *et al.* 1986). However, if it was not by navigation, there is no reason why these islands should not have been settled in any order or at any time in the 3000 years since the colonisation of Remote Oceania began. The archaeological situation is too systematic to allow that. The authors also examine the detail of some simulated drift contact probabilities, but these actually provide no good reason why any one of the Kermadecs, Chathams or New Zealand should have been settled at all by drift, let alone all three.

The structured pattern of archaeological evidence from the islands of the southwest Pacific, at the edge of the tropics and farther south, provides another coherent case of the systematic character of Oceanic colonisation.

The Line Islands

Fanning Island, lying approximately half-way between central East Polynesia and Hawaii in the North Pacific Ocean, provides another independent example, although the only one from this region. Archaeological investigation of Site FAN 1-7 gave a corrected radiocarbon age of 1560 ± 85 years ago, in association with artifacts, including one-piece fishhooks, trolling gear and porpoise tooth pendants (A. Sinoto 1973) that compare closely to early Hawaiian examples of much the same age.

Summary

Evidently the systematic colonisation of the remote Pacific extended to the large islands at the margins of Polynesia. Their small, abandoned satellites provide a secondary level of archaeological corroboration. Further, the fact that the large islands were still occupied at Western contact, but effectively marooned by then, implies other structured similarities in this aspect of their subsequent histories.

7

ISSUES IN THE COLONISATION OF MICRONESIA

Micronesia forms a nearly continuous chain of island groups north of Melanesia and extending east to Polynesia. Of these three conventional regions of Oceania, Micronesia's early prehistory is largely unknown, and its role in Pacific colonisation most problematical. This chapter reviews the prevailing view of Micronesian settlement, considers some practicalities of navigation, and revises some of the issues.

Craib (1983:922) describes Micronesia as comprising nearly 3000 islands with a total land area of 2700 square kilometres spread over 7.4 million square kilometres of ocean. Although there are some high islands, it is coral atolls that typify the area. 'Most of these small islands . . . are uninhabited or uninhabitable' (Terrell 1986:180), yet many have supported human settlement for 2000 years. Standing little more than a few metres in elevation above sea-level within the cyclone belt of the North Pacific Ocean, these atolls are one of the most tenuous successfully occupied habitats on Earth.

The westernmost high island group of Micronesia is Belau, which lies a little less than 500 sea miles east of Mindanao in the Philippines and the same distance north of the Vogel Kop Peninsula of western New Guinea (Fig. 15). From there, north towards Belau, lie half a dozen little islands, which may have formed a dispersed string of stepping-stones at times in the past. Some 230 sea miles northeast of Belau lies the high island of Yap, and another 450 sea miles beyond is Guam, the southernmost of the high islands of the Marianas, which sweep in a 400-mile curve to the north. The Caroline Islands stretch most of the 2000 sea miles east from Belau and Yap to the Marshall Islands, and apart from the high volcanic islands of Truk, Pohnpei and Kosrae, the Carolines are all atolls. South of the Carolines towards Island Melanesia, in considerable isolation, lie the Polynesian Outlier atolls of Nukuoro and Kapingamarangi. The Marshalls, Kiribati and Tuvalu form three substantial links in a scarcely broken chain of island groups – all atolls – which trend south and slightly east, to end 350 sea miles north of Fiji, and much closer than that to the intervening high island of Rotuma. Tuvalu is Polynesian, but its geographic continuity with Micronesia suggests other possibilities in the early years of settlement. The isolated islands of Nauru and Banaba (Ocean Island) stand 150 sea miles apart, approximately 250 sea miles west of Kiribati.

Theories of Micronesian settlement

In earlier theories of the settlement of the Pacific the role of Micronesia was more central than now. Buck (1938) suggested that ancestral Polynesians travelled through Micronesia rather than Melanesia, and, more recently, Howells (1973:252–63) entertained a similar theory on the basis of information available to him at the time. However, in the last 20 years, the identification of Lapita with ancestral Polynesians and the discovery of a string of sites from the Bismarck Archipelago through eastern Melanesia to Fiji and West Polynesia has put the Melanesian route firmly on the map. As for the question of Melanesia as a suitable source for Polynesians, biologically, there is a range of views as discussed in chapter 3. Howells (1979:272) sees Polynesians and Micronesians as somewhat different, but both of Southeast Asian descent. Houghton (in press) suggests both Polynesians and Micronesians came out of Melanesia, in spite of the linguistic difficulties this presents, but Hill and Serjeantson (1989) find clear genetic differences between them. The issue may turn finally on study of skeletal remains, where these are forthcoming. However, on the basis of archaeological evidence alone, while acknowledging Melanesia as a primary colonisation route to the eastern Pacific, it would be premature to relegate Micronesia to the role of an unimportant cul-de-sac.

The current theory of Micronesian colonisation, which rests mainly on linguistics, proposes a twofold entry from both east and west (Bellwood 1978:282). The languages of the Marianas and Belau are of Western Austronesian type and, while not closely related to one another, are most similar to languages of Island Southeast Asia. Yapese and Nauruan appear to be linguistic isolates, while the rest are grouped as Nuclear Micronesian – a sub-group of Eastern Austronesian (Oceanic) – and are related most closely to the southeast Solomons and northern Vanuatu. The implication is that the western high islands were settled from Indonesia or the Philippines, while eastern Micronesia was settled from eastern Melanesia. Separate languages are known within Nuclear Micronesian, but their precise relationships are unclear (Marck 1975:44).

Recently, Blust has made the 'informed speculation' (1988:54) that:

> by perhaps 200 BC . . . AN speakers from the Southeast Solomons settled Kiribati . . . From Kiribati the rest of Micronesia, apart from Palau, Yap, and the Marianas, was settled by a gradual south-to-north and east-to-west movement into the Marshalls, Kusaie [Kosrae], Ponape, and the Carolines (probably in that order), as far as the island of Mapia, some 200 miles north of the Vogelkop Peninsular of Irian. [Blust 1988:58]

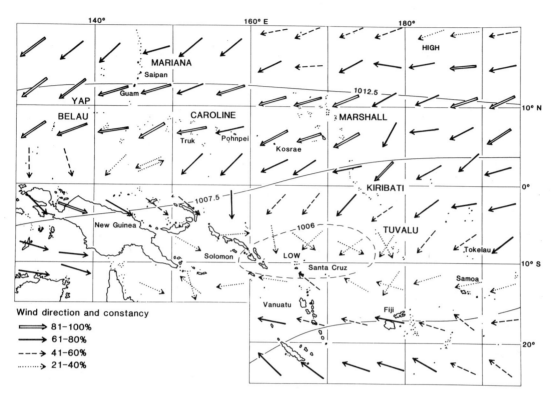

41. The direction and constancy of prevailing winds in Micronesia and Melanesia in January. The northern hemisphere winter is the season of northeasterly trade winds in Micronesia. (Adapted from the *Pacific Islands Pilot.*)

Lastly, according to the model, the Outliers of Nukuoro and Kapingamarangi were reached by Polynesian speakers.

The settlement of Western Micronesia from Island Southeast Asia conforms well enough to general navigational arguments, because, like the separate spread of Lapita, it involved upwind exploration. There is also some support to be found in historical sources.

> Not a few of the canoes that were storm-drifted to the Philippines from the Yap region . . . made successful return voyages. As late as 1910 the *Deutsches Kolonialblatt* . . . wrote of canoes being cast away to the Philippines from the Carolines and returning. There were old people who had 'been five times to the Philippines and made their own way back home, against the prevailing east wind, despite strict German regulations to the contrary'.
>
> It might be supposed that such recent return voyages owed their success to European geographical knowledge were it not for the fact that similar episodes were recorded by Spanish missionaries in the Philippines at a time when the Carolines were virtually a closed book to Westerners. [Lewis 1972:286]

Voyages against the prevailing wind in the trade wind season of the northern tropics would be relatively safe, but difficult (Fig. 41). However, in the northern summer, southeasterly and variable winds would offer some downwind voyages from eastern Indonesia or broad-reaching from the Philippines (Fig. 42). In other words, better winds for the outward passage, but the possibility of a more dangerous outcome if land was not found.

According to theory, in the east of Micronesia, crosswind voyages carried the first colonists across the trade winds from the southeast Solomon Islands or northern Vanuatu. Marck (1975:70–1) suggested that wind patterns would

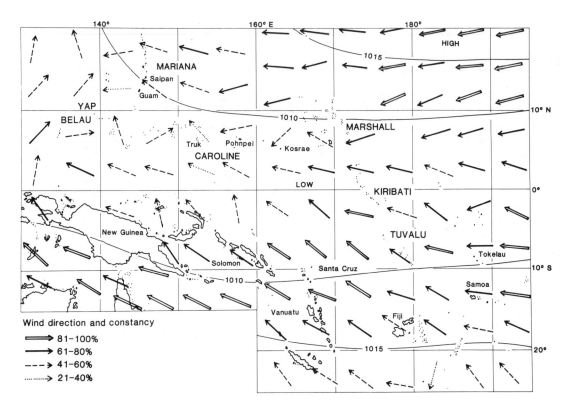

Wind direction and constancy

⟹ 81–100%
⟶ 61–80%
- - -> 41–60%
········> 21–40%

42. The direction and constancy of prevailing winds in Micronesia and Melanesia in July. In the northern hemisphere summer, southeasterly and variable winds offer better conditions for reaching western Micronesia from Island Southeast Asia than in the trade wind season. However, if land was not found, the return could be more difficult. (Adapted from the *Pacific Islands Pilot*.)

point to the Nauru/Kiribati/Marshalls area as the site of initial arrival and would allow a return crosswind voyage. Settlement in the east was followed by expansion west through the Caroline Islands.

In the next chapter a new computer simulation of Pacific colonisation is described in detail, but a small number of experimental voyages are of use to the argument here. Table 1(A) shows a number of simulated exploring canoes sent out over a range of courses from suitable points in the Solomon Islands. Table 1(B) shows comparable fleets sent out from the Reef Islands, which represent a number of possible origins in the vicinity of northern Vanuatu/Santa Cruz. It is sufficient to say here that the canoes are using realistic navigational skills (Strategy Four, as described below). They are sailing in July, which is the best month for eastern Micronesia; they make return voyages, which is the best method, because it allows a canoe a second pass through the target area, as well as greatly increasing the chances of survival. Here the canoes are allowed 18 days each way at an average speed of four knots in their search into the northeast.

The number of canoes is small, but a pattern can be seen in the results. Depending on the course steered, island groups in eastern Micronesia are shown to be accessible, with a high degree of success. Canoes that do not find new islands generally get home, so the enterprise is safe. Various hypotheses of origin receive support. Figure 43 shows the detail of one experimental fleet of 10 canoes sailing from the Solomon Islands at 50° (True). They tack as they meet head winds and resume course as they can. Six canoes reach five islands of the Marshall Islands, one reaches Kiribati. Single landfalls are made on both small, high islands of

Table 1 *Simulated voyages to eastern Micronesia*

1A Voyages from the Solomon Islands

Start	Course	Caroline	Marshall	Nauru	Banaba	Kiribati	Tuvalu	Melanesia	Return	Lost	Total
Buka	0°	8								2	10
Choiseul	10°	8								2	10
Malaita	20°	2	5						3		10
	30°	1	9								10
	40°		9						1		10
	50°		6	1	1	1			1		10
San	60°			1	1	5			3		10
Christobal	70°			1	1	6		1	1		10

1B Voyages from Reef/Santa Cruz Islands

Start	Course	Caroline	Marshall	Nauru	Banaba	Kiribati	Tuvalu	Melanesia	Return	Lost	Total
Reefs	350°	9	2						8	1	20
	0°		9	10						1	20
	10°		15	1	1					3	20
	20°		5	2	6	4			3		20
	30°		8		1	7			4		20
	40°		1	1	1	13	1		3		20
	50°					16			4		20
	60°					11	3		6		20
	70°					7	3		9	1	20
	80°					9	5		6		20
	90°					2	7	5	6		20

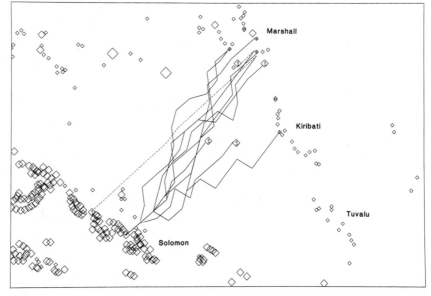

43. The tracks of 10 exploring canoes sailing in a computer simulation that search to the northeast from the Solomon Islands in July, when the trade winds slacken in the northern summer. They sail in winds generated probabilistically according to actual meteorological records. Canoes scatter as they tack when they meet headwinds, and resume course as they can. One canoe reaches each of the isolated but elevated islands of Nauru and Banaba. Within 18 days, six canoes reach five atolls in the Marshall Islands and one other in Kiribati. The last canoe fails to make a landfall, but its safe return to the Solomon Islands is shown by the dashed track.

44. Ten simulated canoes sail a course of 30° from the Reef Islands towards Micronesia. The month is January, the trade wind season of the northern hemisphere, and their tracks curve to the west as the canoes feel the weight of the northeasterlies. One canoe finds Banaba and two reach Kiribati. The rest make seven landfalls in the Marshalls, three of them on the return leg after they turn to come home after 18 days of exploration. Such experiments show the orthodox view of the settlement of eastern Micronesia to be feasible.

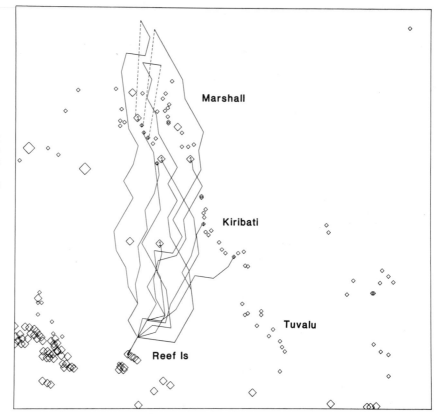

Nauru and Banaba. The one canoe that does not find land returns safely to the Solomons. Figure 44 shows a fleet of 10 canoes sailing from the Reef Islands on a course of 30° in January, often a more difficult time. As they sail into the trade wind season of the northern hemisphere winter, their tracks curve to the north as they feel the weight of the northeasterlies and they scatter as they tack. One canoe reaches Banaba, two reach Kiribati. The rest find seven separate landfalls in the Marshall Islands, three on the return leg of the journey after turning to sail home. Although the results are not shown here, a separate series of simulated voyages with origins in the Marshalls, Kiribati and Tuvalu were sent off on reciprocal courses towards Island Melanesia and most made dependable arrivals. One other possible origin for eastern Micronesia suggested on linguistic grounds (Marck 1975) is Manus in the Admiralty Islands. No simulations were run from there, but one would expect from the pattern of weather for the Carolines to be accessible, but groups further east generally not by direct trips.

The hypothetical routes to eastern Micronesia do not exhaust the feasible ones. Figure 45, which is adapted from Lewis (1972:229, Fig. 47), shows landfall arcs in Rotuma, Tuvalu and Kiribati as seen from northeastern Fiji and Futuna. Therefore a further series of simulated voyages was run up and down this chain of groups between Fiji and the Marshall Islands. Because these groups present wide and close targets, they are not hard

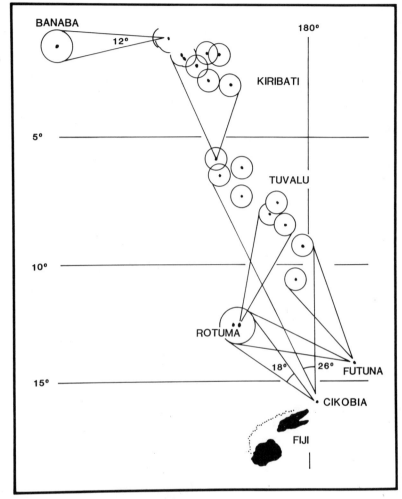

45. A map showing the accessibility of Rotuma, Tuvalu and Kiribati from origins in Fiji and Futuna. The target islands are close, but strung out in line with each other and, as such, they constitute a narrower target arc than Tuvalu and eastern Micronesia present from eastern Melanesia.

to find. However, canoes have to steer within quite a narrow range of courses to achieve a high rate of success. The reason is that the island groups are strung out in a line with each other, trending west of north. By contrast, the same targets are spread in a broad, if broken, arc as seen from starting points in Island Melanesia, although at a greater distance. An eastern route to Micronesia from Fiji or northern West Polynesia runs against linguistic predictions, but is navigationally feasible. Experiments also suggest that canoes that attempted this route, but took the wrong course, could usually survive either by sailing back to their starting island or by running across into Melanesia, which would already be known to them. Figure 46 shows ten canoes on a three-week return voyage from Cikobia, Fiji, sailing at 345°, which is a good course for Tuvalu. Nine arrive, but one does not and runs out of time on the return.

Simulation supports the orthodox view of eastern Micronesian settlement, but raises other possibilities. It would be difficult to choose between them on the basis of present control of geology, chronology, archaeology and linguistics.

46. Ten canoes on a three-week return voyage from northeastern Fiji sail a course of 345° towards Tuvalu. Nine arrive, either on the way north or south, but one unsuccessful canoe trying to return runs out of time. Computer simulation widens the range of possible sources for the colonisation of eastern Micronesia. The figure also plots wind data.

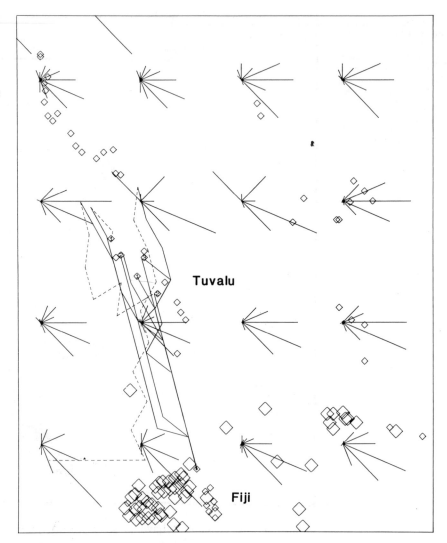

Geological issues

An important area of doubt concerns when the atolls that make up most of Micronesia became available for settlement in prehistory. To consider some general geological issues, many of the island chains of Oceania formed as the Pacific Plate passed across 'hot spots' in the earth's mantle. For example, the Hawaiian islands become progressively younger and larger from the northwest towards the big island of Hawaii, which is still volcanically active (Kirch 1985:24–5). Samoa, near the edge of the Pacific Plate, is older in the east than in the west. It is suggested that some islands on the Plate are sinking; they are all volcanic, even the atolls, which are coral caps on underwater seamounts. Apparently, over long periods, volcanic islands can slip under, leaving their fringing reefs behind, first as offshore barrier reefs around the shrinking islands, and then as atolls, which maintain themselves at sea-level by growth of coral.

47. Although high islands in eastern Micronesia are few, this simulation suggests they could be found by exploring canoes, as well as the many atolls. Here 10 canoes search relatively empty ocean between the Caroline and Marshall Islands. Four canoes find atolls, four find the high island of Kosrae. One canoe returns to the Solomon Islands, and the last did not succeed in leaving them.

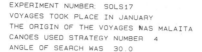

EXPERIMENT NUMBER: SOLS17
VOYAGES TOOK PLACE IN JANUARY
THE ORIGIN OF THE VOYAGES WAS MALAITA
CANOES USED STRATEGY NUMBER 4
ANGLE OF SEARCH WAS 30.0

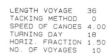

LENGTH VOYAGE   36
TACKING METHOD   0
SPEED OF CANOES 4.00
TURNING DAY   18
HORIZ. FRACTION 1.50
NO. OF VOYAGES   10

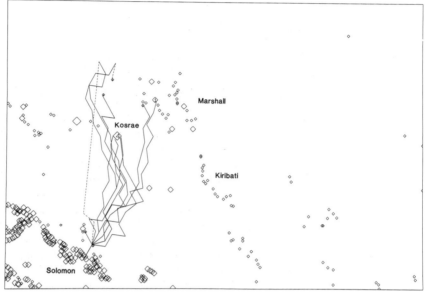

Post-glacial changes in sea-level have affected many islands. Work from the Marshall Islands (Dye 1987), which may apply elsewhere in Micronesia, shows that existing atolls were submerged by the rising post-Pleistocene sea and were still under water when it reached its modern level. With the growth of coral, they returned to the surface, but there was a time lag before they were habitable. The case is complicated by suggestions of a higher sea-level, of a metre or more, lasting until perhaps 1000 B.C. or later, although chronology is uncertain. On the other hand, in a recent review of Pacific data, Clark (1989) emphasises the effect of local variations on wider patterns, and it may be premature to build Pacific-wide models of rising or sinking land and sea into archaeological theories of settlement.

At the base of the Temei site on Vaitupu Atoll in Tuvalu, there is a date of 1840 ± 70 years ago on *Fragum* shell from a sterile layer of beach sand, which suggests the beach dates from at least then (J. Takayama, pers. comm. 1989). One cannot generalise from such slight information, because land formation and modification on atolls are both complex (Leach and Ward 1981).

At all events, it is likely that the atolls of Micronesia were still awash in early Lapita times, but the three high islands of the Carolines were not, and nor were Nauru and Banaba, which stand over 60 m above sea-level. Micronesian islands are easy to reach by simulation, and an earlier theory (Goodenough 1957) that high islands were settled first is only likely to be true if atolls were uninhabitable when this happened. Further, when voyages were first made into this region, high islands were probably found as well as atolls, as shown in Figure 47, which is a simulated voyage of 10 canoes into the relatively open area between the Carolines and

Marshalls. Four canoes reached atolls there, one on its return passage.
Four found Kosrae, a high island in the eastern Carolines, one did not
manage to leave the Solomons, and one canoe returned there. All survived.

Issues of dating

There are obvious problems in dating island sequences in Micronesia.
Bonhomme and Craib have resolved these for Saipan in the Marianas,
and find no compelling evidence for occupation of the group earlier than
1000 B.C. (1987:103). Dates on shell reported by Kurashina (1987) from
Guam, the southernmost island of the Marianas, will probably fall into
line when corrected for the marine reservoir effect, also. However, current
radiocarbon dates for the other western high islands, Belau and Yap, allow
them little more than 2000 years of settlement (Bonhomme and Craib
1987; Masse 1987). In terms of colonisation, it is anomalous that the
Marianas, which are twice the distance from Island Southeast Asia than
Belau and Yap, should be a thousand years older than both. Earlier sites
can be expected in Belau and/or Yap; the earliest of them perhaps even
slightly older than the Marianas.

The high islands of the Caroline group – Truk, Pohnpei and Kosrae – were
evidently settled by A.D. 0–500 (Craib 1983:924; Athens 1987). Spriggs
(1982:7) reinterpreted Pohnpei evidence to suggest a date of c. 250 B.C.,
and there is also the possibility Kosrae has indirect evidence of human
impact on vegetation at approximately 500 B.C. (Athens 1987). There are
dates of 50 B.C.–A.D. 50 from Majuro Atoll in the Marshall Islands (Craib
1983:924). Shun and Athens (1987) have reported comparable dates for
Kwajalein Atoll, also in the Marshalls, of 50 B.C.. Further, while the linguistic
expectation is that dates would be younger from east to west in the Carolines,
this is not shown as yet. Even in the far west there are dates between
A.D. 300 and A.D. 750 from Ulithi Atoll, while most other islands remain
undated.

There is a particular dating problem on Bikini Atoll in the Marshalls,
where the USA tested atom bombs after World War II, in that it has a
date of 3450 ± 60 years ago (Streck 1987) and others that indicate occupation
between c.2500–2000 years ago. The implication of the early and contentious
dates from Bikini is another thousand years at the bottom of eastern
Micronesian prehistory. One curiosity is that one would expect them to
be younger, not older, if contaminated by modern radioactivity (Streck
1987). So, Bikini may be an anomaly or a sign of things to come – together
with the suggestion by Athens (1987) of a possible age for Kosrae of
approximately 500 B.C.

No dates relating to the settlement of Kiribati have been published. For
the Polynesian Outliers Nukuoro and Kapingamarangi, there is evidence
for some 900 years of settlement, which is considerably less than the 3000
known for Tikopia, Anuta and Taumako, other Outliers to the south
(Davidson 1971; Leach and Ward 1981; Kirch and Yen 1982), but these
are not atolls.

The dating situation can be summarised as follows. The Marianas have
a confirmed antiquity of 3000 years. Dates of A.D. 0 for Belau and Yap

probably indicate that there is another 1000–1200 years of prehistory still to be discovered. Dates approaching A.D. 0 for several of the eastern atolls quite possibly suggest they were unavailable for settlement much before then, as described, or, as perhaps implied by the situation at Bikini Atoll, there is a still-undiscovered phase of prehistory in eastern Micronesia earlier than A.D. 0. Beyond that, the existing evidence confirms none of the specific chronology for population movements within Micronesia as predicted by linguistics, apart from the general suggestion that the settlement of eastern Micronesia as a whole should post-date Lapita.

Archaeological issues

Bonhomme and Craib (1987:103) say of the high islands of western Micronesia that, although it is likely that all were settled from the west, there is nothing to suggest that the settlement of Belau, Yap and the Marianas were related in any way (1987:103) and Masse (1987) asserts, in similar vein, that Belau was not a stepping-stone to the rest of Micronesia. But it would be no great surprise if further evidence showed that these western high islands actually were more closely related at the time of colonisation. Belau is the closest target in western Micronesia, and a large one stretching 150 km north and south. In terms of cultural affinities, Craib (1983:923) says it shows more complex influence from Indonesia and the Philippines than do the Marianas, as well it might being so much closer, while Masse (1987) suggests further, that Belau's affinities are more with Indonesia than with the Philippines. Evidently Yap stands apart from the Marianas in language and material culture although Masse (1987) suggests that its early pottery may yet show a closer relationship to the Marianas (and ultimately the Philippines) than to Belau. There is little evidence of early exchange in western Micronesia and, according to Craib (1988a:5), no suggestion of early movement eastward from there to the atolls of the Carolines, although, later on, certain atolls relatively close to Yap and Belau have imported pottery from those islands. In short, there seems to be a great deal left to discover.

There are no clear affinities in the earliest pottery found in the west with specific areas of Island Southeast Asia, although this issue may be influenced by sampling. Almost no decorated pottery sherds are known from Yap, fewer than 1% decorated from Belau and only a fairly low percentage from the Marianas (J. Craib, pers. comm. 1988). It has been thought that the ceramic sequence of the Marianas began about 1000 B.C. with a pottery that was red-slipped but otherwise plain (Marianas Red). Around 500 B.C., a distinctive decorated ware appeared in many sites of the southern Marianas. However, from results of excavations in Achugao on Saipan, Butler and De Fant (1989) have suggested recently that this impressed, incised and lime-filled ware was actually present for the entire early sequence from 1000 B.C. to A.D. 0, in small quantities, and that the decorative style changed with time. This issue is unresolved. Comparisons of the Achugao material with various published sources from the Philippines, Sulawesi, etc., show a lot of generic similarities and support a general Southeast Asian origin for the Marianas (Butler and De Fant

1989:45-6; B. Butler, pers. comm. 1989), although others have suggested the affinities are with the Philippines, in particular (Craib 1988b; Bellwood 1985). The suggestion that Philippines influence on decoration arrived after the earliest period of settlement may no longer hold.

Other kinds of pottery farther east in Micronesia still lack an established ancestry. Pottery, apparently locally made, has been found on the high Caroline islands of Truk and Pohnpei (Craib 1983:924) and most recently on the third high island, Kosrae (J. Craib, pers. comm. 1989), where its absence was formerly attributed either to sampling error or to the poor quality of local clays (Athens 1987). At the time of writing the earliest dated pottery is *c.* A.D. 0 from Fefan in the Truk group and much the same age on Pohnpei (Ayres and Bryson 1989). Fefan pottery has notched rims and incised body sherds, while on Pohnpei decoration is limited to rim and lip decoration by notching, incision and punctation. The relationships of this pottery in the Carolines are unknown, but current opinion is that it is not from the west. Ayres has suggested that Pohnpei ware could be derived from late Lapita ware in eastern Melanesia, although no distinctive Lapita decoration is known and, while this is possible, the situation in eastern Melanesia is still far from clear. For instance, McCoy and Cleghorn (1988) report plain pottery with notched and impressed rims, which is dominant in upper layers of the Mdailu site (SE-SZ-33) on Santa Cruz, but there is Lapita pottery, mainly in the lower deposits, of the same site.

> The co-occurrence of decorated and plain pottery from the fossil beach deposits, though almost certainly mixed to some extent, indicates that the two ceramics are broadly contemporaneous, but whether they represent one or two different traditions is another matter. [McCoy and Cleghorn 1988:113]

The authors take the interim position that there were two traditions, which overlapped and co-existed from as early as 1000 B.C. to approximately A.D. 100 in the region. They refer to the plain pottery and similar ware from the the Reefs, Anuta, Tikopia and Taumako by Green's term Eastern Melanesian Plain Ware, which allows a considerable level of variability within a general 'Lapitoid' series of ceramics and also distinguishes this plain pottery from Polynesian Plain Ware. However, as things stand, the pottery in central Micronesia does not supply prehistorians with an origin or a time for the first settlement there, and, in fact, the first colonists and the earliest pottery could have arrived separately and by different routes.

Writing of the early dates from Majuro Atoll in the Marshalls, Craib said in 1983 that they were not associated with artifacts particularly like those of eastern Melanesia, the supposed origin, and, indeed, he could see no clear archaeological evidence of movement from there at that time (Craib 1983:924). More recently, Davidson (1988:93) finds that eastern Melanesia has a lot to recommend it as the Micronesian homeland, including shell adzes, slingstones, plain pottery, fishhooks, various shell peelers and shell ornaments, which have an antiquity of up to 3000 years in Santa Cruz, for example. However, Davidson (1988) cautions against identifying any particular part of eastern Melanesia as being 'the' homeland and leaves that issue wide open.

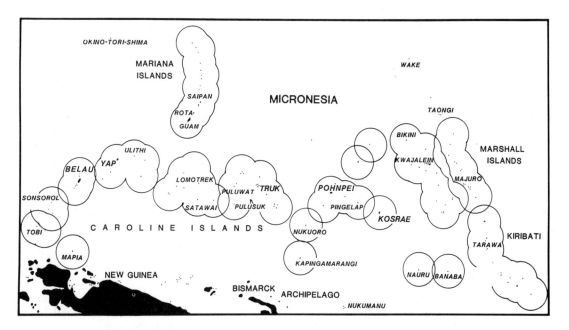

48. A map of language and dialect distributions in Micronesia. An analysis by Marck (1986) showed that islands separated by a voyaging distance of only one night at sea will have mutually intelligible dialects. (Adapted from Marck 1986, Figure 1.)

Linguistic issues

Were it not for linguistic evidence, Micronesian origins would be obscure indeed. However, more difficulties arise here. Archaeology has no data able to confirm south-to-north and east-to-west movements from a source in eastern Micronesia tentatively suggested by Blust (1988) and Marck (1975), nor a number of other linguistic hypotheses. For instance, Marck nominates northern Vanuatu as a possible source of the nuclear Micronesian proto-community (1975:66), and Kosrae, the Marshall Islands and Kiribati are given equal likelihood as the locality of the homeland in Micronesia before wider dispersal (Marck 1975:78). He also suggests this early homeland should not be seen as a closed system and makes the parallel with the early contact sphere inferred for parts of Fiji and West Polynesia (1975:84). Regarding the earlier theory that first settlement was on a high island in Micronesia, he suggests that if it were true, then Kosrae should be the one (1975:95).

Marck (1986) carried out an insightful study, which showed Micronesia to be an excellent example of how patterns of language similarity (or diversity) reflect the history of inter-island contact since settlement. He refers to Gladwin (1970) and Lewis (1972), who both observed that 100 sea miles is about the limit of inter-island voyages that can be made overnight by modern Micronesian sailors. The strategy of these simple voyages is to leave at dusk in good weather and follow star paths, which are the most secure direction-finders, through the night. Then one can make a landfall in daylight on the following day. Such voyages are within the capability of average navigators and constitute a large number of those that are made. When Marck drew 100-mile radii equating with such voyages around Micronesian islands most of the existing languages and dialect groups emerged as the clear pattern shown in Figure 48, which is taken

from Marck (1986: Fig. 1). He concluded that: 'If two islands are separated
by a voyaging distance involving a single night at sea or less in traditional
craft, their dialects will be mutually intelligible. The maximum distance
is about 100 miles in Micronesia' (Marck 1986:256).

To summarise the discussion of geological, archaeological and linguistic
issues, it appears that the colonisation of Micronesia is still open to a
range of possibilities. The orthodox settlement model is essentially a
linguistic one, but the patterns of language reflect late prehistoric contact
spheres more than anything else. Therefore it has been worth inspecting
voyaging issues for any clues they might give to directing future research.

The source of eastern Micronesian settlement

Simulated voyages support the orthodox origin in eastern Melanesia.
However, a route north from Fiji/West Polynesia was navigationally feasible
too, but this does not sit so easily with the conventional view of other
evidence.

The early radiocarbon dates from Lapita sites show a rapid spread from
west to east. If it took as long as 300 years, that would be spanned by
only a dozen human generations, and it could have been less. The first
people in Fiji/West Polynesia probably spoke a language or dialect still
very similar to some others in eastern Melanesia. Prehistorians have generally
interpreted the pattern of linguistic relationships as suggesting orderly
change with the spread of human settlement from west to east. But it
is just as likely that the direction of initial colonisation did not itself
determine the subsequent pattern of language diversification here. One
comparable example has been found in the correspondence of language
and contact patterns in Micronesia. A second is the spread of the western
Melanesian sub-group of Austronesian languages between north coastal New
Guinea and Santa Isabel in the Solomon Islands, obscuring both the pattern
of earlier languages derived from Proto-Oceanic (Ross 1988) and the
linguistic background to Lapita. A similar argument can be made for
archaeological data, and one early example is the similarity of eastern
Melanesia and Fiji/West Polynesia in Lapita times, which was overlain
by later events. In fact, there is a considerable variety of evidence for
contact between parts of Melanesia, Micronesia and Polynesia at different
times in prehistory. Some similarities that have been taken as support
for the conventional view of eastern Micronesian origins can be explained
by a breaking-chain model, which reflects recent interaction rather than
the earliest contact.

We are not constrained to derive the first settlers of eastern Micronesia
from eastern Melanesia, even if that is where they came from. The search
for single origins and discrete homelands has often proved futile. Eastern
Micronesia could have had multiple origins at a time when there was
not much difference between the various colonists. They came by crosswind
voyages from already-settled islands perhaps spread over a wider
geographical range than that envisaged so far.

However, the apparently late settlement of eastern Micronesia presents
us with an important problem and a striking parallel with East Polynesia.

There is no incontrovertible archaeological evidence of settlement prior to A.D. 0, in either region. One wonders if the West Polynesian pause has not doubled in severity. Irrespective of where eastern Micronesia was colonised from, Fiji and West Polynesia were settled 3000 years ago, and it was possible to sail north from there through Tuvalu into Micronesia just as it was towards central East Polynesia. Interestingly, both prongs of this fork cross over from the continental geological regime to the Pacific Plate. Both directions have ecological factors to filter out pottery-making, until larger islands some considerable distance away were reached. The environmental changes were not something explorers knew about in advance. We are confronted with the same questions. Is the absence of sites of c.700–500 B.C. age, a matter of geology, of sampling and archaeological visibility, the difficulties of adaptation, the expanding area of ocean, the discovery of islands but without substantial settlement, or some quite unknown cultural factor that induced Lapita to throw on its brakes? The only new – but unlikely – factor suggested for Fiji/West Polynesia, is that it may have been the first region reached to be empty of preceramic people. The atolls of Micronesia share the same geological uncertainty about habitability as the Northern Cook Islands, but other East Polynesian groups were high as were a handful of islands in eastern Micronesia. The general point is that the apparent or real delay – although now shorter than it was once thought to be – of crossing to the islands of the Pacific Plate, affects eastern parts of Polynesia and Micronesia alike.

The source of Western Micronesian settlement

The orthodox view is that settlement of western Micronesia was by one or more groups of explorers from Island Southeast Asia whose archaeological identity includes the decorated wares of Marianas Red pottery. Like Lapita colonists, they came out of the voyaging corridor that stretched from the Solomon Islands to mainland Southeast Asia. In the period 3500–3000 years ago, voyages were made into Remote Oceania from areas both to the west and to the east of New Guinea. This implies a wide distribution of communities with some kind of inter-relationship and contact. We can now begin to look for specific archaeological evidence of it.

It is generally thought that the colonists of western Micronesia did not penetrate beyond the high island groups of the west into the atoll chain of the Carolines, but if they had the sailing ability to reach Micronesia at all, they surely could have done so. As yet, there is no *archaeological* reason why the whole of Micronesia could not have been first settled from the west. Once again the absence of evidence corresponds with crossing on to the Pacific Plate!

While a Southeast Asian origin of the west is very likely, it may be too soon to dismiss entirely the possibility that it was colonists of Lapita descent from the east, already in Micronesia, who made an original westward crossing themselves to Asia, to open up the route to Island Southeast Asian influences. However, the evidence for this rather outlandish proposition is nil.

Rather, it seems to be the case that different founder populations, whose ancestors had previously shared aspects of their histories in the voyaging corridor approximately 4000 years ago, met again in Micronesia a thousand or two years later. At present it is not possible to suggest where in Micronesia this was, because subsequent interaction has probably blurred whatever linguistic and biological divisions there may have been.

Summary

In spite of increased archaeological activity in Micronesia in the last decade, many fundamental issues in its prehistory remain. There is a very good chance that the first 1000–1200 years is missing from the western high islands of Belau and Yap. Eastern Micronesia could have been discovered between 3000 and 2000 years ago and the high islands settled. One cannot say how much before A.D. 0 atolls were fit for settlement, but they would have been stepping-stones and seamarks for navigation some time earlier. Isolation might have prevented settlement of the high islands alone.

If we accept the Micronesian dual settlement hypothesis, the precise western source of colonists in Island Southeast Asia is an open question, while the origins of eastern Micronesia could have involved multiple settlement from eastern Melanesia and possibly Fiji/West Polynesia. The relations of founder groups who were not conspicuously different will be hard to trace. Much of the evidence normally taken to indicate origins is better interpreted as the record of post-settlement trends, anyway. Answers to such ultimate questions will have to wait for more comprehensive field evidence.

In spite of the uncertainties listed in this chapter, Micronesia fits easily into the general navigational theory of the colonisation of the remote Pacific, which predicts simply that ocean exploration followed the order – against and across the wind. Western Micronesia was settled by an initial search upwind from Island Southeast Asia and the degree to which it penetrated the western Carolines may have been restricted by habitable islands. Archaeologically, we can scarcely distinguish this in time from Lapita's first upwind moves in open ocean farther east. As for eastern Micronesia, after an episode of upwind settlement by Lapita to Fiji/West Polynesia, and perhaps even as early as central East Polynesia was being explored, crosswind voyages peeled off from points along the line of advance. A crude estimate of chronology is that eastern Micronesia should have been reached significantly earlier than the long crosswind voyage to Hawaii. The limiting factor is when atolls presented themselves to the settlers who were already on the scene.

Finally, eastern Micronesia joins East Polynesia in showing an apparent distinction in the settlement, if not in the discovery, of the islands of the Pacific Plate. The same case could apply to the atolls of the western Caroline Islands. Navigational circumstances did not change on crossing on to the Pacific Plate and new islands could have been discovered. However, there was a general change in the process of settlement and/or its archaeological visibility.

8

Voyaging by Computer: Experiments in the Exploration of the Remote Pacific Ocean

In previous chapters, a theory of Pacific voyaging and colonisation was proposed, which contained many elements. It emphasised rationality, in a cross-cultural sense, and assumed explorers understood their own world. It predicted, in a general way, the order in which island groups should be settled and variations in the time that this should take. Then it was measured against archaeological evidence and found to fit tolerably well. However, it remains just another story among others about Pacific colonisation, which have been accumulating for 200 years. Some further testing needs to be done to give it more weight. This chapter summarises the issues and describes a computer simulation undertaken to investigate them.

The first general aim of the simulation was to provide a second level of testing for theoretical propositions about colonisation, to review a host of more specific suggestions about the settlement of particular islands, and to look for possible solutions to current problems. One example was the brief preview of simulation included in the discussion of Micronesia. A second general aim was to use the simulation to try to learn more about the methods of prehistoric exploration and to suggest, specifically, how these might have become more refined during the 2000 or more years that Pacific colonisation continued.

Our starting position is that we know from many thousands of small-boat passages in modern and historical times, and from the evidence of prehistory, that a great many passages in the Pacific were possible. Therefore, we are unable to reject many out of hand. Instead, it needs to be shown that some propositions are more likely than others: that some passages probably required certain kinds of knowledge, which others did not. Measurements can be made of factors such as discovery order, elapsed time and survival rate. Voyages can be compared in terms of whether they were easy or hard, safe or dangerous, simple or complicated. Simulated results and archaeological data together may show the extent to which colonisation was structured. Finally, a special virtue of simulation is that, not only does it generate results that conform to archaeological data, it produces others that clearly contradict them and, to this extent, it helps to choose among options. Inferences can be drawn about cultural matters, such as intention and about classes of navigational knowledge.

General issues in voyaging

Many of these issues are inter-related and can be reviewed in the light of the simulation results.

1. A key proposition is that as the Pacific was settled there was both a need and the opportunity for navigation methods to develop to meet changing conditions. A major objective of the simulation is to discover what people needed to know by when.
2. Colonisation, while fast, was directed towards safety rather than speed, and loss of life was less than often proposed.
3. Voyages were conventionally two-way, and there was feedback of information. (In fact it will transpire that 'three-way' voyaging was necessary in some cases.)
4. The settlement of islands was probably multiple.
5. There was a general directional trend of exploration, which led first upwind and, later on, across and down it.
6. The order of discovery was affected by the order of ease of return.
7. Colonisation was a continuous process without systematic cultural pauses. There may have been geographical reasons for variation in the elapsed time of island settlement, but cultural ones have yet to be confirmed.
8. Colonisation of the remote Pacific proceeded until most of its islands had been found and its continental margins touched.
9. The relative order of colonisation is important to this theory, but, at present, it is more loosely tied to an absolute chronology. There are several archaeological problems over dating still to be resolved, but the essence of this argument does not derive from them.

A large number of specific suggestions about the settlement of particular island groups have arisen in the discussion. As it happens, the simulation supports many, contradicts some, and adds a lot of information to what has gone before. The various points will be covered when the relevant experiments are discussed.

COMPUTER SIMULATION METHODOLOGY

A simulation of prehistoric exploration of the remote Pacific was set up at the University of Auckland by the author, in collaboration with Philip

Quirke and Simon Bickler (Irwin *et al.* 1990), using an IBM 4341 as host computer, linked to a graphics system that included an IBM 5085 computer, a high-resolution screen, digitising tablet and plotter. Programmed data includes a map of the Pacific Ocean that extends from Papua New Guinea to the American coast and shows islands as sighting circles of radii of 10, 20 or 30 nautical miles, according to elevation. A zoom function allows enlargement of particular parts of the display. Stored data record wind, by 5° ocean squares, for the months of January, representing midsummer, and July midwinter (the same wind information as Levison, Ward and Webb used in their pioneering simulation (1973), and originally taken from data held by the Marine Division of the Meteorological Office, Bracknell, England, for use in preparing the monthly meteorological charts for the Pacific Ocean). We are glad to have continuity with their experiments. During simulated voyages a canoe receives a wind selected by probabilistic methods, on each new day, according to the wind records of its ocean square.

The rules by which voyagers travel in the simulation require no abilities of crew and canoes that exceed those described for traditional Pacific navigation; nor do they include information and techniques that could have been obtained only *after* island groups were settled. The rules within the computer program include the following:

1. Canoes can start a voyage from any island, if necessary waiting for up to 30 days for a fair wind before they do so.

2. A voyage can last for any period between one and 90 days, and the crew check for new land every hour after the first three days.

3. Canoes sail at selected average speeds.

4. They can steer a course at sea that may be selected at random, or by the navigator (i.e. the operator).

5. When a canoe faces a headwind, it tacks by choosing the optimal tight-reaching course closest to the desired one, but cannot sail closer to the wind than 75°, which is about as high as comfortable passage-making can be made at sea. When a fair wind blows, the canoe returns to its chosen course.

6. However, in parts of the Pacific where the same headwind might blow day after day, a canoe will steadily diverge from its preferred course. In this case it has the option of taking the non-optimal (losing) tack, to bring it back closer to its initial rhumbline course, every 2nd, 3rd or nth day.

7. Canoes can make one-way or return voyages. The return course can be selected by the navigator, or according to a latitude-sailing option. In the second case, the canoe, which has kept the equivalent of a dead-reckoned position, can select a course that will probably return it to the latitude of the starting island, while still upwind of it, and then run downwind along the latitude. If forced away from the latitude by adverse weather, the navigator will try to return to it, but can make a course correction only once each 24 hours, at night, when he can see the stars.

In the experiments described here, latitude estimates can fall anywhere within 30 nautical miles on either side of the real latitude, which is equivalent to a 1° error in estimating the angle of reference stars in the sky. The program is interactive: canoes can be seen to move out and back across the screen while islands respond visibly to being hit by changing colour. An experiment can include any number of voyages whose statistics are recorded; and the screen can be plotted as required.

Sailing strategies

Initially, four strategies with variants were tested to see if they could produce the archaeologically observed pattern of colonisation, especially in terms of the order and elapsed time of settlement of islands and groups, both as the pattern currently stands and as corrected for expected sampling error (Irwin 1989). It was possible to see how different methods affect the rate of survival or death at sea, and, at the same time, to see when strategies produce clear patterns of results that are *not* found archaeologically. Later, a fifth strategy was added.

These strategies are a kind of shorthand required by this investigation. It is not suggested that any sailors think or thought in terms of a specific number of such models. Yet, on the other hand, it is clear that aspects of the strategies do relate to the ways in which sailing boats behave, and also to the way in which sailors think about managing them. The large body of ethnographic information on indigenous sailing, plus the author's own experience, suggests their use is justified here, and still apply to parts of the Pacific. The kind of concepts that prehistoric explorers might have considered explicitly will be discussed with the results of the simulation.

The first two strategies represent a control. If they produce the pattern of observed colonisation, then we could no longer support a survival theory of exploration based on search and return, first upwind and then across and downwind. Strategy 1 is the simplest. A starting island, average speed and voyage duration are selected by the operator, and the computer then sends off voyages in randomly selected directions which the canoes try to steer. There is no return. Figure 49, an experiment that began in Samoa, shows that this strategy will not do. The chance of reaching East Polynesia is low, and most would-be settlers die at sea. Making headway east against the trade winds can be seen to be much more difficult than sailing any course with a westerly component.

Strategy 2 sends out voyages in directions selected by the navigator (operator) and, again, there is no return. Figure 50 shows 20 voyages sent out during the summer monsoon from the southeastern end of the main Solomon Islands chain on a relatively short 200 sea mile voyage towards Santa Cruz, which presents a large target of 30°, and most of the canoes arrive safely in this very easy case. This example creates many sites where they have not been found archaeologically, in the Tuvalu group.

The effect of one-way voyaging is that any canoe that navigates competently towards a large target through normally predictable wind systems has a very good chance of finding land. However, any innocents who sail abroad in the wrong direction into empty ocean, without returning in good time, will almost certainly die. It will be shown that this situation applies in many parts of the remote Pacific, where return voyaging makes such compelling sense it is hard to conceive of it not being done.

Strategy 3 tests the efficacy of return voyages and allows study of crosswind

1 A Mailu canoe at speed in Amazon Bay, Papua New Guinea. (*Photograph by the author, 1973*)

2 Crew stowing the sail at nightfall in the anchorage at Mailu Island, Papua New Guinea. (*Photograph by the author, 1973*)

3. Canoes preparing to leave the village at Mailu Island to visit the New Guinea mainland. (*Photograph by the author, 1973*)

4 Canoes drawn up on the beach at Amazon Bay, Papua New Guinea. (*Photograph by the author, 1973*)

5 A traditional Massim canoe leaving Tubetube Island, Papua New Guinea. (*Photograph by the author, 1980*)

6 A canoe under sail as it leaves Tubetube Island, Papua New Guinea. (*Photograph by the author, 1980*)

7 A traditional Louisiade Archipelago sailing canoe at Moturina Island, Papua New Guinea. (*Photograph by the author, 1985*)

8 The author's yacht *Rhumbline* and a small canoe at Bagaman Island, Louisiade Archipelago, Papua New Guinea. (*Photograph by the author, 1985*)

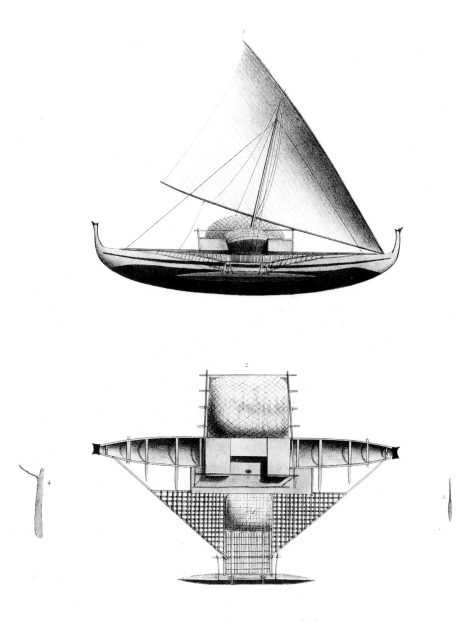

9 Plan of a canoe recorded in the Caroline Islands during the voyage of *L'Astrolab*, 1826–29 (D'Urville 1833).

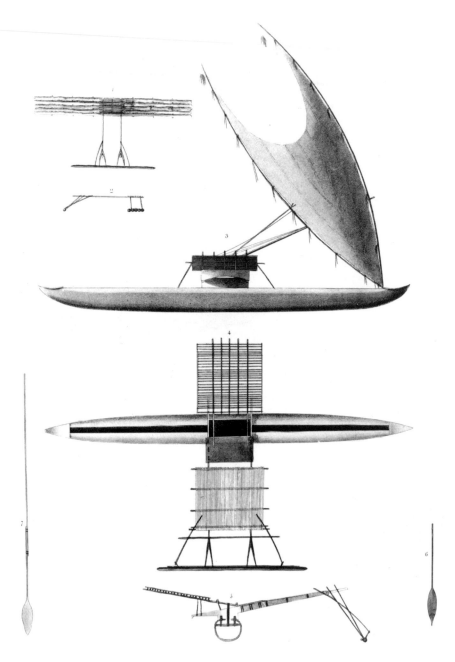

10 Plan of a canoe recorded at Vanikoro in the southeast Solomon Islands during the voyage of *L'Astrolab*, 1826–29 (D'Urville 1833).

11 A Fijian canoe with D'Urville's ship *L'Astrolab* on its voyage of 1826–29 (D'Urville 1833).

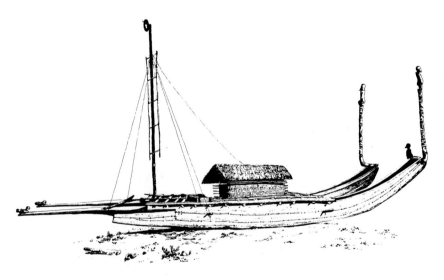

12 Sketch of a Tahitian double-canoe by Webber made during Cook's third voyage in 1777.

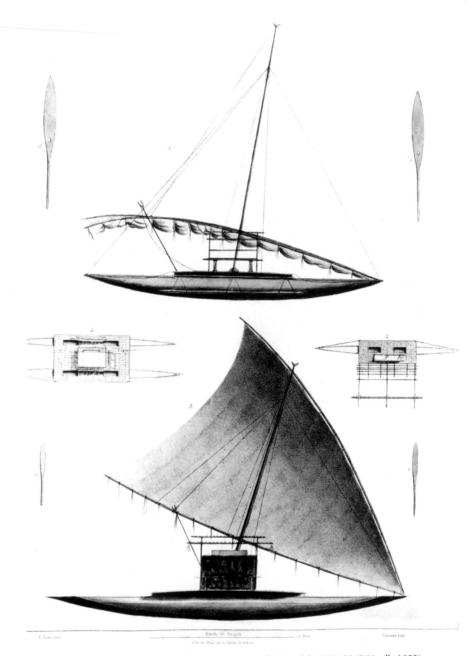

13 Plan of a canoe recorded in Tonga during the voyage of *L'Astrolab*, 1826–29 (D'Urville 1833).

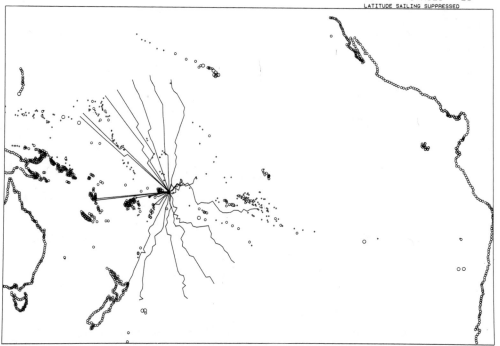

EXPERIMENT NUMBER: SAMOA
VOYAGES TOOK PLACE IN JULY
THE ORIGIN OF THE VOYAGES WAS MANU'A
CANOES USED STRATEGY NUMBER 1

LENGTH VOYAGE   30
TACKING METHOD   2
SPEED OF CANOES 3.00
TURNING DAY   30
HORIZ. FRACTION 0.67
NO. OF VOYAGES   25
LATITUDE SAILING SUPPRESSED

49. Computer simulation by Strategy 1. One-way navigation in random directions from Samoa was evidently not the way to settle East Polynesia. (Reprinted by permission of the editor, from Irwin, Bickler and Quirke 1990.)

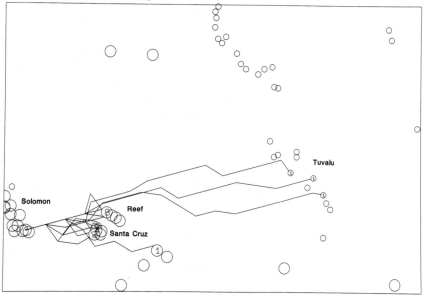

EXPERIMENT NUMBER: REMOTE OCEANIA 1
VOYAGES TOOK PLACE IN JANUARY
THE ORIGIN OF THE VOYAGES WAS SOLOMON IS
CANOES USED STRATEGY NUMBER 2
ANGLE OF SEARCH WAS   75.0

LENGTH VOYAGE   30
TACKING METHOD   0
SPEED OF CANOES 3.00
TURNING DAY   30
HORIZ. FRACTION 0.67
NO. OF VOYAGES   20

50. Computer simulation by Strategy 2. One-way voyaging can produce settlements when directed towards substantial island targets, in this case Santa Cruz to the east of the Solomon Islands. However, simulated results do not always conform to archaeological patterns. (Reprinted by permission of the editor, from Irwin, Bickler and Quirke 1990.)

51. Computer simulation by Strategy 3. Twelve canoes search upwind from Pitcairn towards Easter Island (solid track) and one is successful. The rest attempt a return course (dashed track), but five crews die at sea. (Reprinted by permission of the editor, from Irwin, Bickler and Quirke 1990.)

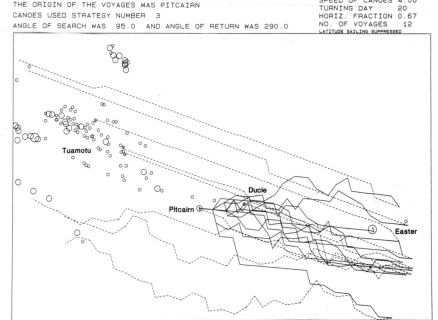

EXPERIMENT NUMBER: EASTER5
VOYAGES TOOK PLACE IN JULY
THE ORIGIN OF THE VOYAGES WAS PITCAIRN
CANOES USED STRATEGY NUMBER 3
ANGLE OF SEARCH WAS 95.0   AND ANGLE OF RETURN WAS 290.0

LENGTH VOYAGE   50
TACKING METHOD   3
SPEED OF CANOES 4.00
TURNING DAY   20
HORIZ. FRACTION 0.67
NO. OF VOYAGES   12
LATITUDE SAILING SUPPRESSED

voyages of exploration to such places as Hawaii and New Zealand. Normally, a canoe sets out as in Strategy 2 following a selected course. Depending on the wind, it may tack, reach or run until the time of the outward voyage has elapsed. If land has not been found, the navigator, who has a dead-reckoned estimate of position, then selects a course that he will try to maintain throughout the return voyage, which lasts until land is reached or time runs out and the canoe is lost. Return sailing restricts the time and range of outward exploration, but has the advantage of sweeping through the same stretch of ocean twice and increasing the chance of a discovery there. In Strategy 3, if a canoe manages to get back to the latitude of its starting island it has, as a further option, the ability to run west in search of it, by latitude sailing with the prevailing wind.

As an example, Figure 51 shows the tracks of 12 canoes that sailed according to Strategy 3 east from Pitcairn towards Easter Island, a small and distant target. Their outward course of 95° (solid track) takes them to the vicinity of Easter by Day 20, the turning day, but only one canoe finds it. Then the others choose a course of 290° for their return (dashed track), which will carry them down, not only towards Pitcairn, but in the direction of the large island screen of the Tuamotus, which was presumably known and mentally mapped. The latitude sailing option is suppressed. The month is July and trade winds offer a considerable range downwind. By the 50th day, one canoe has returned to Pitcairn, two have found small Ducie Island upwind of it, and three canoes have made successful landfalls in the Tuamotus. However, five canoes of the twelve were lost

52. Computer simulation by Strategy 4. Ten canoes from Pitcairn search empty ocean north of Easter Island and one luckily finds Sala y Gomez, its tiny neighbour. The other crews attempt to return by latitude sailing and all succeed, except for one which dies at sea. (Reprinted by permission of the editor, from Irwin, Bickler and Quirke 1990.)

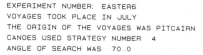

EXPERIMENT NUMBER: EASTER6
VOYAGES TOOK PLACE IN JULY
THE ORIGIN OF THE VOYAGES WAS PITCAIRN
CANOES USED STRATEGY NUMBER 4
ANGLE OF SEARCH WAS 70.0

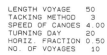

LENGTH VOYAGE 50
TACKING METHOD 3
SPEED OF CANOES 4.00
TURNING DAY 20
HORIZ. FRACTION 0.50
NO. OF VOYAGES 10

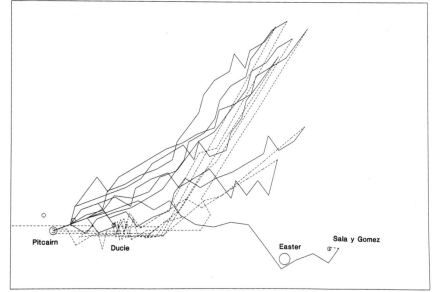

at sea, and it is arguable whether such a high proportion of loss could normally be sustained.

In Strategy 4 the outward leg of a journey is similar to previous ones, but the return presents the most 'intelligent' feature of the voyaging algorithms, intended to establish where, in the settlement of the Pacific, a conceptually equivalent skill was required. When a canoe turns for the trip back, the computer (i.e. navigator) sets the course by reference to the angle between the turning point and a dead-reckoned estimate of the position of the starting island. The canoe then tries to return safely by intercepting the latitude of the starting island, while still upwind of it, and to make its landfall by sailing west along it. The fraction of the distance between the longitude of the turning point and that of the starting island, towards which the canoe sails before beginning its latitude run, can be varied, so the ability of canoes to return can be examined. (This is referred to as the 'horizontal fraction'.) A successful return is by no means assured, because position estimates become uncertain and canoes have to face vicissitudes of wind and weather. Sometimes, canoes already to leeward of their starting island, and also north or south of it, can attempt to return by Strategy 4 by first climbing back to windward of it, and then turning west.

In the example in Figure 52, 10 canoes have – unknowingly – set off from Pitcairn to search empty ocean north of Easter Island. By chance, one of them finds Sala y Gomez, Easter's tiny neighbour, just after starting its return trip. Eight other canoes return, either to Ducie Island (5) or

53. Computer simulation by Strategy 4. Ten canoes from Pitcairn choose a suitable course for Easter Island and four find it. The others return by latitude sailing, except for one, which loses contact with the latitude during adverse weather. (Reprinted by permission of the editor, from Irwin, Bickler and Quirke 1990.)

EXPERIMENT NUMBER: EASTER9
VOYAGES TOOK PLACE IN JULY
THE ORIGIN OF THE VOYAGES WAS PITCAIRN
CANOES USED STRATEGY NUMBER 4
ANGLE OF SEARCH WAS 95.0

LENGTH VOYAGE   50
TACKING METHOD   3
SPEED OF CANOES 4.00
TURNING DAY   20
HORIZ. FRACTION 0.60
NO. OF VOYAGES   10

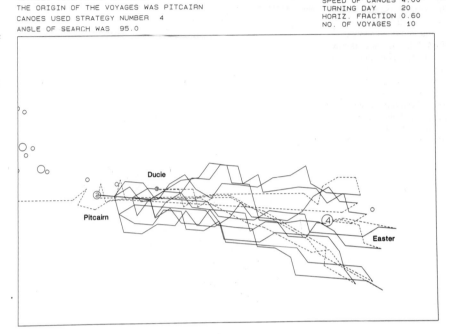

Pitcairn (3), as shown. Several are forced to tack to hold the chosen latitude; one canoe loses contact and misses Pitcairn to be lost at sea. The example (Fig. 52), illustrates the general point that an explicit strategy of latitude sailing allows one to search and survive in difficult circumstances.

In Figure 53, 10 canoes from Pitcairn have followed the precise upwind course (95°) most likely to carry them out to Easter Island, although the odds against finding it still appear to be high. Four lucky canoes find the new island, five return safely to Ducie (3) and Pitcairn (2), but one misses the return target and sails into empty ocean. In reality, all would not be lost for this last navigator; he would realise eventually he had overshot and, knowing of previously discovered land farther west, would have another chance to survive by turning northwest to cross the Tuamotu screen.

One suggestion that was made about fixing the position of new land is supported already by these preliminary experiments. Figures 51–53 show that upwind voyages that follow wind-shifts are more difficult and erratic than downwind voyages, which are simpler, faster and more systematic. In fact, the return voyage from a new discovery could fix its position more easily than the outward one, and a case has been made that to close a voyage with a return was necessary to secure a new discovery (Irwin 1989). This is just one aspect of the feedback of information thought to have accompanied the exploration of the Pacific.

It will be explained that these four strategies, which were anticipated by the author before the simulation was set up, were not able to cope with all situations, and needed to be supplemented by another.

EXPERIMENTS IN ·THE COLONISATION OF THE PACIFIC

Although key elements of the simulation are probabalistic, navigators and their canoes have the ability and intelligence to do almost anything, within broad limits. For this reason many thousands of feasibility trials were run in order to find suitable general conditions for the experiments that are described here. This preselection reduced the number of voyages needed to the tens of thousands, and allowed comparison of voyaging by different methods and strategies, in different seasons, directions, and for different periods of time.

FROM THE SOLOMON ISLANDS INTO REMOTE OCEANIA

This experiment considers the fortunes of the first explorers to pass from Near into Remote Oceania. This account of Experiment 1 considers more details of methodology than the ones that follow to illustrate the procedure. Three starting locations were used to prevent voyages leaving in different directions from simply discovering other parts of the Solomon Islands and going nowhere. All canoes sailed at the modest speed of 4.0 knots, which gave an effective but reasonable daily average of 96 sea miles. All of the voyages were navigated: canoes tried to maintain their course and on meeting a head wind took the best tack. However, at this stage they were not sophisticated enough to change tacks, from time to time, to avoid being taken away from their target if the same headwind persisted. Voyages were made in January and July representing summer and winter. Most outward voyages lasted for 15 days, because trials showed that 15 days gave sufficient range to reach islands in the region, but some were repeated over 28 days, to see how the results changed. All return voyages sailed for 35 days (five weeks), turning on day 15, to give three weeks for the return. Five weeks were not considered too much for human endurance at this early period of colonisation. Canoes were sent out at 10° intervals, which provided a fair coverage of the ocean, especially as their tracks scattered, and 25 canoes were sent in each direction, because that number appeared to represent larger fleets. Canoes were not sent out around the full 360° degrees of the compass rose, because the author, who had seen the map, already knew that many directions were superfluous. Even so, the range of angles chosen was generous.

Experiment 1 had eight parts and a total of 4300 canoes. Run 1A left the Solomons by Strategy 2 at 4.0 knots for 15 days in January on courses 0–230°. Run 1B was the same in July. Runs 1C and 1D were repeats over 28 days. Run 1E used Strategy 3, over 35 days in January (turning day

Table 2   *Simulated voyages from the Solomon Islands*

Starting Island: Solomon Islands	January																							
Angle	0	10	20	30	40	50	60	70	80	90	100	110	120	130	140	150	160	170	180	190	200	210	220	230
returned																								
died	56	52	52	52	28	48	40	36	12	4	4	24	4	8	12	8	24	52	92	100	24	0	0	0
lived*	44	48	48	48	72	52	60	64	88	96	96	76	96	92	88	92	76	48	8	0	76	100	100	100
Solomon					8																			
Caroline	36	44	40	44	12																			
Nukuoro	4	4	8																					
Kapingamarangi	4																							
Marshall				4	28	12																		
Nauru					24	28																		
Banaba						8	4																	
Kiribati						4	32																	
Santa Cruz							8	28	68	72	8													
Tuvalu							16	36	20	8														
Tikopia										16	84	56	8	12										
Vanuatu											4	4	76	80	60	12								
Rotuma												4												
Fiji												4	12											
Futuna												8												
Loyalty															28	36	20							
Hunter																4								
New Caledonia																40	56	48	8					
Australia																					76	100	100	96
Papua New Guinea																								4

Note: All scores are percentages; 25 boats sailed per angle
* Lived score is returned plus found new land

54. The results of Experiments 1A and 1B, which were one-way voyages from the Solomon Islands. Fleets of canoes were sent out at 10° intervals, and the percentage success is shown by direction for January and July, representing different seasons. Island groups are shown by the target arcs through which they were hit. Islands in eastern Melanesia were high success targets, and Micronesia was easier to reach in July than against the stronger northeast trades of January. Virtually all canoes that steered towards Australia arrived safely. Canoes that sailed into empty ocean were usually lost at sea.

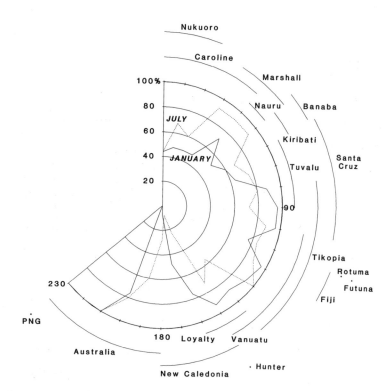

15), latitude sailing was suppressed. Run 1F was the July equivalent. Runs 1G and 1H were the Strategy 4 equivalents: latitude sailing was permitted and the horizontal fraction was 0.5.

The results of Run 1A are shown in Table 2. Island groups were hit across a range of adjacent courses, which showed navigated voyages produce coherent results. Voyages followed rather different tracks because conditions varied. Figure 54 compares overall results of Runs 1A and 1B, which were Strategy 2 (one-way) voyages in summer and winter. It can be seen that the islands of eastern Melanesia from Santa Cruz round to New Caledonia presented a continuous high success target. Micronesia was not such a successful target, but almost all canoes that headed towards Australia arrived safely. Most of those which sailed between New Caledonia and Australia were lost at sea.

There were differences between summer and winter (Fig. 54). In July, more voyages got to Micronesia, and especially to the Marshall Islands and Kiribati. Voyages in the northeastern sector of the experiment sailed into the Northern Hemisphere and July, which is summer there, is the time of slackening in the northeast trades, which may explain the higher success. Conversely, in January, which is southern summer and the time of the northwest monsoon, the southeast trades ease and there are periodical north and west winds, which allowed more successful voyages towards eastern Melanesia and especially to New Caledonia and the Loyalty Islands, which lie in the southeast. The fortunes of islands that overlap one another's target arcs differed with the season, as in the case of Santa Cruz, which in July intercepted many voyages that reached Tuvalu in January, although the sum for the two groups remained much the same.

55. The results of
Experiment 1A are of
one-way voyages from
the Solomon Islands in
the southern summer.
Successful voyages
are shown by island
destination. It can be seen
that island groups often
overlap and affect one
another.

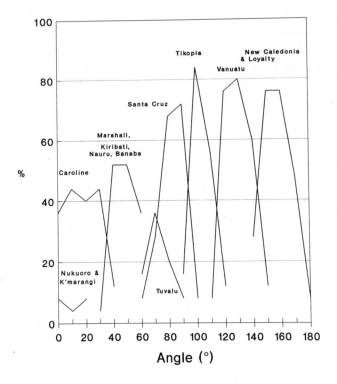

56. For comparison with
Figure 55, this shows the
results of Experiment
1G – return voyaging by
latitude sailing (Strategy 4),
also in the southern
summer. The success rate
for finding new land by
return voyaging follows a
similar pattern to one-way
voyaging in the previous
example, but is sometimes
higher. This is because
Strategy 4 canoes that did
not find land on the way
out have a second chance
on the return.

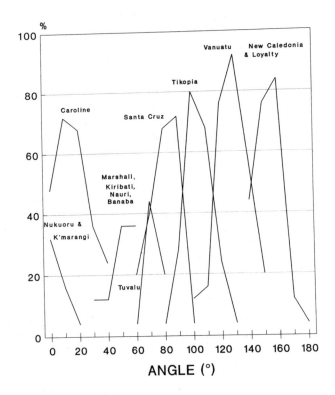

In January, the time expected to be best for sailing east from the Solomons, a few voyages reached islands quite far in the east. Three reached Fiji, two Futuna, and one each to Hunter and Rotuma; in July four got to Rotuma. Increasing the voyaging range to 28 days (Runs 1C and 1D) left the pattern substantially unchanged. More of the distant islands appeared in the results and in January included 15 voyages to New Zealand, five to Lord Howe, four to the Phoenix group, two to Howland, Futuna and Samoa, and one each to Futuna, Niuatoputapu, Tokelau, Palmerston and the Kermadecs. But if we remember that this was out of 600 directed and long voyages, the number is not large. Canoes can slip through the Melanesian net, but not many did.

Different strategies are compared in Figures 55 and 56, which show the frequency of success by islands and groups, according to the direction sailed. One obvious point is that island groups often overlap and affect one another. The comparison is between summertime voyages by Strategy 2 and Strategy 4 respectively (Runs 1A and 1G), in other words one-way voyaging and return voyaging by latitude sailing. The outward legs of both were the same and, structurally, the results should have been, too. However Strategy 4 canoes, which did not find land on the way out, had another chance on the return. In the case of a broad archipelago, of scattered islands, a second pass increased discoveries, and this accounts for the higher success rate visible in the figure, especially in the Caroline Islands.

Figure 57 compares survival by strategy and helps us to decide what kinds of voyaging skill were appropriate for this first offshore passage into Remote Oceania. Distinctions are made between canoes that found new land, ones that did not but returned, and those that did neither. Strategy 2 navigators did well when there was land to be found, but not where there was not. Strategy 3 navigators had a good return rate, except where they sailed into open ocean in the south between Island Melanesia and Australia. The death rate for Strategy 4 navigators was negligible.

Prehistoric issues

Experiment 1 raises the question of why there is no Lapita in Micronesia or Australia, if they can be reached so easily in just a fortnight. An explanation suggested for Micronesia is that its atolls were not in existence in a habitable form at the time. But the three high islands of the Carolines were, and so were Nauru and Banaba, west of Kiribati. It is possible, as discussed, that some of these were found but not settled, perhaps because of isolation. The case of Australia is more difficult to argue away. Even if colonists failed to stay or to survive local competition, they took with them a conspicuous material culture, and it is not impossible there are sites to be found, perhaps in areas of the northern coast or Barrier Reef islands.

Lapita sites are conspicuous in eastern Melanesian islands, and these lie upwind from the Solomons, whereas both Micronesia and Australia lie generally across the wind. It follows that an initial upwind direction of search, as hypothesised here, could be the answer, and that sites do not occur in Micronesia or Australia because people did not search through such a wide and unsafe arc so early. As it happens, the reason to search

57. A comparison of survival by strategy for voyages from the Solomon Islands. Success rates are shown for canoes that found new land, for those that returned, and for those that did neither. Not surprisingly, one-way voyages are more dangerous than two-way ones. Returns by latitude sailing are safest.

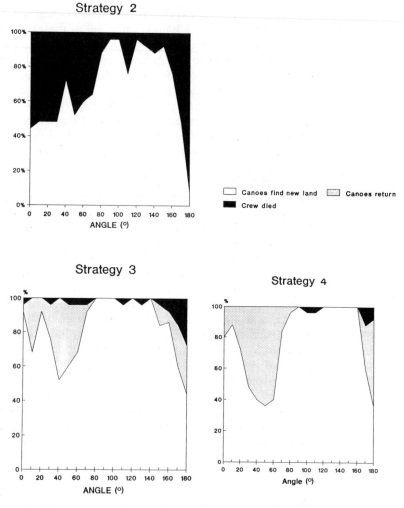

upwind – to have a safe trip home – is not so pressing in this case, because Melanesia is a very substantial target upwind. One might argue that it was the intention to return that directed exploration upwind, but the results of this experiment actually show it was possible to colonise eastern Melanesia by one-way voyages; not as successfully as by two-way voyages, but quite well enough to succeed. This could be seen as a reason for leaving the door ajar if not wide-open, to the idea of pre-Lapita, aceramic settlement of the islands as far east as New Caledonia. However, this question is considered again.

Melanesian islands were reached a few days sooner than Micronesia and Australia, but it is unlikely that they made the difference between life and death for the crews. Santa Cruz and Vanuatu were reached more quickly than New Caledonia, and the results suggest the latter may not have been the first offshore island settled, even if it followed quickly behind.

Finally, it was possible for a handful of voyages of a month or more to reach islands as far afield as Fiji, Samoa and New Zealand from the Solomons. However, the chance of sailing through the gaps in the Melanesian screen, and not being intercepted by islands there was actually very small: for practical purposes we may dismiss it.

FROM EASTERN MELANESIA TO FIJI/WEST POLYNESIA

Canoes were sent on a total of 10,600 voyages from three locations – Santa Cruz, central Vanuatu and the Ile des Pins at the eastern end of New Caledonia – in January and July, by Strategies 2, 3 and 4. The length of one-way voyages was increased to 18 days and the return leg of two-way voyages was 12 days, allowing a month for the round trip. Canoes still travelled at the same speed, but they could now tack on every third day that they continued to meet the same headwind, which is not unreasonable, as they were trying to go in a particular direction. They sailed courses from 40–180°.

Santa Cruz was the most successful origin for canoes that reached Micronesia, and many voyages going east were intercepted by Tikopia (which also included its two neighbours Anuta and Fataka). As mentioned already, this fits evidence for fleeting use of Tikopia in the mid-second millennium B.C. (Kirch and Yen 1982:314). Tikopia may have been a staging post in the earliest offshore expansion by Lapita some 500 years before there is evidence of more substantial settlement there. From New Caledonia, many voyages that took southerly courses reached New Zealand and its neighbours, in fact, more than to any other single island group in the east, although apparently they did not do so in Lapita times. Fiji was the tropical group in the east that received most hits (Tables 3 and 4).

Of the voyages that reached tropical islands in the east, central Vanuatu was the best origin for Rotuma, Fiji and the more northerly islands of West Polynesia, in summer, when canoes had the benefit of the monsoon. The Ile des Pins was the best origin for Fiji and southern parts of West Polynesia, in winter, presumably with some benefit of winter westerlies. Hunter Island captured many canoes leaving the Ile des Pins, but being small and volcanically active, probably served as little more than a navigational aid. An earlier suggestion that Vanuatu was a better origin than New Caledonia is not supported.

Fiji and West Polynesia offer rather smaller and more distant targets than the route crossed already to eastern Melanesia, and of the 375 voyages from New Caledonia sailed under Strategy 2, shown in Figure 58, only 74 got there. Almost the same number (70) were caught by other islands of eastern Melanesia, 100 reached New Zealand and other high latitude islands, and the rest disappeared in eastern waters. Two-way voyaging was safer than one-way, but, even then, it was not safe to sail south of the tropics except towards a large target. From Vanuatu, 106 voyages reached Fiji and West Polynesia by one-way voyaging, and Figure 59 compares the results of Strategies 2 and 4. Figure 59 under-represents successful returns: many canoes were trapped by other islands of Vanuatu on their way out, so no returns were counted.

Table 3   *Simulated voyages from Vanuatu*

Starting island: Vanuatu   January

Angle	50	60	70	80	90	100	110	120	130	140	150	160	170	180
returned	0	0	0	0	0	0	0	28	36	64	68	60	4	4
died	40	40	44	40	8	12	8	40	44	20	4	12	16	0
lived	60	60	56	60	92	88	92	60	56	80	96	88	84	100
Vanuatu								**28**	**36**	**64**	**68**	**60**	**4**	**4**
Tuvalu	52	32	8	4										
Tikopia														
Tokelau		12	8	4	4									
Phoenix	4													
Howland	4													
Niuatoputapu						4								
Futuna			8	12		12	4			12				
Hunter								8	8					
Rotuma		16	24	20	16									
Loyalty												20	72	96
New Caledonia														
Uvea			4	8		8								
Swain's			4	8										
Fiji					44	52	72	16	4					
Samoa					24	8	8							
Tonga					4	4	8							
Kermadec								8	8		4			
Norfolk											4	4		
New Zealand										4	20	4	8	

Note: All scores are percentages; 25 boats each angle

Table 4 *Simulated voyages from New Caledonia*

Starting island:	New Caledonia	July													
Angle	40	50	60	70	80	90	100	110	120	130	140	150	160	170	180
returned	0	0	0	0	0	0	0	0	0	0	0	0	0	0	0
died	0	32	24	16	4	16	56	64	84	76	56	32	4	24	32
lived	100	68	76	84	96	84	44	36	16	24	44	68	96	76	68
New Caledonia															
Vanuatu	92	44	24	4											
Tuvalu		8	12												
Tokelau		4	12												
Phoenix			4												
Futuna			4												
Hunter				24	12	32	24	20		4					
Rotuma	8	12													
Uvea					4										
Swain's															
Fiji			20	52	80	28	16								
Samoa				4											
Tonga						24	4	8							
Kermadec								8	16	20					
Norfolk													8	4	32
New Zealand											44	68	88	72	36

Note: All scores are percentages; 25 boats sailed per angle

58. The success rates of Strategy 2 and Strategy 4 voyages in winter from New Caledonia shown by direction and island target. Return voyages were more successful than one-way trips, but it was not safe to sail south of the tropics except towards a substantial target.

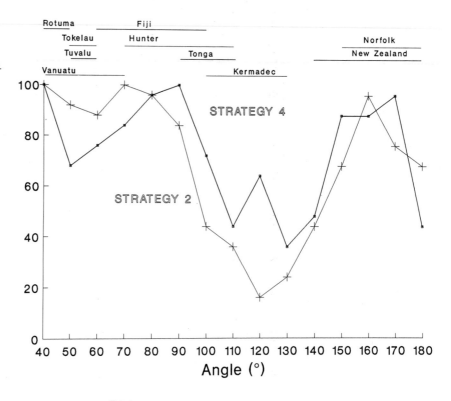

59. The success rates of Strategy 2 and Strategy 4 voyages in summer from Vanuátu, shown by direction and island target.

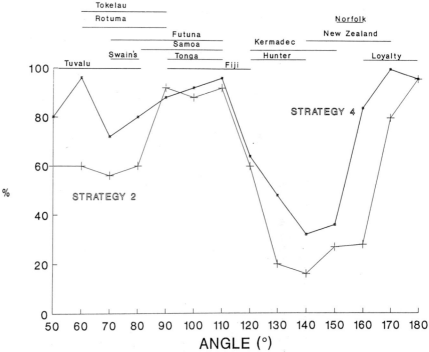

FROM WEST POLYNESIA TO EAST POLYNESIA

A total of 4400 canoes left from American Samoa in the north and Tongatapu in the south, in summer and winter, using the same sailing methods. The length of outward voyages remained 18 days, but round-trips were increased to 35, allowing 17 for returns. They covered an arc wide enough to encompass all East Polynesia, and examples of the results for part of this are shown in Tables 5 and 6. Samoa was the better origin for East Polynesia, except for Niue and New Zealand, and summer the best time to leave: 49 canoes of the 325 voyages shown in Table 5 reached the Northern Cook Islands and 44 reached the Southern Cook Islands whereas only 25 got to the Society Islands, four to the Tuamotus and none to the Marquesas. This confirms the suggestion that the closer parts of East Polynesia were easier to reach, and could be expected to show this archaeologically. Winter sailing from Samoa was quite successful also, with 34 canoes reaching the Southern Cooks and 11 to the Society Islands. From Tonga, summer sailing produced the best overall results, but as many canoes were able to cross the southern part of the tropics to the Southern Cooks in winter. In Table 6, a dozen canoes reached the Northern Cooks, 35 got to the Southern Cooks, five to the Society Islands and one to the Austral Islands.

The cost of sailing east had increased. The success rates by one-way and return voyages were now farther apart. Figure 60 shows a January fleet from Tonga, by Strategy 4, which stayed mainly within the tropics. It can be seen that about half of the people would have died if there had been no return, but this example cuts it to 14%. There is no evidence for a pause between West and East Polynesia, but there is the suggestion of a navigational threshold between the tropics and higher latitudes.

To check the result for the Marquesas, which are still claimed as a likely early direct origin in the east (Bellwood 1989; Davidson 1989), an experiment was set up to give every chance of reaching them from West Polynesia. Canoes were sent out in summer in what had proved to be the three best directions, with 35 outward days to find the target. 12% did reach the Marquesas, but the Northern Cooks claimed 15%, the Society Islands, 24%, the Southern Line Islands 13% and the Tuamotus 7%. The Marquesas remained a long shot.

VOYAGING IN CENTRAL EAST POLYNESIA

To explore the discovery of central East Polynesia, and to provide a range of competing departure points for the islands of marginal East Polynesia, four experiments from six starting islands employed some 15,900 canoes.

Table 5   *Simulated voyages from Samoa*

Starting island:	Samoa	January	Strategy 2															
Angle	**40**	**50**	**60**	**70**	**80**	**90**	**100**	**110**	**120**	**130**	**140**	**150**	**160**	**170**	**180**	**190**	**200**	**210**
returned	0	0	0	0	0	0	0	0	0	0	0	0	0	0	0	0	0	0
died	92	44	32	56	48	48	40	24	40	44	92	96	100	96	80	36	72	32
lived	8	56	68	44	52	52	60	76	60	56	8	4	0	4	20	64	28	68
Samoa																		
Tonga																	8	48
Phoenix	4																	
N Line	4	4																
S Line		4	12	4	16													
Pukapuka		36	28	4														
Penrhyn		8	8															
Manihiki		4	12															
Suwarrow			8	16	12	8	4											
S Cook				4		4	28	36	52	40	8	4						
Society				12	24	40	·16	8										
Tuamotu				4														
Palmerston							4	24	8	12								
Austral							8	8		4								
Niue														4	20	64		
Kermadec																	20	20

Note: All scores are percentages; 25 boats sailed per angle

Table 6 *Simulated voyages from Tonga*

Starting island:	Tonga	January																	
Angle	30	40	50	60	70	80	90	100	110	120	130	140	150	160	170	180	190	200	210
returned	24	4	8	0	0	0	0	0	0	0	0	0	0	0	0	0	0	0	0
died	8	32	48	52	56	24	28	56	76	100	100	100	100	100	96	76	60	20	4
lived	92	68	52	48	44	76	72	44	24	0	0	0	0	0	4	24	40	80	96
Tonga	**24**	**4**	**8**																
Niuatoputapu	4	4																	
Samoa	64	56	16	16															
Swain's		4																	
Niue			16	16	12	28	16	12	8										
Penrhyn			4																
Manihiki			4	4															
Suwarrow			4	4															
Palmerston				4	12	8	4												
Society				4	12	4													
S Cook					8	36	52	32	12										
Austral									4										
Kermadec															4	4	24	32	8
New Zealand																4	16	48	88
Chatham																16			

Note: All scores are percentages; 25 boats sailed per angle

60. The results achieved by fleets of eastbound canoes sailing from Tonga in summer. About half of the crews would have died if there had been no return, but this two-way experiment reduces losses to 14%. Voyages from West Polynesia to East Polynesia were more costly than those before. Courses to the southeast were more difficult than easterly ones.

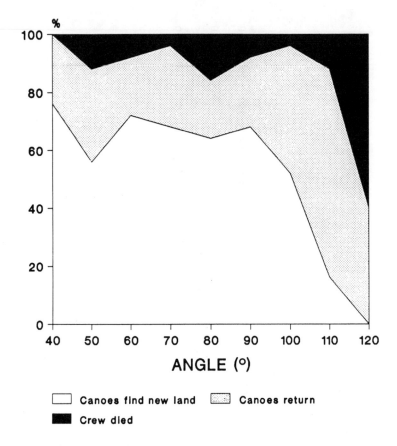

Canoes find new land   Canoes return
Crew died

Voyages from the Southern Cooks

Summer and winter voyages set off from Atiu, in a wide arc from 0–270°, to allow voyages to Hawaii in the north, New Zealand in the south, and back to West Polynesia (and beyond) in the west. Trials showed that while parts of East Polynesia could be reached quite quickly, it required 21 days to get to New Zealand, a day or two more to Norfolk Island, and 30 for Hawaii. Accordingly, 30 days were set for outward voyages and another 30 for the return, making a round trip of two months. But while the range of canoes was increasing, their average speed (4 knots) and tacking method (every third day of the same headwind), did not.

The broad pattern of results for central East Polynesia were similar for January and July, which is to be expected as many voyages followed reaching courses across the southeast trades, as well as waiting for other winds to make progress against them. Table 7 shows that in January the largest number of voyages (78) reached the Society Islands, while 29 got to the Tuamotus, which are partly concealed behind them. A further 31 canoes reached the Austral Islands, and it would appear that there is little reason to suppose that much time separated the date of first discovery of these groups. A number of landfalls were also made among the scattered islands of the Northern Cooks and, the three clusters of the Line Islands, but in numbers that suggest their first discovery was more gradual and piecemeal.

Table 7 *Simulated voyages from Atiu (Southern Cooks)*

Starting island: **Atiu**   January

Angle	0	10	20	30	40	50	60	70	80	90	100	110	120	130	140	150	160	170	180	190	200	210	220	230	240	250	260	270
returned	0	0	0	0	0	0	0	0	0	0	0	0	0	0	0	0	0	0	0	0	0	0	0	0	0	0	0	0
died	68	32	44	44	64	28	52	8	0	8	44	40	88	92	100	100	100	100	96	92	100	68	76	0	36	80	64	0
lived	32	68	56	56	36	72	48	92	100	92	56	60	12	8	0	0	0	0	4	8	0	32	24	100	64	20	36	100
S Cook																			4	8								
N Line	4	20	16	8																								
Jarvis	8	4	4		4																							
Manihiki	20	8	4																									
Ctr Line		8		12																								
Penryhn		20	8	12	4																							
Hawaii		8	20	12	8																							
S Line				8	8	16	4																					
Society			4	4	12	56	44	60	76	44	12	4																
Tuamotu								28	20	28	20	16																
Austral								4	4	12	12	36	12	8														
Rapa										4	8	4																
Pitcairn										4																		
Henderson											4																	
Bounty																						4						
New Zealand																						4	24	80	28			
Chatham																						24						
Kermadec																								20	36			
Norfolk																										12		
Lord Howe																										8		
Hunter																											4	
Tonga																											32	88
Vanuatu																												4
Loyalty																												4
Fiji																												4

Note: All scores are percentages; 25 boats sailed per angle

Only four canoes found Rapa, more isolated than the Austral Islands, and one each to Pitcairn and Henderson far in the east, and it seems likely such outliers were found some time after the large central targets. Finally, it can be seen that New Zealand was within range of outward voyages. Survival rates for voyages from Atiu were only 42% for Strategy 2, 63% for Strategy 3 and 76% for Strategy 4. Many of the simulated deaths occurred during voyages south into empty ocean, but there is no archaeological evidence yet from high latitude islands to prove that many early voyages actually tried to go that way.

Voyages from the Society Islands

These again followed a 0–270° arc for wide coverage, and again the patterns for January and July showed many similarities. The Tuamotus provided the best target from the Society Islands, followed by the Austral Islands, again confirming that these three central groups were discovered, if not settled, quickly. However, only six canoes of the 700 shown in Table 8 reached the Marquesas, partly concealed by the Tuamotus, which suggests they were as hard to reach directly from here as was New Zealand! Similarly, only 15 voyages reached Rapa. Islands like this, which outlie at some distance from central East Polynesia, could have been brought within the range of communication only if accurate methods of latitude fixing by the stars were known by this stage. Simulation suggests the need for knowledge of this kind was becoming more pressing. As for survival rates, these were better than from the Southern Cooks, quite possibly because the Society Islands are surrounded by more islands.

Voyages from the Australs

Another 1950 canoes left the Australs in January and July by Strategies 2–4, on courses 0–120°, using the same sailing methods for 14 days out, and 30 days for the round-trip. Results for Strategy 2 sailing in summer are shown in Table 9, where it can be seen that the great majority of successful voyages shot straight into the Tuamotus and Society Islands. Rapa received most of its hits in January, but these were still only 14 of the 325 that set out. Voyages reached Mangareva in both summer and winter, but were so rare as to suggest it was more likely settled via the Tuamotus than from the Australs. No simulated voyage had reached Easter Island by this stage. The probabilities for reaching Pitcairn and its small neighbours were also negligible, and the few successes occurred in winter, presumably with help from the westerlies of sub-tropical origin. One normal feature of the strategies with return voyages was that success rates for remote islands increased as canoes made their second pass among them.

Voyages from the Tuamotus and Mangareva

This was essentially the one experiment. Two starting locations were needed to allow most canoes to escape in 36 directions (0–360°) from this broad

Table 8   Simulated voyages from Raiatea (Society Islands)

Starting island:	Raiatea	January																									
Angle	0	10	20	30	40	50	60	70	80	90	100	110	120	130	140	150	160	170	180	190	200	210	220	230	240	250	260	270
returned	0	0	0	0	0	0	0	0	0	0	0	0	0	0	0	0	0	0	0	0	0	0	0	0	0	0	0	0
died	32	32	68	96	92	88	60	20	12	4	20	36	64	52	52	60	88	52	92	100	92	76	0	0	0	0	16	0
lived	68	68	32	4	8	12	40	80	88	96	80	64	36	48	48	48	12	48	8	0	8	24	100	100	100	100	84	100
Society									**12**	**8**	**24**	**8**	**4**	**4**														
S Line	24	20	12		8																							
Hawaii	44	48	20	4																								
Tuamotu						12	36	76	64	84	56	56																
Marquesas							4	4	12	4																		
Austral													12	24	28	48	12	48	8		4							
Rapa													20	20	20													
New Zealand																							40	8				
Chatham																					4	24						
S Cook																							60	84	100	100	12	
Kermadec																								8				
Tonga																											56	76
Niue																											4	
Palmerston																											12	
Niuatoputapu																												4
Fiji																												20

Note: All scores are percentages; 25 boats per angle

Table 9 *Simulated voyages from the Australs*

Starting island: Austral January													
Angle	0	10	20	30	40	50	60	70	80	90	100	110	120
returned	0	0	0	0	0	0	0	0	0	4	0	0	0
died	4	16	8	0	0	8	4	4	16	56	76	80	76
lived	96	84	92	100	100	92	96	96	84	44	24	20	24
Austral										4			
Society	88	44	52	16	8	4							
Tuamotu	8	40	40	84	92	88	92	92	80	40	8	4	
Marquesas							4						
Mangareva								4	4				
Rapa											16	16	24

Note: All scores are percentages; 25 boats sailed per angle

Table 10 *Simulated voyages from the Tuamotus*

Starting island: Tuamotu Islands July Strategy 2												
Angle	returned	died	lived	Tuamotu	Marquesas	Oeno	Henderson	Pitcairn	Ducie	Rapa	Austral	Society
0	0	4	96		96							
10	0	16	84		84							
20	0	68	32		32							
30	0	96	4		4							
40	0	100	0									
50	0	100	0									
60	0	100	0									
70	0	92	8			4	4					
80	0	96	4				4					
90	0	76	24				12	12				
100	0	68	32			8	12	12				
110	0	64	36			4	12	16	4			
120	0	84	16			8		8				
130	0	84	16					16				
140	0	96	4					4				
150	0	96	4					4				
160	0	100	0									
170	0	100	0									
180	0	100	0									
190	0	100	0									
200	0	100	0									
210	0	100	0									
220	0	96	4							4		
230	0	100	0									
240	0	88	12							12		
250	0	80	20							20		
260	0	68	32							4	28	
270	0	48	52								52	
280	16	72	28	16							12	
290	100	0	100	100								
300	84	8	92	84								8
310	92	8	92	92								
320	100	0	100	100								
330	0	100	0									
340	0	100	0									
350	0	92	8		8							

Note: All scores are percentages; 25 boats sailed per angle

61. Strategy 3 and 4 canoes sail out around the compass from two origins in the archipelagos of the Tuamotu Islands and Mangareva. The inner result line shows percentages of canoes that succeeded in finding some other land. The effect of diminishing targets in an expanding ocean in this part of the Pacific is clearly seen in the narrow arcs within which land was found. The shaded outer part of the figure shows the percentages of canoes lost at sea. Between these two zones can be seen the percentages of canoes that failed to find land, but got back safely. The very large atoll cloud of the Tuamotu archipelago represented a broad target in central East Polynesia, which could provide staging posts for voyages between central groups of high islands, or which could be found fairly reliably by canoes that had ventured out in various directions into the Polynesian margins.

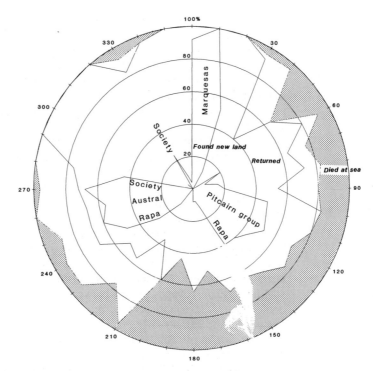

island cloud. One was from the vicinity of Fangatau Atoll in the northeast (for courses 330–350° and 0–50°), and the other was Mangareva (60–320°), at the southeast extremity of the wider archipelago. Strategies 2–4 were compared by season; outward journeys were 14 days long and round trips a month.

Table 10 shows the July one-way voyages of Strategy 2. Canoes successfully escaped the origin except between 280–320°, where there was nowhere much else to go, anyway. Voyages north between 350° and 30° gave the best results so far for reaching the Marquesas, and the probabilities were even better in summer (not shown). This confirms an earlier suggestion that the Marquesas were probably not settled by a direct upwind voyage from the west, but by reaching across the trade winds from a more southerly immediate origin in a longer and more indirect route.

Winter was the best time for easterly voyages from Mangareva to the Pitcairn group, which, for the first time, became a practical proposition. Their settlement can be associated to some extent with sub-tropical westerlies. Rapa and the Australs were reached from Mangareva in a narrow target arc.

Figure 61 is a rather dramatic depiction of the effect of two-way voyaging from this region. Firstly, it can be seen that successful voyages to new islands occurred within quite restricted arcs, and these are bigger than they would be in one-way voyaging because canoes have been able to make the second pass. Evidence for the erratic tracks of some returns is found in the diverse directions from which Rapa and the Societies were reached.

A second main point is that return voyaging was clearly necessary here, and earlier, if ocean exploration was not to be very substantially suicidal.

Only a quarter of the crews survived one-way voyages in this experiment. However, a very large percentage of unsuccessful two-way canoes were able to return safely. In Figure 61, the perimeter of the return circle is made up of either Strategy 3 or Strategy 4 voyages, whichever gave the best results for a particular point of sail. Strategy 3 navigators simply tried to return on a reciprocal course, sometimes corrected by the dead reckoned estimate for leeway, but without the benefit of latitude sailing, in this example. They have worked best, here, for returns from the west, where canoes were already downwind of their origin and not in a position to use latitude sailing without a long upwind climb to windward of it first. Without the option of latitude sailing, they lacked the precision it gives to homing in on a specific target, but in this case the target was very wide.

Thirdly, there is support for the suggestion that the Tuamotu/Mangareva archipelago presented a very large target screen in central East Polynesia. This was one that could be returned to or one that could be aimed at on voyages from outside. The atolls of the Tuamotus did not offer the same potential for dense settlement as the high islands of the Society Islands, Mangareva, Marquesas and Austral Islands, but it did offer a huge staging post on voyages to and between these surrounding groups. Crews could locate the island screen, rest, find food, reorientate themselves if necessary, and sail on.

There are implications in these voyaging probabilities for patterns of post-settlement diversification in central East Polynesia. For instance, the Society Islands, NW Tuamotus and Austral Islands were very accessible to one another, with a firm link to the Southern Cooks. The Marquesas and Mangareva (and islands probably settled from them, including Hawaii and Easter Island) could be expected to be more remote from subsequent cultural and linguistic changes.

THE POLYNESIAN MARGINS

Conventionally, the Polynesian margins include Easter Island, Hawaii and New Zealand, but in voyaging terms and in the matter of discovery, Rapa, the Marquesas and the Pitcairn Group were also quite hard to reach, if not as far away. It has been suggested that the three clusters of the Line Islands were sometime satellites or intermediaries of Hawaii, as easily hit on the way in as out, and the Kermadecs and Norfolk stand in a similar relationship to New Zealand.

Simulated voyages to and from the margins were more selective in terms of direction and strategy, than earlier ones, because of what had been learned by explorers already. They include six experiments sailed back from starting points at the margins, and involve a total of 7175 canoes.

The Marquesas

It was found possible for the simulation program to force a small number of canoes upwind to the Marquesas directly from Samoa, but the chance that it was first colonised from there must be rated as extremely low, unless

Table 11 *Simulated voyages from the Marquesas*

Starting island:	Marquesas	July		Strategy 2																				
Angle	0	10	20	30	40	50	60	70	80	90	100	110	120	130	140	150	160	170	180	320	330	340	350
returned	0	0	0	0	0	0	0	0	0	0	0	0	0	0	0	0	0	0	0	0	0	0	0
died	100	100	100	100	100	96	96	100	100	100	100	100	12	36	16	28	20	24	32	88	8	84	100
lived	0	0	0	0	0	4	4	0	0	0	0	0	88	64	84	72	80	76	68	12	92	16	0
Marquesas																							
Tuamotu													76	56	84	64	76	76	68				
Mangareva													12			4	4						
Henderson														4									
Pitcairn														4		4							
Hawaii																				12	92	16	
America						4	4																

Note: All scores are percentages; 25 boats sailed per angle

it was by a remarkable event beyond the scope of this simulation. Canoes began to arrive more naturally from the Society Islands, but still in small numbers. However, the Marquesas are partly obscured from the Society Islands by the Tuamotus, which are closer and, significantly, in a more accessible direction across the wind. The results here favour them as the source, as described already.

Some 3450 voyages were sent out from the Marquesas and results of the first fleet of 575 are shown in Table 11. These sailed out for a month in selected directions by Strategy 2; 125 reached the Tuamotus in a fairly substantial arc of 70°, and 5 got to Mangareva at the southeastern extremity of the wider archipelago. Three canoes got to the Pitcairn group, and two (out of the experiment total of 3450) even reached America, to indicate what is possible, but rare. Of interest are the 30 canoes, 5% of the starters, which reached Hawaii, very successfully, but in a narrow target arc. In this one-way experiment only 29% of the crews survived, again emphasising the compelling sense of return voyaging.

The effect of return voyaging was to increase the rate of success in finding land as the canoes went out and back. The Central, Southern and Northern Line Islands accounted for 34 successes (6%) in the January experiment of Strategy 3, while Hawaii increased to 54 (9%). Values for the Pitcairn Group were 3%, and other islands in central East Polynesia were hit as the canoes tried to find their way home.

Easter Island

The most likely source of those tested was Pitcairn. One-way simulated voyages sailed out from Pitcairn for 21 days, while two-way voyages were allowed 30 days for the outward leg and a further 20 back. Winter was the better season, but Easter Island was usually hit only by voyages sailing in a 30° arc. The success rate achieved by sailing in the very best direction was only about 30% for Easter Island, with just a few more percentage points for its tiny neighbour Sala y Gomez.

One feature of return voyages was that, for the first time, Strategy 4 voyages, which used latitude sailing as the explicit strategy of return, were very much more successful than returns that did not use it. Easter Island is far upwind of the starting island, Pitcairn, which is a small target itself to find on the way home with only a few small scattered neighbours, and, if they were all missed, Mangareva and the Tuamotu group were still some distance away. Table 12 shows the situation.

Table 12   *Voyages from Pitcairn towards Easter Island (percentages)*

	Experiment 10-A, D and F, courses 30-150°, 975 canoes				
	Find Easter	Find other	Return	Live	Die
Strategy 2	1.5	3.1	0	4.6	95.4
3	4.3	30.8	4.3	39.4	60.6
4	4.6	30.2	43.0	77.8	22.2

The success rate was low for all strategies, although better for the return ones. However, the death rate for Strategy 3 returns was 60%, whereas for Strategy 4 it was only 22%. This is strong evidence that some conceptual equivalent to latitude sailing was a necessary part of the repertoire of deep-sea exploration. Further, because it appeared in voyages out from central East Polynesia, presumably it was carried to other discoveries made from there, including the Marquesas, Hawaii and New Zealand.

Two experimental fleets totalling 800 canoes were sent back from Easter Island, half each in summer and winter, in just an 80° arc sufficient to cover the groups of central East Polynesia. The first were two-way return voyages of Strategy 4, which sailed in a risky downwind direction for 25 days, and, if they failed to find land, set themselves the still more difficult task of finding their tiny and isolated origin, far upwind, in another 35 days. Because they knew where they were going and wanted to get there, they were able to tack every second day against the same headwind. The outcome was that 54% found some land, another 7% returned to Easter Island, while 39% died in the attempt. It is interesting that even 7% success for Easter Island is better than achieved by the canoes that first set out to find it (4.6%); the difference is that now they had a dead-reckoned estimate of its position as well having knowledge of its latitude. All the same, these were high losses by the normal standards of Strategy 4, and they are a consequence of return voyages ending in a largely empty area of ocean.

The second fleet began to explore a different strategy and did much better, because none of the canoes that did not find land tried to return, even though these were two-way voyages. They sailed out from Easter Island by Strategy 3 for the same 25 days, and, if they had not found land when time expired, they deliberately turned north or south to intercept the Tuamotus, which they already knew existed. Whether canoes turned north or south depended on the bearing of their outward track, and where the dead-reckoned position placed them at the end of it. Latitude sailing was suppressed, so that success depended upon the interception. Of this fleet, 94.5% found land and 5.5% died.

Table 13   *Simulated voyages from Easter Island*

Starting island:	Easter Island	January	Strategy 3					
Angle	250	260	270	280	290	300	310	320
returned	0	0	0	0	0	0	0	0
died	0	0	0	0	4	0	0	48
lived	100	100	100	100	96	100	100	52
Easter								
Ducie				4				
Mangareva				8	4			4
Marquesas						4	96	8
Pitcairn				32				
Henderson				20				
Rapa	20	32	28					
Austral	8	4	4					
Tuamotu	68	64	68	36	92	96	4	40
Society	4							
boats out of bounds:					1			12

Note: all scores are percentages; 25 boats per angle

The results support the earlier independent suggestion that, as the colonisation of the Pacific progressed and as its geography became known, canoes that sailed downwind would often return by a different route or through a different island. This is one clear case where this extra strategy was required, and there are others. The possibility began as a deduction, but with this empirical support we may refer to it, in a general way, as Strategy 5. It means that there was something akin to a 'three-way voyage': going from A to B to C and with a final leg back to A again, if one wished to take it. Places A and C were known at the outset; B might have been known or not, depending on whether it was a voyage of exploration or a later one over a known track. This example also shows the effectiveness of the central East Polynesian net, and especially the Tuamotus, to catch incoming canoes that knew of it already.

The details of the January section of this experiment are shown in Table 13. The Tuamotus were hit through a wide arc and other groups in more narrow ones. The 35 days of the second leg allowed those unfortunates who missed land to sail north or south completely out of the experimental area of the Pacific.

South America

Five hundred canoes sailed east from Easter Island on bearings between 50° and 140°, which previous trials had shown to cover the most suitable range of courses for America. Success rates between 50% and 70% were achieved, and controlled Strategy 4 returns to Easter Island and Sala y Gomez brought survival up to 95%, except for canoes that searched far to the south. Generally, South America was easier to reach in winter, but survival for the crews who did not make it was better in summer. The Juan Fernandez and St Felix islands off the coast of South America accounted for about 5% of canoes, and .08% (four canoes) reached the Galapagos, which does not make a prehistoric Polynesian landing on the latter at all likely.

While two canoes (out of 3450) originating from the Marquesas reached South America in an earlier experiment, the southern tropics appear to be a much better bet. Easter Island is a likely origin, but it is also likely that South America was reached directly from farther downwind, for example from Mangareva or the Pitcairn Group, with the extra time needed to reach Easter Island's longitude. In round figures, the choices are between a one month voyage from Easter Island and a two-month voyage that sailed past Easter Island, which was hard to locate at the best of times. However, I prefer Easter Island as the source, because a return to Easter Island was safer than one farther downwind.

Returns to Easter Island from South America were shown to be fairly dependable. To see what would happen to the relatively few canoes from South America that missed it, a fleet of 250 was sent from South America, in the appropriate direction, but without the knowledge of Easter Island's latitude (under Strategy 3); only 6% found it and the rest sailed past. Of the latter, 56% found other land in central East Polynesia, but the others did not. However, other experiments have shown that with knowledge of the latitude of the Tuamotus and other nearby groups, the success rate could have been high.

Hawaii

The probable origins of settlement on Hawaii emerged from earlier experiments. No simulated voyage reached Hawaii from Samoa, but from Atiu in the Southern Cooks, between 8% and 20% of canoes that sailed courses between 0° and 40° by Strategy 2 did so (Table 7), and there were even more successes in two-way voyages. From Raiatea in the Society Islands, they increased to between 4% and 48% for the same courses (Table 8) and still higher for two-way voyages. It should be borne in mind that the most effective target arc from the Society Islands was small, and these voyages must be regarded as quite difficult, at least in terms of this simulation. Results were better from the northern Tuamotus, but best of all from the Marquesas – farthest to the east and upwind. Fine-grained results are shown in Figure 62, where 100 canoes sailed each direction between 310° and 350°, at 5° intervals, summer and winter. These were one-way voyages, and it is clear that Hawaii was a good target for those who chose the right direction. The results of experimental voyages in replica canoes at sea are relevant here, because they show that dead-reckoning errors do not accumulate during voyages of this length, but rather cancel each other out: canoes generally could have held their chosen courses. The results of Figure 62 also demonstrate, yet again, the numerical argument in favour of return voyaging. Further, with latitude sailing, which is believed to have existed by this stage, Hawaii would have been an even easier target after discovery: canoes could have increased their margin of safety

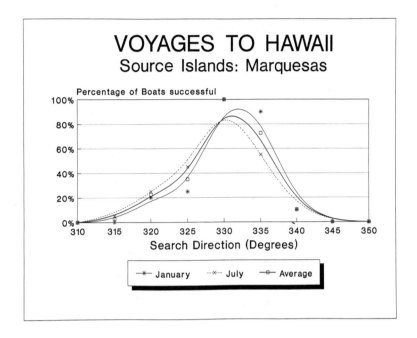

62. Fleets of 100 canoes sail at 5° intervals on courses from 310° to 350° from the Marquesas towards Hawaii, in both summer and winter. Canoes that choose the best direction, within some 10° of angle, are very successful. This diagram also confirms the point that explorers who sail out into empty ocean are well advised to return in good time. (Reprinted by permission of the editor, from Irwin, Bickler and Quirke 1990.)

by holding a track upwind of the rhumbline course until arriving at, and running along, the destination latitude.

With regard to returning from Hawaii, 1350 canoes set off under various circumstances. For most of this century, commentators have mentioned the feasibility of canoes sailing north from the Marquesas, but back to the Tuamotus/Societies, because the Marquesas lay too far upwind for an easy return. This is borne out by the results, shown in Table 14, of a Strategy 4 experiment that allowed 28 days for outward legs and 52 days in which to get back to Hawaii again, if the need arose. Canoes that sailed at 130° did have to return, except for one that reached the Marquesas. At 140°, 36% got there and 44% came back, but others were beginning to reach the Tuamotus, which was the dominant place of arrival in central East Polynesia and, west of there, overlapped with the Society Islands. Thus Hawaii appears to represent another application of the 'three-way' voyage. Figure 63 clearly shows the circumstances involved. It is a plot of a simulated Strategy 4 voyage of 10 canoes south from Hawaii, in January, at 150°. The canoes can be seen to reach steadily across the northeast trades towards the Marquesas. They cross the doldrums and meet the southeast trades, as headwinds, and can no longer lay their course. Their tracks sag to the west; nine canoes make their landfalls in the Tuamotus, but one does not. It returns to the latitude of Hawaii, then turns west and runs downwind to find it. All survive. This clearly illustrates the rationale of this application of a 'three-way' voyage.

On various courses as far as 190° (Table 14), other islands of East Polynesia including the Lines and the Cooks were hit. More westerly courses took canoes successfully to West Polynesia and Micronesia, destinations from which they could not hope to return.

Table 14 *Simulated voyages from Hawaii*

Starting island: **Hawaii**   **January**

ANGLE	130	140	150	160	170	180	190	200	210	220	230	240	250	260	270
returned	96	36	4	0	0	0	0	0	0	0	0	0	0	0	0
died	0	0	0	0	8	4	20	8	8	8	28	4	12	20	40
lived	100	100	100	100	92	96	80	92	92	92	72	96	88	80	60
Hawaii	**96**	**36**	**4**												
Marquesas	4	44													
Tuamotu		20	96	92	8										
Society				8	52	8	28								
Jarvis					4	4									
N Line						48	16						4		4
Ctr Line						4									
S Line					28										
S Cook						28	4								
Penrhyn						4									
Manihiki							28								
Suwarrow							4								
Pukapuka								4							
Niue								36							
Samoa								48	20						
Tokelau								4	32	4					
Uvea									12						
Niuatoputapu									28						
Tuvalu										72	48				
Rotuma										8					
Phoenix										8					
Kiribati											24	92			
Banaba												4			
Marshall													4	24	
Caroline													80	56	
Mariana															56

Note: All scores are percentages; 25 boats sailed per angle

63. Connections between central East Polynesia and Hawaii were probably made by 'three-way voyages'. The best starting point for Hawaii was in the Marquesas, farthest upwind. However, it can be seen in the simulated tracks of 10 canoes trying to return to the Marquesas that they are unable to lay the course once they reach the southeasterly trades, which become headwinds on the return journey. A landfall in the Tuamotu or Society islands is more feasible. Such a triangular link with Hawaii has long been proposed.

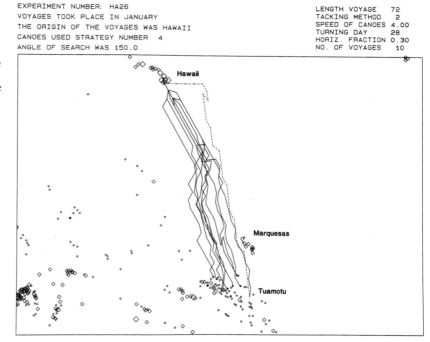

```
EXPERIMENT NUMBER: HA26                              LENGTH VOYAGE    72
VOYAGES TOOK PLACE IN JANUARY                        TACKING METHOD    2
THE ORIGIN OF THE VOYAGES WAS HAWAII                 SPEED OF CANOES 4.00
CANOES USED STRATEGY NUMBER  4                       TURNING DAY      28
ANGLE OF SEARCH WAS 150.0                            HORIZ. FRACTION 0.30
                                                     NO. OF VOYAGES   10
```

Of the courses from 160° to 190°, 33 canoes (33%) reached various of the Line Islands, many apparently on their outward track from Hawaii. Two which left on 250° and 270° appear to have made their way back as far as the Northern Lines from somewhere in Micronesia. We have confirmation of the suggestion that they could be hit from Hawaii as well as from the south. There are implications for the chronology of settlement of the Lines, which are almost entirely undated archaeologically (but not quite). If it were found that Hawaii was as good a target in the north as the Lines, or better, then we could not tell from which direction the Lines themselves were first settled, Hawaii or somewhere in the south. The figures confirm the suggestion. The Line Islands were hit in small numbers by canoes from Samoa (Table 5). From the Southern Cooks, Hawaii and the Line Islands showed roughly the same low frequency. The parity was much the same from the Society Islands (Table 8), although the numbers became more significant. However, the results for the Marquesas, the most probable source of Hawaiian settlement, suggests it attracted twice as many landfalls as its probable intermediaries. We would therefore expect some of the Line Islands to have been discovered at about the same time as Hawaii, from both directions, but whether they were also settled as early is quite another matter.

New Zealand

According to various experiments, New Zealand was accessible from several island groups to the north. Information extracted from experiments from New Caledonia, Tonga and the Southern Cook Islands is shown in Tables 15–18.

Table 15   *Voyages from New Caledonia in July; Strategy 2; 18 days (percentages)*

Angle	Kermadec Is	Norfolk	New Zealand
100	4		
110	8		
120	16		
130	20		
140			44
150			68
160		8	88
170		4	72
180		32	36

Table 16   *Voyages from Tonga in January; Strategy 2; 18 days (percentages)*

Angle	Kermadec Is	New Zealand
170	4	
180	4	4
190	24	16
200	32	48
210	8	88

Table 17   *Voyages from Tonga in January; Strategy 4; 18 days (percentages)*

Angle	Kermadec Is	New Zealand	Norfolk
180	16		
190	44	16	
200	60	28	
210	4	88	
220		92	
230		12	4
240		4	48
250			8

Table 18   *Voyages from the Sthn Cook Islands in January; Strategy 2; 18 days (percentages)*

Angle	Kermadec Is	New Zealand	Norfolk	Chatham Is
210		4		24
220		24		
230	20	80		
240	36	28		
250			12	

The chances of reaching New Zealand were very high within fairly narrow target arcs. New Caledonia gave best results for July, while Tonga and the Southern Cooks were better in January, but, in all cases, results for the other season were respectable. Fiji is not shown, but is as feasible an origin.

64. New Zealand can be reached reliably within a series of narrow target arcs from New Caledonia (as shown), Fiji, West Polynesia and East Polynesia. The absence of archaeological evidence for settlement of New Zealand during the first 2000 years of deep-ocean exploration suggests directions in which explorers chose not to sail.

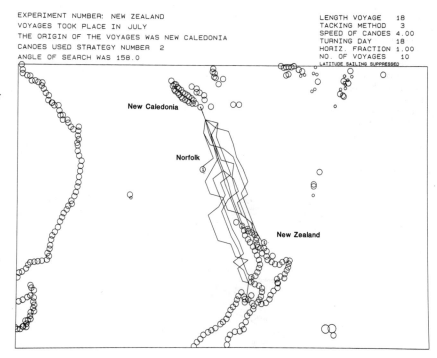

```
EXPERIMENT NUMBER:  NEW ZEALAND                          LENGTH VOYAGE    18
VOYAGES TOOK PLACE IN JULY                               TACKING METHOD    3
THE ORIGIN OF THE VOYAGES WAS NEW CALEDONIA              SPEED OF CANOES 4.00
CANOES USED STRATEGY NUMBER  2                           TURNING DAY      18
ANGLE OF SEARCH WAS 158.0                                HORIZ. FRACTION 1.00
                                                         NO. OF VOYAGES   10
                                                         LATITUDE SAILING SUPPRESSED
```

New Caledonia

Norfolk

New Zealand

The results are no surprise, as New Zealand's closest large neighbour is New Caledonia. Figure 64 is a plot of a one-way voyage of 10 canoes from New Caledonia, and all of them can be seen to arrive safely except the one that went to Norfolk Island. New Zealand also lies closer to Fiji and West Polynesia than it does to the closest part of East Polynesia, the Southern Cook Islands.

It is also most interesting that it appeared to be no harder to reach New Zealand from eastern Melanesia, than it was to cross from there to Fiji and West Polynesia! However, this applies only to those canoes that steered the best course for New Zealand.

Compared with Norfolk Island and the Kermadecs, New Zealand is the bigger target at the greater distance, and, all things being equal, it could be expected to have been settled as early, and is therefore a possible source of early settlement of its smaller northern neighbours. In this respect the simulation supports previous suggestions.

All or any of these southern islands could have been discovered in Lapita times, or at any time since. The obvious reason against this for New Zealand is latitude, to which the simulation is neutral. The North Cape of New Zealand is 34°S. and well below the tropics. Sailing in cooler conditions in a different weather regime may have deterred explorers. However, Norfolk Island and the Kermadecs are both at 29° S., which is less than 2° (120 sea miles) south of Easter Island and Rapa, which were both occupied. By Polynesian standards, Norfolk Island and the Kermadecs are not very small; they are also high and visible from some distance. Quite possibly they were discovered early, but not settled then, but the question arises of whether there is any suggestion of a wider pattern into which they fall.

65. East Polynesia can be reached in approximately 35 sailing days from New Zealand, and many voyages are intercepted by the Kermadec Islands. Closer destinations in the tropical Pacific can be reached more quickly. The conventional wisdom that New Zealand's prehistory lies exclusively with East Polynesia could be reviewed once again.

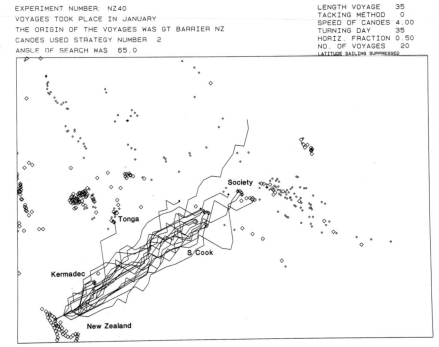

EXPERIMENT NUMBER: NZ40
VOYAGES TOOK PLACE IN JANUARY
THE ORIGIN OF THE VOYAGES WAS GT BARRIER NZ
CANOES USED STRATEGY NUMBER 2
ANGLE OF SEARCH WAS 65.0

LENGTH VOYAGE 35
TACKING METHOD 0
SPEED OF CANOES 4.00
TURNING DAY 35
HORIZ. FRACTION 0.50
NO. OF VOYAGES 20
LATITUDE SAILING SUPPRESSED

With regard to return voyages from New Zealand to the tropics, in Experiment 14, 700 canoes sailed north from the Three Kings Islands at the northern tip of New Zealand, by Strategy 4. Only 29 failed to find land and returned, and 68 were lost at sea, giving a success rate of 86%. One fleet showed that it was possible to sail to eastern Melanesia in under 21 days, with success rates up to 70%, provided they took the best courses, which covered about 30° of arc. The best course for Norfolk Island, in a narrower arc, gave up to about 20% success. Fiji and West Polynesia (especially Tonga) jointly had high success rates within some 30° of arc. East Polynesia needed voyages of 35 days to give an assurance of arrival there. The best targets were the Southern Cooks, which received up to 36% of hits on the very best course, and secondarily the Australs, but more than half of the voyages in this general direction were intercepted by the Kermadecs, which would have made an excellent staging post on the way (Figure 65). Combined values for the Kermadecs and all destinations in East Polynesia gave successes of about 90% or more within the best 30° target arc in summer, and better than 70% in winter.

The situation is that navigators who knew where they were going could return to Melanesia and both West and East Polynesia. The odds would be much worse for those who did not. Current orthodox archaeological thinking is that New Zealand's prehistory lies entirely with East Polynesia, but voyaging considerations suggest a wider range of possibilities.

The Chatham Islands

Table 18 showed that 24% of canoes leaving the Southern Cooks in January on a course of 210° reached the Chatham Islands, which was the best

Table 19   *Simulated voyages to Chatham Islands*

Experiment 15	To the Chathams														
	Strategy 2, January				Strategy 2, July				Strategy 4, January				Strategy 4, July		
Angle	NZ	Chatham	died	lived	NZ	Chatham	died	lived	NZ	Chatham	died	lived	NZ	Chatham	died	lived
110	0	60	40	60	0	40	60	40	28	64	8	92	24	68	8	92
115	0	52	48	52	0	72	28	72	24	64	12	88	20	76	4	96
120	0	40	60	40	0	44	56	44	32	28	40	60	40	32	28	72
125	0	20	80	20	0	32	68	32	20	48	32	68	44	24	32	68
130	0	12	88	12	0	16	84	16	20	16	64	36	28	20	52	48
135	0	0	100	0	0	8	92	8	12	12	76	24	20	20	60	40
140	0	0	100	0	0	0	100	0	0	4	96	4	4	4	92	8

Note: All scores are percentages; 25 boats sailed per angle

experimental result (and an exceptional one) achieved from outside New Zealand, but very much worse than the general chances of reaching New Zealand. Table 19 shows results of 700 canoes that left the southeastern coast of the North Island of New Zealand to explore the chances of sailing on to the Chathams. Canoes had 14 days for the outward journey, and 21 for the return, where applicable. The Chathams were found most satisfactorily on courses of around 110-115°. Return voyages that missed the Chathams and passed to the north (not shown) had a better chance of returning the farther north they sailed, whereas those that missed them to the south, had an increasingly certain chance of dying (Table 19). The situation does not offer good prospects for continuing interaction. Figure 66 gives three examples of canoes that sailed north of the optimal course, plotted against the background of January wind data.

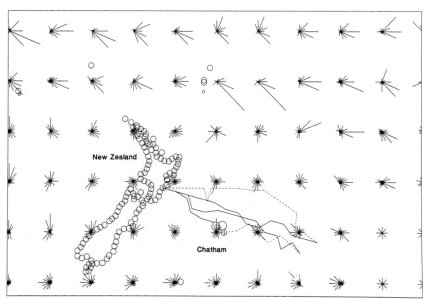

66. Three simulated canoes sail a course south of east from the North Island of New Zealand on a map that plots wind data for January. Return voyages to the North Island are feasible, but difficult from southern latitudes. In terms of navigation, the settlement of the Chatham Islands represents the most difficult voyaging achieved by prehistoric humans anywhere in the world, and the archaeological evidence is currently the youngest in Polynesia.

New Zealand

Chatham

RANDOM VOYAGING

The one strategy not discussed so far is Strategy 1, in which canoes are given a course, at random, by the computer program. But having got it they do not sail at random: they do their best to maintain that course until they find land or run out of time. As Experiment 16 shows, fleets of 100 canoes were sent out on one-way voyages, in both summer and winter, from the Solomon Islands, Vanuatu, Samoa, the Cook Islands, Mangareva and the Marquesas, to see how they fared in the major crossings involved in the colonisation of the remote Pacific. Not surprisingly, most of the Pacific islands were reached. There was a tendency for voyages leaving an origin in the west of the Pacific to remain on that side of the ocean and vice versa, and canoes that sailed in empty ocean had fewer successes. But the outcome did not resemble the archaeological evidence for colonisation in the Pacific, and the results do not need to be considered in detail. However, they do show something that has been understood since the early history of enquiry in this subject. Canoes, on occasion, can sail from anywhere to almost anywhere else, for one reason or another, by intention or accident, with or without a destination in mind, and with some chance of success. This element can never be removed from general theories of Pacific exploration. The success rates of these voyages without return are shown in Table 20.

Table 20   *Random outward voyaging (percentages)*

	Solomon Is	Vanuatu	Samoa	Cook Is	Mangareva	Marquesas
January						
success	88	85	68	44	27	44
died	12	15	32	56	73	56
July						
success	86	86	50	43	30	49
died	14	14	50	57	70	51

Summary

Many of the propositions about the theory of colonisation, as listed at the beginning of the chapter, have been substantially corroborated by computer simulation of voyaging. For example, one important conclusion is that navigational skills and exploration strategies did become more refined as the colonisation of the Pacific proceeded, as suggested. A review of these issues is presented in the final chapter. Secondly, the simulation has produced detailed information on the feasibility and relative ease of various passages in the South Pacific, which relate to the direction and order of island settlement. This can be compared with archaeological evidence and a summary is given in the final conclusions.

There are new insights into the intentions and choices of Pacific explorers, in so far as the computer simulation has identified feasible directions in which people chose *not* to sail. New Zealand, Norfolk Island and the Kermadecs joined a wider group of islands shown to have been within range of early settlement. They include Australia, the high islands of the Carolines, Nauru and Banaba, and the atolls of Micronesia, if they were available. These islands constituted a very broad arc of possible destinations for the first explorers who entered the remote Pacific. However, the only part with evidence of Lapita settlement is eastern Melanesia/West Polynesia where, significantly, *all* of the large islands show it. The pattern is more than can be explained by the sum of particular arguments about sampling for each apparently empty island. Also, arguments about problems of adaptation could scarcely apply equally to them all. But one thing that does distinguish the colonised islands from the other accessible ones is their direction. They lie in the east and generally upwind, and the ease and probability of returning from there was greater.

Finally, while the settlement of the Pacific has a demonstrable coherence, the experiments in simulated voyages by Strategy 1, in which courses were chosen at random but sailed competently, show that the accidental element in colonisation cannot be left out of the equation. Unusual and accidental things undoubtedly happened sometimes. The pioneering computer simulation by Levison, Ward and Webb (1973) proved that the remote Pacific was settled with *intention*. This study builds on their conclusion by approximating navigational *method* within the context of a continuing and rational tradition of ocean exploration and colonisation.

9

VOYAGING AFTER COLONISATION AND THE STUDY OF CULTURE CHANGE

In archaeological time and on a world scale, the colonisation of the remote Pacific was an explosive expansion that touched the continents of Australia and America and then withdrew as voyaging declined to the extent described at European contact. Although prehistorians will continue to fine-tune the results of radiocarbon dating, the broad chronological pattern of evidence will remain.

The colonisation of this island world by sailing canoes was necessarily influenced by various natural factors and probabilities, which are reflected in outline by aspects of archaeological evidence, such as the order of island settlement. Many theories about the variability seen at contact among Pacific people in language, biology and culture associate this in some way with the nature of the founder populations, and it is presumed that diversification was an integral part of colonisation. However, sometimes the very speed of it may have outstripped presumed changes, and some patterns are clearly the result of post-settlement change, which took place in the context of ongoing voyaging. Since voyages of exploration were conventionally two-way, new and initially small settlements would be influenced by further contacts. The voyaging tradition that established founder populations maintained links between them. We can expect that islands began to diverge faster, in isolation, from the time effective communication between them slowed or ended, rather than when contact between them began. While colonisation set part of the Pacific pattern, it has yet to be realised how continuing voyaging provided another dimension to post-settlement change.

Further, it appears that the context of diversification of island populations was as systematic, in its own way, as colonisation, and that both have general predictive value for local prehistories, even though these were individual and idiosyncratic as well. The issue to be considered here is how changes in voyaging influenced island prehistories after settlement. One point that is clear at the outset is that once all of the islands were known, voyaging was no longer constrained by survival sailing, and islands could have been reached again according to their accessibility.

CONDITIONS AFFECTING POST-COLONISATION CHANGE IN POLYNESIA

This issue is investigated in Figure 67, which compares the relative ease of reaching each of the islands or groups of Polynesia and Fiji by plotting the relevant distances and target angles of expanded sighting radius, from their closest inhabited neighbour at the time of European contact, which

67. The decline in voyaging after settlement followed the general pattern of accessibility. Here, the islands of Polynesia and Fiji are plotted according to their distance and angle of target from their nearest occupied neighbours at the time of Western contact. Accessibility identifies groups that shared aspects of their prehistories. These include the empty and abandoned islands, the marooned margins of Polynesia, shrinking prehistoric interaction spheres and the voyaging spheres of the contact period.

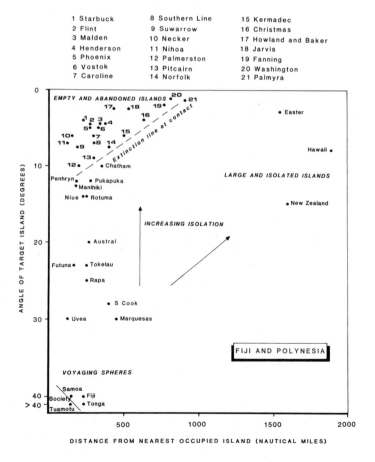

1 Starbuck	8 Southern Line	15 Kermadec
2 Flint	9 Suwarrow	16 Christmas
3 Malden	10 Necker	17 Howland and Baker
4 Henderson	11 Nihoa	18 Jarvis
5 Phoenix	12 Palmerston	19 Fanning
6 Vostok	13 Pitcairn	20 Washington
7 Caroline	14 Norfolk	21 Palmyra

is chosen ahead of the closest island, because the former is the nearest source of information or support. The more distant and small the island target, the less accessible it is, and it appears that the decline in voyaging followed the general pattern of accessibility. One might object that these variables are not independent of each other: that a large island at a greater distance can present the same angle as a smaller, closer one, and the angle of an island target increases as one approaches it. However, experimental voyages by modern replica canoes have shown that navigational errors in traditional methods of dead-reckoning tend to cancel each other out rather than accumulate during a voyage, and the ability to maintain an accurate course does not change with increasing distance. It follows that any islands that present the same angle of target have the same chance of being hit, irrespective of distance and size, from the point of origin of the respective voyages.

Although other variables, especially size and resources, must have influenced settlement, Figure 67 shows that accessibility alone has distinguished groups of islands that shared important elements of their prehistories. There are some that were once occupied but then abandoned, while the rest maintained varying levels of isolation or outside contact. The pattern applies to the time of Western contact, but was evidently the result of changes in prehistory; earlier periods would have shown coherent stages in the development of that situation.

THE 'MYSTERY' ISLANDS

More than a score of islands that were small targets at some distance from their nearest neighbours were found to be empty or abandoned, having been occupied some time previously. These include the so-called 'mystery islands' of Polynesia (Bellwood 1978), but they retain little mystery here. There is an unambiguous extinction line, which must have been advancing with increasing isolation. Islands with evidence of former settlement include Pitcairn Island and Henderson in the Pitcairn group, Necker and Nihoa in Hawaii, Howland in the Phoenix Islands, Washington, Fanning and Christmas in the Northern Line Islands and Malden in the central group, Palmerston and Suwarrow in the Cook Islands, and the sub-tropical islands of the Kermadecs, and Norfolk Island. The possiblity of settlement has been raised also for Phoenix, Sydney, Canton and Hull in the Phoenix group, and Caroline in the Southern Line Islands, while it remains an open question for several other empty islands still to be investigated archaeologically.

Figure 67 identifies these islands without reference to their size or resources, but both have been used previously to explain their abandoned state. Suwarrow, Necker and Nihoa are all less than 1 km², Howland, . Palmerston and Pitcairn no more than 5 km², Washington less than 10 km² and the remainder between 30 and 40 km². However, Christmas Island (which has various estimates) is more than 320 km², or twice the size of Easter Island (Douglas 1969). The volcanic islands of Nihoa, Necker and Pitcairn lack fringing reefs and have limited seafood, while several of the atolls that have extensive reefs are short of water and good soils, including Howland, Malden, Washington, Christmas, Palmerston and Suwarrow. Christmas Island, although large, is virtually all barren sand flats less than three metres above sea-level. On the other hand, Washington has a freshwater lake and better soil, but it shows no signs of greater utilisation than some others. Pitcairn has fertile soils, and the descendants of the *Bounty* mutineers who arrived in 1790 provide a historical case of strikingly rapid population growth there (Terrell 1986), although they suffered from occasional droughts and food shortages. In 1856 the Pitcairn population moved to Norfolk Island, where most of them stayed and continued to increase. This island, which is also volcanic and about six times larger than Pitcairn, could probably have sustained a permanent population, while Raoul in the Kermadecs, although steep, arguably might have done the same.

Apart from local environmental factors there are biogeographical properties that affect islands (MacArthur and Wilson 1967, Terrell 1986, Keegan and Diamond 1987), such as distance, area and configurational effects on human as well as other animal populations. The quality that all of these mystery islands conspicuously share is that, compared with islands that remained occupied, they were less accessible from their neighbours by indigenous navigation. When voyaging declined, they were affected first, as one would expect.

In the Pacific Islands, extinction applied variously to the people themselves, the domestic animals they took with them, and the native populations they found. Distributions of introduced pig, dog and fowl in the remote Pacific are patchy, but will become more coherent as sampling effects are overcome. The early settlement of islands was accompanied by a wave of extinctions of endemic land birds and local exterminations of seabirds; data comes from islands as widespread as New Caledonia, Tikopia, New Zealand, the Chathams, Fiji, Cooks, Marquesas, Hawaii, Norfolk and Henderson (Steadman and Olsen 1985, Keegan and Diamond 1987). Degradation of forest was another consequence of human occupation on many islands (Keegan and Diamond 1987:79).

As a group, the empty islands whose locations are shown in Figure 68 played a systematic part in Pacific prehistory. Archaeology and computer simulation suggest that both small and large islands were settled at much the same time, when colonists entered their part of the ocean. Fanning, one of the Line Islands between central East Polynesia and Hawaii, has a date similar to the settlement of Hawaii, and Norfolk and the Kermadecs have age estimates close to New Zealand's. These small, intermediary islands could have been found by voyagers on their way in or out from the larger distant ones, and resettled or simply used as staging posts while interaction lasted. While the evidence is sketchy, the interpretation favoured for Norfolk Island is that after settlement from somewhere in East Polynesia it received secondary influences very possibly from New Zealand, while the Kermadecs have evidence of continuing or renewed settlement at *c.* A.D. 1600 and demonstrated contact with New Zealand at some point during the sequence.

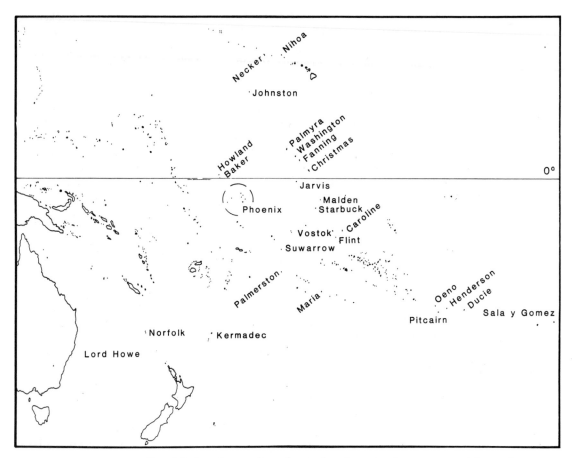

68. The location of the widespread 'mystery' islands of Polynesia, which were empty at contact, but often show traces of earlier occupation. While many are small and could have suffered 'ecological crunches', it seems they played a more systematic part in Pacific prehistory. It is likely that they were discovered when colonists first entered their part of the ocean. Some acted as intermediaries between the margins and the centre. But they were never successful 'stand-alone' islands, and their abandonment will calibrate the decline of voyaging.

Considering the quality of samples there is almost a surprising coherence in the data.

The case seems to be that these small islands were not successful stand-alone settlements, and their emptying calibrates the decline of voyaging in several parts of the Pacific. The scattered islands of the Pitcairn group may be another example. None has early evidence that reflects on the time Easter Island was settled, in which they may have had a role, but there is some evidence for settlement on both Pitcairn and Henderson between c.A.D. 1100–1400. No archaeological remains have been found on Oeno or Ducie, but the computer simulation suggests they were surely hit. Pitcairn is 375 sea miles east of Mangareva, but Easter Island is another thousand beyond. Pitcairn and Henderson are just over 100 sea miles apart, which makes this a fairly comfortable overnight passage. A likely pattern is that, as communications here became difficult to sustain, they withdrew from east to west; Easter Island was cut off first, Henderson and Pitcairn remained in mutual support until both were abandoned at about the same time. One can imagine the lights of settlement flickering out in this stretch of the Pacific and only Easter's was left burning alone, perhaps less brightly, far in the east.

Palmerston and Suwarrow are relative isolates within the Cook Islands and present no difficulties of interpretation. The Phoenix Islands, like some other cases, may be best seen as a single settlement system spread over several adjacent islands, in which most were used but some lived on more than others, until their location far from the sea-lanes of prehistory became too isolated for them to continue. Nihoa and Necker were the last two sometime-occupied islands on a string that stretched northwest from Hawaii to nowhere, and their falling into disuse simply reflects the shortening range of internal voyaging in the Hawaii group, although not necessarily any change in its frequency. Two radiocarbon dates reported from Nihoa are A.D. 1436 ± 200 and A.D. 890 ± 90, although what it is they date is uncertain (Kirch 1988b).

Clearly these widely scattered islands, whose inhabitants were usually unknown to each other, were subject to similar external constraints. Many of them shared similar internal stress factors, and among those suggested are water and food shortage, natural disasters, illness, homesickness, lack of women, and warfare (Diamond 1985). Steadman and Olsen (1985) suggest extermination of local bird populations as a reason, and make an argument for Henderson Island, whose rugged coral surface is considered to be unsuitable for gardening or domestic animals and where there is no evidence for either (Diamond 1985), while two species of large pigeon became extinct and breeding colonies of storm petrels were wiped out. The force of this argument depends on the self-sufficiency of Henderson Island, but if it was substantially a satellite of Pitcairn, which has a better subsistence base, then it might normally have had a small, fluctuating population, with people commuting across to fish, collect birds and turtles, etc. Such activities are widespread in the Pacific. Many satellite and seasonal atolls in the Tuamotu group today, and also some near Mangareva, were reported as empty at contact, but have evidence for former use (Emory 1939). One reported change in the Henderson Island sequence is from imported basalt adzes and pearl shell fishhooks in the lower excavated deposits to an absence of quality industrial imports in the upper layers (Kirch 1988b), which could suggest increasing local difficulties, but the change may relate to the time when settlement on Pitcairn was winding down as well.

Pitcairn and Henderson Islands may also have been part of a wider contact sphere. Gathercole (1964) found a basalt flaking floor and many unfinished adzes on Pitcairn Island. There is a suggestion that it served as a quarry island, but this is unconfirmed. Gathercole has repeated the claim that the timber of Pitcairn was the finest in the southeast Pacific, which implies its value for canoe-building. The evidence does not call for a model of exchange of industrial items as elaborate as some ethnographic Melanesian ones, but we can envisage a measure of specialisation that lasted while there was the external exchange to support it.

Terrell (1986:92-3) has suggested that these small islands could suffer periodic 'ecological crunches' brought on by events such as droughts and cyclones, when populations fell to levels from which they could not recover alone. It was not simply a question of too many people with not enough to eat; one can allow the longer-term effect of diet on factors such as fertility. With all these solid reasons why such islands should become empty, the issue arises of the extent to which settlement was permanent at all (Emory 1934, Terrell 1986), and it can be said that there is no archaeological evidence that shows clearly that many, or even any, were occupied for long periods, although it is certainly possible.

At all events we find these widespread islands to be diverse. The cases of distant stepping-stone islands and nearby economic satellite islands have been mentioned, plus those engaged in wider networks of exchange. A 'hostile-resources' model can be applied to many. The possibilities do not stop there as, for example, on Necker and Nihoa Islands, where the evidence for religious sites is so abundant that it has been seen at one extreme as a sign of the desperation of the marooned inhabitants and at the other as the product of some religious 'cult' or 'pilgrimage' voyaging.

What all of these islands have in common is a primary factor of external inaccessibility. Together, they tell us something new about the dynamics of Pacific settlement. When voyaging declined those islands that were not voluntarily abandoned were left to suffer their diverse fates alone. It is interesting that the islands with radiocarbon dates that may bear on the length of settlement point shakily towards the middle of the second millennium A.D., or a little before, and it would be of great interest to obtain a finer chronology from various parts of the remote Pacific.

It has been remarked that these islands tell us something about the marginal limits of oceanic subsistence and settlement; for instance, that they 'should provide ideal cases for examining the evolutionary or adaptive plasticity of Polynesian culture in the face of relatively extreme or harsh selective pressures' (Kirch and Green 1987:439). However, to be interpreted correctly, these individual and often isolated islands must be seen as part of a system of settlement wider than themselves.

The extinction line in Figure 67 was probably still moving at the end of prehistory, and it is clearly suggested which might have been the next islands to fall. The scattered atolls of the Northern Cooks, which were still settled, presumably would have joined Palmerston and Suwarrow, their empty neighbours, and one might suggest this line may have been drawing closer to the Chatham Islands, too; not necessarily so close as to threaten oblivion (except possibly in the very long term), but certainly close enough to have an influence. The point must be made very clearly that the extinction of human groups under difficult circumstances is neither uncommon nor the consequence of their intrinsic inability to survive. The issue is a general one of adaptation, and a case can be made for the Chatham Islands that this occurred at several levels. They were at such a high latitude that Neolithic Polynesians adapted to a hunting and gathering economy, while other aspects of their culture may also have changed in the direction of material and social simplification. This apparently included the shift towards a less ranked society (Sutton 1980). Moreover, the Chatham Islanders had apparently given up warfare as an instrument of politics and were not in a position to compete effectively with Maori immigrants in historical times. Such factors have been explained quite plausibly in local terms, but they should be seen in the wider context of the Pacific, where many island societies in restricted environments underwent changes that in more extreme cases had ended in extinction.

THE MAROONED MARGINS OF POLYNESIA

The second group of islands in Figure 67 is made up of the three points of the Polynesian Triangle – Easter Island and the archipelagos of Hawaii and New Zealand – which were solitary but still occupied at the end of prehistory. Easter Island lay in an inaccessible direction upwind, New Zealand was far outside the tropics, and Hawaii, which was the most accessible of the three, being closest to the equator in a cross-wind direction from central East Polynesia, was still 3500 km from its nearest occupied neighbour. This fits Davidson's (1984) view that archaeological evidence suggests Easter Island has been isolated since settlement, that New Zealand did not share later East Polynesian developments to any extent, while Hawaii may have had some continued contact. These islands were large and varied enough not to need outside reinforcement, and by contact their inhabitants no longer made long passages offshore. Kirch (1985:66) describes Hawaiian canoes as no longer capable of ocean-going navigation. In New Zealand double-hulled sailing canoes were rare, and Easter Island craft were described as small patchwork constructions of short planks sewn together (McCoy 1979:160) or reed rafts.

Hawaii is more than 16,000 km² in area, and New Zealand is half a million, but it is interesting that the smallest of the group, Easter Island, which is only 160 km², lies closest to the extinction line. Easter Island had a naturally impoverished and fragile biota susceptible to degradation following human alteration of the environment. In the first thousand years of settlement, Easter Island developed an elaborately ranked society, and its stylised megalithic art and architecture are renowned. Yet, by the end of prehistory the island was deforested, the population had declined and was readjusting to cope with resource scarcity (McCoy 1979); most of its fabulous statues had been thrown down and contemporary reports tell of a skirmishing population under stress. Where the changes would have led finally is a matter for conjecture, but in terms of the cultural trajectories of larger East Polynesian groups, Easter Island had already peaked and declined. Its inhabitants were coping with an island far different to the one they first settled and, by then, it may not have had the trees for canoe hulls for anyone who wanted to leave.

SHRINKING CENTRAL EAST POLYNESIAN CONTACT SPHERES

Several moderately isolated central East Polynesian groups appear to have been formerly part of contact spheres that contracted in late prehistory. These include the Cook Islands, Australs, Rapa, the Marquesas and possibly

Mangareva, while Pitcairn Island, as discussed already, not only dropped
out but went under.

One line of archaeological evidence for this consists of raw materials
and finished items that formerly moved among them. Pearl shell, which
was a preferred material for making fishhooks, has a restricted distribution,
and in East Polynesia occurs abundantly in the Northern Cooks, Tuamotus
and Mangareva, in limited quantities in the Australs and is generally scarce
in the Society Islands and absent in most of the Southern Cooks and
Pitcairn Island. Kirch (1986) says that pearl shell items in the Marquesas
were probably from the Tuamotus. Walter (1988) reports it from the Anai'o
site on Ma'uke dated c. A.D. 1300-1400, where it was used for a number
of purposes as well as hooks, and he believes it came in from outside
the Southern Cooks. Kirch finds the pearl shell data from Mangaia match
Walter's from Ma'uke (P. Kirch, pers. comm. 1989). Pearl shell was imported
to the Pitcairn group in the same general time range, and has been reported
from Henderson. Recently, two potsherds of probable Tongan origin have
been found in Ma'uke (Walter and Dickinson 1989), and another from
Atiu still to be described. Further research is likely to bring many more
instances of exchange to light, including the movement of industrial stone.
Such materials are merely the bare bones of contact, and we can expect
that there were numerous social and political links, intermarriages and
so on, whose traces are left in kinship and tradition.

In a discussion of settlement patterns in the Southern Cooks, Walter
(1990) describes a number of twelfth- to fourteenth-century coastal villages
that were located by reef passages, which he relates to the importance
of external contacts at the time. Later on, settlement became more dispersed,
and its focus shifted inland.

Another line of evidence of declining overseas sailing is the geographical
knowledge that Polynesians had of islands beyond their sailing range at
the time of Western contact, which could be taken as retained from a
formerly wider sphere. This was the interpretation G. Forster put on the
example of Tupaia, the navigator from Raiatea in the Society Islands who
sailed with Cook and who was able to name many islands, 74 of which
were mapped. However, he had personally visited only a minority of near
ones (Lewis 1972). Similar information was collected from Tahiti by Spanish
navigators and in the Marquesas by the missionary Crook. Contacts had
declined in the Australs and among the Southern Cooks, where the
missionary Williams was unable to obtain sailing directions to locate
Rarotonga, although he knew of its existence (Walter 1990). In the Santa
Cruz group of eastern Melanesia, voyaging as decribed in the nineteenth
century had evidently declined since Quiros' visit in 1606 (Lewis 1972:298).
Another interpretation of this knowledge, which is less likely, is that it
was carried by accidental voyagers, but the archaeological evidence for
the movement of material items counts against it.

CONTACT PERIOD VOYAGING SPHERES

The final group of islands to be seen in Figure 67 consists of large targets
close together, which were, predictably, the voyaging spheres described

at contact. One consists of the Society and northwestern Tuamotu islands, which are interpreted as the shrunken core of once-wider central East Polynesian contact spheres. The other is West Polynesia and Fiji, which was a very different case, because it was in a phase of expansion and reaching out to neighbouring islands of intermediate accessibility, such as Niue, East Uvea, East Futuna, Rotuma and farther afield.

Beyond Polynesia, another voyaging sphere survived in the mainly atoll-archipelagos of Micronesia, whose islands were too small to be viable without a flow of trade goods and information and reinforcement for local populations periodically exposed to cyclones and tidal waves. Here, islands were accessible to one another, and there were ecological reasons for keeping in touch. However, in Remote Oceania voyaging spheres were exceptional cases at contact and should not obscure the more general pattern of absence of long-distance offshore sailing (Irwin 1980:328).

THE POLYNESIAN OUTLIERS

The Polynesian Outliers are communities on small islands scattered along the windward fringes of Melanesia and Micronesia, with the exception of Rennell and Bellona (Figure 69). They are located outside the Polynesian Triangle, and identified primarily because they speak Polynesian languages and show other Polynesian affinities. While they are grouped as Outliers, they have characteristics that set them apart from one another, as well as from their Melanesian and Micronesian neighbours, with whom they also share a variety of archaeological, cultural and biological features. They occupy mostly small islands, many of which are atolls, but others are high volcanic or raised coral.

There has been a long interest in the Outliers. Originally they were seen as relict populations left behind during west-to-east migrations of Polynesians, until Buck (1938:46–7) suggested they might have sailed back from Polynesia afterwards. The pattern of winds and currents supports this suggestion, and the simulated voyages of Levison, Ward and Webb (1973) showed it could be achieved easily by drift from West Polynesia. Recent archaeological work on several of the Outliers now shows that elements of both of these hypotheses may be correct, and also that the prehistories of these islands are probably complex and involve multiple contacts (Bayard 1976, Davidson 1971, 1974, Kirch 1984a, Kirch and Rosendahl 1976, Kirch and Yen 1982, Leach and Ward 1981, Terrell 1986).

The very term Polynesian Outlier, which may have been first used by Buck in 1938 (Bayard 1976:1), firmly relates these islands to Polynesia, but gives no hint of how they became or remained Outliers, and one wonders whether there is any other shared characteristic apart from their Polynesian affinity that distinguishes them from their Melanesian or Micronesian neighbours.

This question is investigated in Figures 70–72, which plot the Outliers and the islands of Melanesia and Micronesia by reference to their distances and angles of target from their nearest occupied neighbours. Islands are treated individually, except where they are so close together as effectively

69. The Polynesian Outliers are communities on small islands scattered mainly along the windward fringes of Melanesia and Micronesia, identified by their Polynesian languages and other affinities. Originally it was thought they were left behind by Polynesian immigrants on their way east, and later it was suggested they might have sailed back afterwards as Polynesian emigrants. Archaeology shows them to have complex prehistories and finds elements of support for both hypotheses.

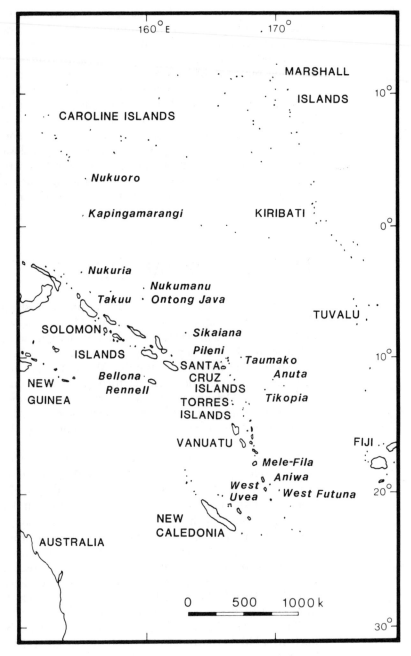

to be one; expanded sighting radii are used to calculate target angle; the highest point of an island more than 300 m in elevation is taken to be visible from 30 sea miles, one above 150 m from 20 sea miles, above 75 m from 15 sea miles and those lower than that from within a radius of 10 sea miles. Information was taken from British Admiralty charts INT506, 602, 604, 605 and 763. Each of the Outlier islands is considered, together

70. When all of the islands in the vicinity of the Solomon Islands are plotted by accessibility, the Polynesian Outliers stand unambiguously apart from Melanesian neighbours. The Outliers are a good example of the delicate balance between settlement and society in so far as they are close enough to Melanesia and Micronesia not to be abandoned, but far enough from them to retain their Polynesian character. As such, they could be as easily described as Micronesian and Melanesian Outliers – of Polynesian speakers!

Key: 1. Buka, Bougainville, San Christobal, 2. Uki, Vanguna, New Georgia, Rendova, Gizo, Vella Lavella, Shortland, Santa Ana, 3. Choiseul, 4. Savo, Guadalcanal, 5. Nggela, Treasury, 6. Ulawa, Malaita, 7. Tagula.

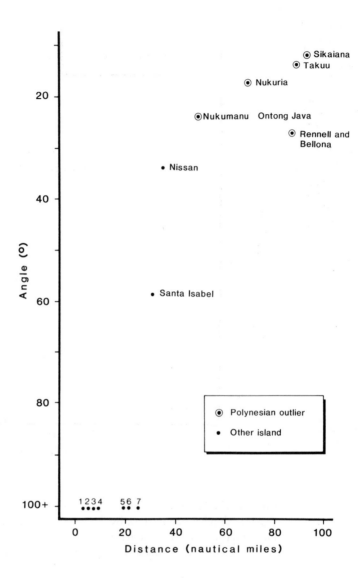

with the Melanesian or Micronesian groups that lie closest. Figure 70 shows the Solomon Islands and the related Outliers, which stand unambiguously apart from their non-Outlier neighbours, although treated alike in this analysis.

Figure 71 shows the islands of Santa Cruz and Vanuatu, and again the Outliers stand apart, as do a few non-Outliers, including Erromanga and Aneityum in the more scattered southerly part of Vanuatu, close to the Outliers West Futuna and Aniwa, and also the Torres Islands, which lie to the north of it (Fig. 69). This also immediately raises questions of their possible history of Polynesian contacts. For instance, there is already a suggestion that the Aneityum chiefly system results from Polynesian influence (Spriggs 1986:18). One of the anomalies of Outlier location is that the tiny islets of Mele and Fila are located almost within a stone's

71. When islands in the region of Vanuatu are plotted by accessibility, the Polynesian Outliers stand apart as do some other islands. Efate is a medium-sized Melanesian island with an Outlier entourage. Other Melanesian islands that stand out reveal Polynesian traits. Many Melanesian islands may have had complex histories of Polynesian and other outside influence, but the evidence for it survives best with isolation.

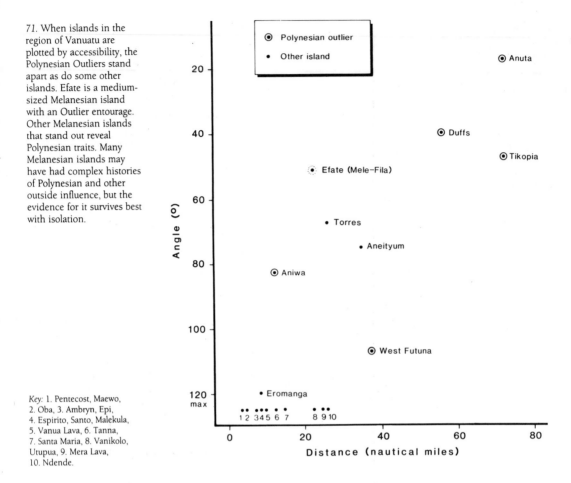

Key: 1. Pentecost, Maewo, 2. Oba, 3. Ambryn, Epi, 4. Espirito, Santo, Malekula, 5. Vanua Lava, 6. Tanna, 7. Santa Maria, 8. Vanikolo, Utupua, 9. Mera Lava, 10. Ndende.

throw of the larger non-Outlier Efate in the Vanuatu chain, while the small Outlier-island Emae is close by. However, in Figure 71, Efate and its Outlier entourage are seen to stand apart as one, which shows the consistency of this case, and simultaneously raises questions for the culture history of Efate.

The Loyalty Islands are some distance from New Caledonia, but West Uvea, which is an atoll Outlier, is no more remote than the others of this group. But they are larger high islands, and here size and ecological difference may be an issue, as it may be also in the case of the high non-Outlier Ndende in the Santa Cruz group, as compared with the much smaller and lower Reef Islands and Duff near by.

Figure 72 includes the Caroline Islands, Belau and Yap, and although these islands are notoriously dispersed, the two Outliers, Nukuoro and Kapingamarangi unerringly are among the most isolated of all. Further, it can be shown that in the region of the eastern Micronesian groups, where there are no Polynesian Outliers, the three islands that are less accessible than others are Nauru, which is a linguistic isolate, Banaba and Rotuma.

72. In the Caroline Islands of Micronesia, Nukuoro and Kapingamarangi are two Polynesian Outliers. Here they are seen as being among the most remote islands in the group.

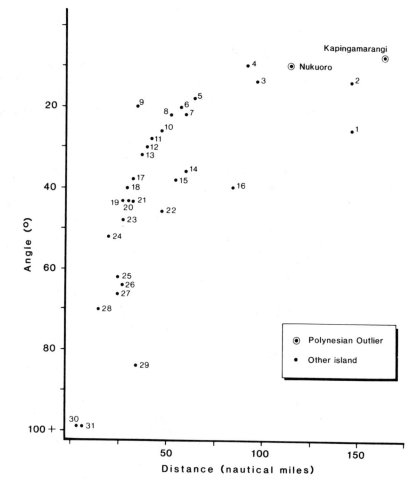

Key: 1. Kosrae, 2. Belau, 3. Sorol, 4. Oroluk, 5. Faraulep, Gaferut, 6. Pingelap, Mokil, 7. Ngulu, Kama, 8. Pikolet, 9. Ngatik, 10. Fais, 11. Sonsorol, 12. West Faya, 13. Satawal, Tobi, Helen, 14. Yap, 15. Namauito, 16. Pohnpei, 17. Ifalik, 18. Ulul, 19. Namoluk, 20. Pulo, Anna, Merir, 21. Woleai, 22. Ulithi, 23. Pisaras, Magur, 24. Olimarao, 25. East Faya, 26. Nomoi, 27. Hall, 28. Pulawat, Pulap, 29. Truk, 30. Lamotrek, Elato, 31. Losap, Nama.

Issues in Polynesian Outlier prehistory

It is revealed that, with few exceptions, the Outliers are all geographic isolates among their non-Polynesian neighbours, which provides the main common factor other than the linguistic and cultural afffinities that link them together. Their systematic relationship is actually with Melanesia and Micronesia, not Polynesia, and confirms an earlier assertion that there is almost a case for renaming the Outliers. The survival of Polynesian traits, notably language, occurred because they outlie from Melanesia and Micronesia, while their spatial relationship to Polynesia is immaterial. They may be regarded as Melanesian or Micronesian Outliers – of Polynesian speakers (Irwin 1980:331).

Island size is also an issue in the survival of Outlier communities, and the suggestion has been made that some Polynesians travelling with the prevailing winds would have been bound to pass between Outlier-islands to reach the main Melanesian chains. However, no such communities have been found on the large islands. A likely explanation is that the smaller the island, the greater the impact of the migrants, and the essence of the question, therefore, is not arrival but survival. Outlier communities once existed that now do not (Irwin 1980:331). Polynesian communities may never have become established on large Melanesian islands, but they may have lasted longer on more of the islands of intermediate size and isolation, perhaps in Vanuatu, where Mele, Fila and Emae show Polynesian inroads, and a number of other possible candidates suggest themselves in Figure 71.

Whereas Polynesians disappeared from the mystery islands of Polynesia without replacement, in Melanesia some communities with links to Polynesia may have been replaced without conspicuous archaeological trace. Further, it is clear that Outlier communities have survived on their own islands when in contact with larger ones at a distance, as shown by Tikopia, which, at various times in its 3000-year prehistory, was probably in intermittent contact with at least the Solomons, West Polynesia, the Banks and Vanuatu (Kirch 1988a, Kirch and Yen 1982, Flannery et al. 1988), which is not to imply its inhabitants were equally or conspicuously 'Polynesian' all that time.

The circumstances of Outlier survival do not contribute much to the question of when and why they arose. Some early archaeology on them failed to find evidence for decisive cultural replacement, and it now appears that throughout their sequences there have been strong affinities between Outliers and their Melanesian or Micronesian neighbours, with more sporadic inputs from Polynesia (Terrell 1986:119). Major recent and current archaeological studies are showing that Outliers such as Anuta, Tikopia and Taumako all have long prehistories, which are complex and involve diverse external contacts (Kirch and Yen 1982; J. Davidson, pers. comm.), while Kirch also notes that each Outlier must be considered on its own merits (1984a:218). The extent to which Outlier prehistory is marked by migration and cultural replacement is yet to be shown.

Linguistically, the Outliers have their closest ties with Samoa and with islands west of there, including East Futuna and Tuvalu (which may be a kind of large Polynesian Outlier in Micronesia, itself), and suggestions have been made that they can also be divided into southern and northern geographic and linguistic groups (Terrell 1986:115), although these are by no means clear-cut (P. Ranby, pers. comm. 1990). Models of settlement relationship have been based on linguistic similarity, but Leach and Ward (1981:95) have suggested this will inform us only about the end of a complex prehistory. However, at a more general level, it may be worth noting that the primary language link is with Samoa, which may suggest an earlier phase of a wider West Polynesian contact sphere prior to the situation at the time of contact, when Tonga appeared to dominate foreign affairs and to influence the language of some neighbours, and sometimes even to overlay an early influence by Samoan.

Finally, it can be suggested that study of the Outliers is making the boundaries of Polynesia, Melanesia and Micronesia even less useful as prehistoric categories (Golson 1961; Green in press), and Terrell (1986) has suggested that whereas the Outliers have been considered marginal to the mainstream of Pacific prehistory 'it is becoming increasingly clear that what transpired . . . was very much part of what happened during prehistory on a much larger scale in the Pacific' (Terrell 1986:120).

Patterns of Permanent and Intermittent Settlement in Polynesia

Differences between the settlement and use of islands have been coherent on a wider scale in historical times, and this almost certainly applied in prehistory too, although we can expect the patterns to have altered with voyaging frequency. Figure 73 is a graph of the 76 islands of the Tuamotu group, which are divided into those that are more or less

73. Differences between the settlement and use of islands are coherent on a broad scale. The 76 islands of the Tuamotu group divide into those that were permanently or intermittently settled, according to accessibility. Islands that do not follow the pattern usually can be explained in terms of special local circumstances.

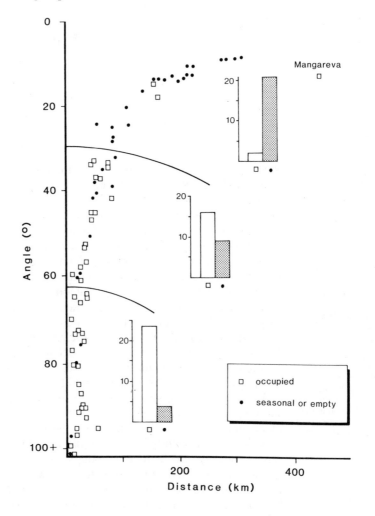

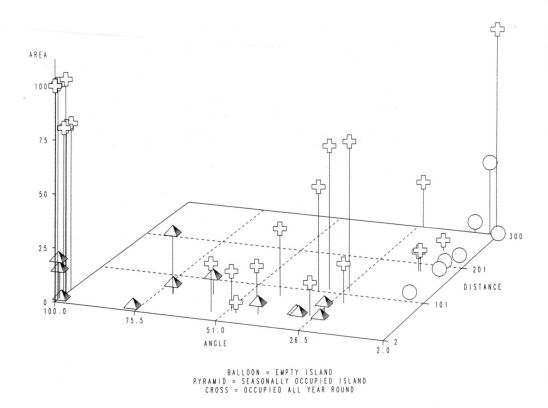

BALLOON = EMPTY ISLAND
PYRAMID = SEASONALLY OCCUPIED ISLAND
CROSS = OCCUPIED ALL YEAR ROUND

74. Central East Polynesian islands of the Cook, Austral, and Society islands, the Marquesas, Pitcairn, Rapa and Easter are plotted by both accessibility and area. (1) Large, accessible and occupied islands in the left foreground have an understorey of smaller intermittent ones; (2) intermittent islands are generally smaller than permanent ones, as they become less accessible towards the right of the diagram; (3) small, empty islands are found in the inaccessible right side of the diagram; (4) at the extreme of isolation in the top right, only Easter Island is large enough to stay occupied.

permanently settled and those that are used seasonally, occasionally or not at all. Data have been gathered from various sources, including Douglas (1969) and the *Pacific Islands Pilot* (vol. III, 1982); their quality is patchy, but nevertheless it is clear that islands that are more accessible are occupied more often than ones that are more remote. Further, the anomalous islands, which are shown as seasonal or empty and lie in accessible parts of the group, usually have particular local circumstances to account for the absence of settlement. Among the eight most accessible empty islands six are very small, and of these, one has no lagoon (Akiaki) and two have no boat passage into the lagoon (Hiti and Reitoru). Of the two large accessible empty islands, one (Toau) is described as having poisonous fish in the lagoon (*Pacific Islands Pilot* vol. III, 1982:125) and one remains unexplained. Further, of the two least accessible occupied islands, one (Tatakoto) is described as one of the most fertile atolls in the eastern part of the Tuamotu group (*Pacific Islands Pilot*, vol. III, 1982:111). Such consistency is impressive.

A wider example is shown in Figure 74, where, as well as the accessibility variables, island area is added to a three-dimensional plot, and the pattern of occupied, intermittent and empty islands is coherent. This analysis includes the 51 islands listed in Table 21 from the Pitcairn, Cook, Rapa, Austral, Society and Marquesas groups; Easter Island is included, but the Tuamotus, which have been considered already, and marginal New Zealand and Hawaii are not. (In fact, Figure 74 shows less than the 51 islands because some are obscured by others.) The results in Figure 74 show (1) large accessible islands in the left foreground with an understorey of smaller

Table 21 *Accessibility and size of 51 East Polynesian Islands*

Group	Island	Distance	Angle	Area	
	Easter	1450	2.5	160.0	
Pitcairn	Ducie	555	2.0	0.8	*
	Henderson	375	4.5	35.0	*
	Pitcairn	300	9.0	5.2	*
	Oeno	230	6.0	0.7	*
Cook	Mangaia	110	25.0	70.0	
	Rarotonga	110	31.0	67.0	
	Ma'uke	30	50.0	18.0	
	Mitiaro	22	55.0	22.0	
	Atiu	16	100.0	28.0	
	Takutea	16	78.0	1.3	+
	Manuae	50	25.0	6.0	+
	Aitutaki	50	45.0	18.0	
	Palmerston	200	7.0	2.6	*
	Suwarrow	190	7.5	0.4	*
	Pukapuka	240	12.0	5.2	
	Manihiki	180	12.5	5.2	
	Rakahanga	180	12.5	4.0	
	Tongareva	180	12.0	10.0	
Rapa	Rapa	300	25.0	22.0	
	Marotiri	48	26.0	0.3	+
Austral	Raivavae	100	33.0	20.0	
	Tubuai	100	33.0	49.0	
	Rurutu	80	42.0	31.0	
	Rimatara	80	23.0	18.0	
	Maria	118	8.0	1.3	*
Society	Tahiti	8	100.0	1003.0	
	Moorea	8	100.0	132.0	
	Mehetia	64	60.0	10.0	+
	Tetiaroa	30	42.0	6.4	+
	Maiao	40	28.0	15.0	
	Huahine	20	100.0	78.0	
	Raiatea	3	100.0	200.0	
	Tahaa	3	100.0	100.0	
	Borabora	10	100.0	37.0	
	Motuiti	10	100.0	20.0	+
	Maupiti	25	48.0	5.0	
	Maupihaa	40	32.0	2.6	+
	Manuae	40	32.0	2.5	+
	Motuone	38	31.0	2.5	+
Marquesas	Fatu Hiva	35	100.0	78.0	
	Motane	12	100.0	15.0	+
	Tahuata	2	100.0	52.0	
	Hiva Oa	2	100.0	241.0	
	Fatu Huku	16	100.0	1.3	+
	Ua Pou	24	100.0	100.0	
	Ua Huku	25	100.0	78.0	
	Nuku Hiva	24	100.0	338.0	
	Eiao	54	71.0	32.0	+
	Hatutaa	55	71.0	18.0	+
	Motu One	55	71.0	6.0	+

* Empty island   + Seasonal or intermittent island

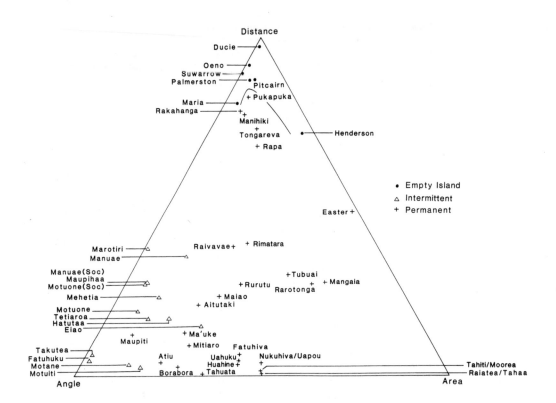

75. Fifty islands of central East Polynesian groups are plotted by both accessibility and area. Empty islands are small and inaccessible; intermittent islands are small, but rather more accessible; the rest are occupied. The implication is that we can expect both discontinuous and continuous archaeological sequences in Polynesia. Even within island groups there will be cases of delayed settlement and environmental impact. Allowing for sampling error, such differences should be systematic.

intermittent islands; (2) intermittent islands generally continue to be smaller than permanent ones as islands become less accessible towards the right of the diagram; (3) the inaccessible right side of the diagram is the location of small empty islands; (4) at the extreme of isolation in the top right corner, only Easter Island is large enough to remain occupied. The same information is transformed into a ternary plot in Figure 75. It can be seen that variable patterns of settlement are predictable in Polynesia both overall, and also when taken group by group.

The underlying factors can be taken as constraints that affect islands today and most probably in prehistory also. Accordingly we can expect to find some islands with uninterrupted prehistoric sequences, and others with broken or intermittent ones. We can expect some islands to have been settled, in an archaeologically conspicuous way, later than others. Even within island groups there may be apparently different settlement dates and possible delays in local bird extinctions and other forms of environmental impact. As the prehistory of island groups in tropical East Polynesia becomes better known, we can expect such variations, but need not regard them as necessarily anomalous. Allowing for sampling error, they should be systematic. To the operation of such general factors other local ones can be added, such as the relative difficulty of landing and living on *makatea* islands. There are other obvious issues, such as the inability of small early populations to use all islands of groups equally, and the ever-present likelihood of functional differentiation between sites.

76. The groups of islands that are identified by accessibility can be used to summarise some of the major themes of Pacific prehistory. Clearly, some of the circumstances of change are systematic, even if they are not necessarily the causes of change.

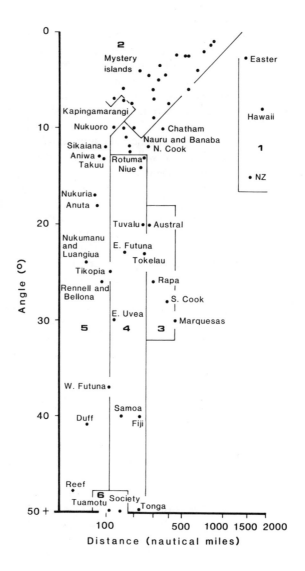

SUMMARY OF VOYAGING RELATIONSHIPS AND IMPLICATIONS FOR PREHISTORY

The various strands of argument are brought together in Figure 76, which is a graph of the remote Pacific showing the positions of most of the islands, once again, by their distance and angle of target from nearest occupied neighbour at the time of contact. This simple diagram can be used to summarise some of the major themes of Pacific prehistory. Some six accessibility groups are apparent as follows:

1. In Group 1 the three points of the Polynesian Triangle, which are farthest apart on the map, come together here as the three least accessible islands. They were large enough to survive prehistory, but what an uninterrupted future may have held for Easter Island is uncertain.

2. The 'mystery' islands were not quite so inaccessible, but they were too small or environmentally limited to remain occupied. The time of their abandonment will calibrate the decline of voyaging in their respective parts of the Pacific Ocean.

3. Group 3 includes those islands of central East Polynesia that fell into isolation probably only a couple of centuries before the Spaniards routinely began to cross what seemed to them a largely empty ocean.

4. The islands of Fiji, Tonga and Samoa and their neighbours Niue, Rotuma, East Futuna, East Uvea, Tuvalu and Tokelau are more accessible in general and also to one another, such that varying degrees of contact were being maintained between them at the time of contact.

Although they are not shown, the Micronesian archipelagos would fall into Group 4, too, and traditional inter-island sailing still takes place today between some of these islands. The late survival of voyaging here has been partly explained by the fact that almost all eastern Micronesian islands are atolls, which are among the most precarious human habitats on earth. Also in the area of Group 4, but not shown in Figure 76, are the archipelagos of the Solomons, Vanuatu and New Caledonia. Voyaging was not taking place between them at the end of prehistory, but they were evidently in intermittent contact with the Polynesian Outliers, and especially those that were close.

5. Group 5 islands shown in Figure 76 are all Outliers. They were far enough away from Micronesia and Melanesia to remain Polynesian, but close enough to remain occupied. As such they are a delicately balanced example of Oceanic settlement trends at the time of Western contact. The most precariously situated Outliers are in Micronesia and almost merge with the abandoned islands. Their closest neighbours are in the Carolines, so it is no surprise to find the reflection of this in material culture, just as the Outliers in Melanesia mirror their locations. Moreover, there is sufficient accessibility between the Outliers and West Polynesia to accommodate the archaeological contacts displayed sporadically through their sequences and also the linguistic connections, perhaps first with Samoa and latterly with Tonga, which probably fall mainly within the last thousand years. At all events, there is reason to believe that voyaging skills persisted in this region from first settlement until European times and were never lost. However, it will be a painstaking task for archaeology to fill in the picture of the history of this communication.

6. In central East Polynesia, Group 6 is made up of the Society and northwestern Tuamotu Islands, the remnant of a former voyaging sphere. Whether the tide would have turned for voyaging here or whether all East Polynesian societies would have become entirely alone cannot be told.

The main point to be made is that patterns of mutual influence following settlement have been more systematic, and individual island prehistories rather less independent of one another than we have thought. Further, it is clear that this pattern relates to the issue of diversification much more than to colonisation. The relative ease with which islands can be reached, after their positions are known, is not the same order in which they were first settled, because, until then, the order of colonisation was affected by the difficulty of return as well as the ease of advance.

PATTERNS OF VARIABILITY AND CHANGE IN POLYNESIA

Until now there has been no independent navigational theory of Pacific colonisation and change. Instead, such theories have been attached *ad hoc* to the patterns of language, culture and biology, as described since the time of Western contact. But while such patterns are indeed coherent, they do not explain themselves. Now that argument might be reversed: an explicit theory of colonisation might interpret these data better than they can provide an adequate theory of colonisation.

We have seen already that some broad similarities between the prehistories of groups of islands conform to their relative accessibility. In so far as this affected colonisation and, more particularly, post-settlement external contact, we have identified an important *circumstance* of change, although not necessarily a *cause*. It is also clear that patterns of contact changed systematically and differentially. Polynesian society was apparently not as insular as its islands, even though it commonly appeared to be, at the end of prehistory, to landlubber anthropologists.

Figure 77 summarises the linguistic information and shows a standard model of Polynesian language relationships as used in various theories of origins (chapter 5). Biological attributes of prehistoric and modern Polynesian populations have been used to construct comparable patterns

77. A standard model of Polynesian language relationships.

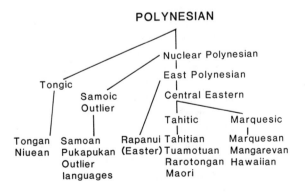

78. An example of a model of biological similarity among Polynesian samples according to a study by Pietrusewsky 1971. (Adapted from Howells 1979, Figure 11.3.)

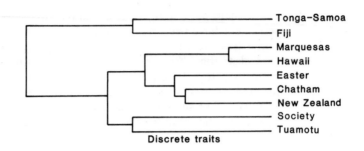

of similarity, and one example is in Figure 78, from Howells (1979). Some differences and many points of similarity can be seen among such schemes, and these include the most recent studies of genetic data (Hill and Serjeantson 1989; L. Smith, pers. comm. 1989). The situation reflects a general acceptance by scholars that the people of Triangle Polynesia represent a valid 'unit of historical analysis', as Kirch and Green put it (1987:474), but what is less clear is how this is to be explained. A popular model has been that many islands received small and similar founder populations, which subsequently developed and diverged from one another in a state of substantial isolation. This seems due for review.

A mutual accessibility model for Polynesia

The previous analysis of accessibility showed islands that were similarly accessible without specifying which particular islands were accessible to one another. In order to investigate how far mutual accessibility of the second kind is predictive of the patterns of similarity seen in biology, language and culture, there is need for an accessibility model that can be compared explicitly with them. In order to do this, three experimental matrices were formulated, which contained coefficients of similarity between all pairs of Polynesian islands that expressed both distance and angle of island target combined into a single similarity value. These matrices were then used as the basis for a cluster analysis to extract the overall pattern. The method was as follows:

1. A preliminary matrix was made up of the distances between every pair of the 13 island groups included in the study. To normalise the data, each value was converted to a percentage of the greatest distance. Then, to turn this distance matrix into a closeness matrix, each value was subtracted from 100%.

2. Corresponding matrices were made of values for the angles of expanded island target between each pair of island groups, and these were then converted to percentages, again by calculating each value as a percentage of the highest. It is obvious that pairs of islands seldom present the same angles of target to one another, so three matrices were made taking (1) the minimum angle between island pairs, (2) the maximum angle between island pairs, and (3) the mean angle between island pairs.

3. Pairs of closeness and angle matrices were then combined into single accessibility matrices by mutiplying each value in the one by the corresponding value in the other and taking the square root.

At this point, three accessibility matrices were available for clustering procedures. For example, one could model minimum accessibility if it was thought that the minimum value for accessibility between islands pairs would be the factor that effectively limited interaction. Alternatively, one could take the maximum or mean values, but, as it transpired, the results of all three followed the same general lines. The matrix of minimum accessibility is shown in Table 22.

Table 22   *A Minimum Accessibility matrix for Polynesia*

		1	2	3	4	5	6	7	8	9	10	11	12	13
Tonga	1		.44	.32	.18	.22	.18	.24	.09	.16	.10	.11	.03	.23
Samoa	2	.44		.27	.23	.17	.15	.17	.10	.19	.11	.19	.05	.24
S. Cook	3	.32	.27		.23	.54	.30	.46	.14	.38	.18	.15	.08	.24
N. Cook	4	.18	.23	.23		.23	.15	.21	.11	.18	.14	.11	.05	.10
Society	5	.22	.17	.54	.23		.41	.98	.22	.71	.21	.20	.09	.20
Marquesas	6	.18	.15	.30	.15	.41		.54	.20	.34	.15	.13	.10	.12
Tuamotu	7	.24	.17	.46	.21	.98	.54		.34	.63	.21	.21	.11	.24
Mangareva	8	.09	.10	.14	.11	.22	.20	.34		.23	.21	.08	.14	.08
Austral	9	.16	.19	.38	.18	.71	.34	.63	.23		.33	.19	.06	.21
Rapa	10	.10	.11	.18	.14	.21	.15	.21	.21	.33		.05	.10	.09
Hawaii	11	.11	.19	.15	.11	.20	.13	.21	.08	.19	.05		.03	.09
Easter	12	.03	.05	.08	.05	.09	.10	.11	.14	.06	.10	.03		.00
N.Z	13	.23	.24	.24	.10	.20	.12	.24	.08	.21	.09	.09	.00	

Figure 79 is an average linkage cluster analysis of minimum accessibility values for the 13 islands and groups shown in Table 22. The islands most accessible to one another are the Society and Tuamotu groups, which were an ethnographic contact sphere, and next to join this central East Polynesian cluster in order of descending similarity are the Austral, Southern Cook and Marquesas groups. At the bottom of the diagram, Tonga and Samoa form a West Polynesian cluster. Then, at approximately the same level of similarity as between central East and West Polynesian groups, come Mangareva, Rapa, the Northern Cook Islands, New Zealand and Hawaii. Finally, Easter Island is shown as being most remote of all.

Without going into details, it is clear that this model, which is regarded here as reasonable, but arbitrary, bears points of similarity with a number of published summary diagrams of Polynesian linguistic and biological relationships including those shown in Figures 77 and 78, and provides another factor that may be implicated in the development of such patterns of variation. It should be remembered, however, that accessibility affected both colonisation and subsequent voyaging, but, of the two, colonisation was further constrained by factors mentioned elsewhere, and the model might be taken as more representative of post-settlement contact.

Figure 80 is a close proximity analysis following the method of Renfrew and Sterud (1969) based on the same minimum accessibility matrix (Table 22), and it can be seen to conform tolerably with the map of the Pacific,

79. An average linkage cluster analysis of mutual accessibility values for 13 Polynesian islands and groups. Such a model is comparable with similarity studies of Polynesian culture, language and biology.

80. A close proximity analysis of mutual accessibility among Polynesian islands, which bears many specific points of similarity with patterns in biology, language and culture. To take one example, it is close to the first major ethnological study of areal differentiation in Polynesian culture made by Burrows (1938). With clear evidence of correspondence between human patterns and island accessibility, it must be accepted that Polynesian communities on different islands influenced one another in prehistory. Indeed, it seems that Polynesian societies were not as discretely divided as their islands, although they often appeared to be at contact.

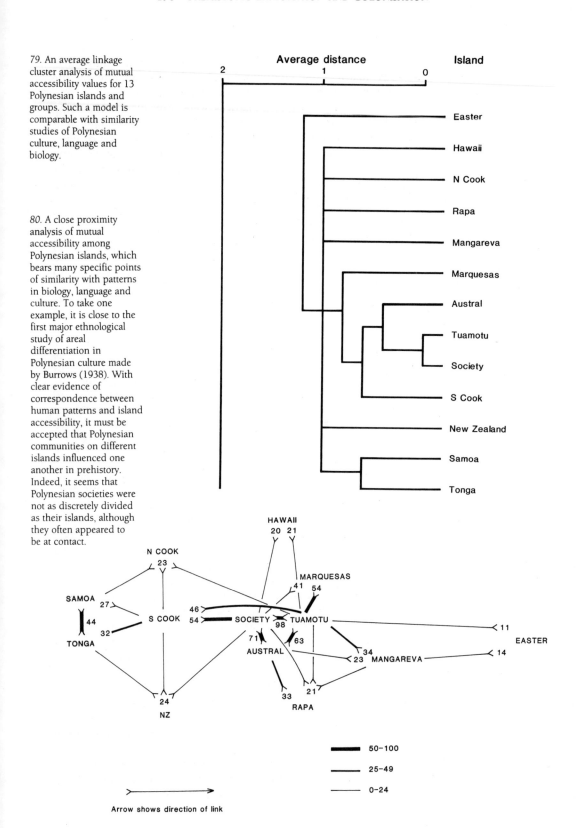

as indeed it should. Some of the details are of interest: West Polynesia stands apart, as it does in language, culture and biology. However, the Northern Cook group is as close to West Polynesia as to the rest of East Polynesia, and it is noted that the language of the westernmost island, Pukapuka, is Samoic, while those of the others belong to East Polynesian.

Although there is a close language relationship between the Southern Cook Islands and New Zealand Maori, which is usually related to the discussion of New Zealand's origins, the Southern Cook Islands can be seen to be more accessible to West Polynesia than New Zealand is. This is clearly reflected in biological similarities between Southern Cook Island and West Polynesian samples (Katayama 1988), while New Zealand biological affinities lie with East Polynesia. New Zealand is just as accessible to the Society as to the Southern Cook Islands, which, again, conforms to the expectations about origins, which derive especially from language.

Figure 80 could also be taken to imply that, after the settlement of East Polynesia, Easter Island became an early isolate, as it is linguistically (although not earliest settled). The Marquesic and Tahitic language sub-groups are perceptible in the diagram too, in so far as the members of the former – Hawaii, the Marquesas and Mangareva – are all peripheral, while the Society, Austral and Cook islands, which belong to the latter, are more mutually accessible or 'central'. One could hypothesise that the Tahitic sub-group may have maintained a relatively higher frequency of contact as they mutually diverged as a group from proto-Central Eastern Polynesian, to which the Marquesic sub-group retains more similarity. (Uncertainty regarding Austral languages is due to changes in historical times.) The separation of the two sub-groups could have been assisted by the attenuated string of the eastern Tuamotus, which provided the most probable link between them, acting as a filter, and to the kind of atoll islands there which were unable to support any intensity of settlement.

The Society Islands lie in the core of East Polynesia in terms of accessibility, but it is anomalous and curious that they are least like their East Polynesian neighbours as far as shared vocabulary goes (Clark 1979:262). This is conventionally explained by the tabooing of words homophonous with the names of chiefs as exemplified historically in the case of Pomare (Clark 1979:265-6). However, it is interesting that this most striking 'black hole' in Polynesian language (shared cognate) similarity occurs in a centre of gravity, rather than a periphery, and may mark a developing cultural elaboration there, precisely where one might – not unreasonably – expect to find it.

My purpose in making these observations is to show a selection of the parallels that one might make between accessibility and other general descriptive patterns in Polynesia. Indeed, the results conform well with the first major ethnological study in areal differentiation of culture by Burrows (1938), who distinguished Western and Central-Marginal Polynesia. In this scheme Central Polynesia had the Society Islands as its nucleus and included the Cook, Austral and Tuamotu islands. Marginal Polynesia comprised Hawaii, the Marquesas, Mangareva, Easter Island and New Zealand, all of which have been found in this study to be relatively inaccessible within Burrows' Central-Marginal area, now commonly known as East Polynesia. Burrows based his study on the distribution of numerous material and cultural traits, and it is still largely, if not entirely, acceptable at that level of description. He noted (1938:91): 'What really stand out from these comparisons are not sharply-defined cultural sub-areas within Polynesia, but two main centers, western Polynesia and central Polynesia.' This observation is closer to the recent idea of variable interaction spheres than to the view of Polynesia as a museum of separate migrations in antiquity, which prevailed before the 1930s and still casts a shadow on the 1970s and 1980s.

EXTERNAL CONTACTS AND CULTURAL CHANGE IN POLYNESIA

With clear evidence of correspondence between cultural patterns and accessibility, it is hard to reject the possibility that East Polynesian communities on different islands influenced one another at times in the past. Yet recent work on the development of Polynesian societies has been evolutionary in approach and sees them as working out their cultural inheritance on islands that were fairly closed systems, as indeed many were at the end of prehistory. Similarities are seen to arise partly because they were all working from the same 'social blueprint', which arrived in Polynesia with Lapita, while differences are related to diverse environments. However, there is some hard evidence for contact in the form of imported pearl shell and pottery, as discussed, and we can expect it to increase and perhaps include the movement of industrial stone and other durables. As for the wider implications of such contact, we can briefly raise two examples: the 'Archaic' artifact assemblages of the first millennium A.D. and the development of complex stratified societies in the second.

As discussed in chapter 5, the East Polynesian 'Archaic' assemblage, which included numerous forms of tanged adzes, harpoons, fishing gear and ornaments, was thought to typify first settlement, until it was realised that characteristic items were missing from the earliest sites, as in the case of Hawaii (Kirch 1986). Walter (1990:14–15) suggests that the origins of most of these artifacts may lie outside East Polynesia, and, for all we know, they could have arrived in a piecemeal fashion. Nevertheless, by the end of the first millennium A.D. we find a wide community of shared items and ideas in tropical East Polynesia and in New Zealand. Until this time, new islands were still being settled, probably both within already discovered archipelagos and beyond them.

A striking feature of the assemblage is its diverse range of adze forms, which was also a characteristic of the Lapita cultural complex (Green 1979). Such assemblages disappeared by a process of simplification in the number of forms – to mainly quadrangular cross-sectioned adzes in New Zealand (Duff 1956), and to different forms elsewhere. Various suggestions have been made to explain these changes. Best (1977) saw the change in New Zealand adzes as related to a different set of functions, which affected both raw materials and technology. Standardisation of forms has also been taken as evidence of craft specialisation, which developed in late prehistory.

With regard to the issue of early diversity, Kirch (1980) suggested that early assemblages could be seen as reflecting experimentation and innovation in the face of environmental constraints. A suggestion made by Bowdler, in the very different context of Australian and Southeast Asian stone tools associated with early modern humans, which are described as generally amorphous and expedient in form, may have a parallel application in Neolithic Oceania. Diverse suites of artifacts found in Lapita and its descendant 'Archaic' may have operated similarly, as 'a sort of travelling survival kit' (Bowdler 1990) with the flexibility to adapt to different conditions. At some time after the settlement of the high latitude islands of New Zealand and the Chathams, the Archaic, in so far as it can be considered an assemblage, disappeared everywhere. Until then its persistence reflects a community of ideas, and its function, in part, a flexible mode of adaptation to different environments and raw materials.

To turn to the second example, on several of the larger groups of Polynesia, economic intensification, political integration and increased social complexity were well advanced, and in East Polynesia this applied especially to Hawaii and the Society Islands. In their displays of high rank, associated taboos and ritual, chiefly architecture and a developing bureaucracy, they were approaching the level of the state. Large resource-rich islands had more stratified societies than more restricted ones. Sahlins (1958) originally related social differentiation to environmental factors that led to different modes of adaptation while Goldman (1970), focusing on the same institutions, stressed status rivalry in the development of a range of chiefdoms.

Most of the recent and current theories accept that Polynesian societies had a common origin in an ancestral culture, which, on linguistic grounds, is thought to have included hereditary leadership and the existence of other specialists such as navigator. Various island groups experienced 'parallel evolutionary processes' (Kirch and Green 1987:442), but as internal developments in substantially closed systems. Among the factors that are invoked commonly are population increase, intensification of wet and dry-land agriculture, competition, political integration and social transformation. There are numerous schemes, which differ in significant ways, concerning Hawaii in particular (e.g. Cordy 1981; Earle 1980; Hommon 1976; Kirch 1984b).

All of this is as may be, but one continuing difficulty is that we have no clear evidence in portable artifacts or in architecture for early distinctions of rank in Polynesia (R. Green, pers. comm. 1990). Archaeological evidence for rising population and intensifying production systems is found in the second millennium A.D., and increasingly through it. The same can be said of ceremonial structures, such as the *heiau* of Hawaii and the *marae* of central East Polynesia, which imply more elaborate religious sanctions to developing political power. While these were complex and varied at the time of contact, the available evidence suggests they became so, increasingly, through time.

A modified view of East Polynesian prehistory is suggested by inter-island accessibility and supported by computer simulation and raises the possibility of mutual influence. Perhaps an appropriate social model might be something like the Peer Polity Interaction, which Renfrew found to be a factor in the emergence of some Old World states (Renfrew and Cherry 1986). Here similarities between societies are seen as the result of interaction, but not according to a model of influence from the more complex situation to the simpler one. The source of change is not seen as external to the wider region, but nor is it uniquely situated in any single polity, which is a position often overlooked by evolutionist and diffusionist alike. The theory has it that polities of comparable scale will exist in the same region, and that similar changes will tend to develop in several at once. Transformations will occur with internal competition of various kinds, which may involve external imitations and the transmission of innovations. While we need not argue a specific application in East Polynesia, we find broadly parallel changes in social complexity and, to take a material example, the striking elaboration of associated religious structures, especially in Hawaii and the Society Islands.

Although archaeologists favour a first settlement of Hawaii from the Marquesas, one strand of evidence for later contact may be the elements of language and the Hawaiian traditions relating to 'Kahiki', which have long been interpreted as evidence of secondary settlement from Tahiti. Instead, these may actually record much more recent contacts, perhaps lasting until around the mid-second millennium A.D.

Easter Island diverged from the East Polynesian mainstream, in settlement and possibly society, long before European discovery, because of relatively high isolation and, latterly, ecological degradation. Similarly, we can ask whether social change in New Zealand followed a different direction from its East Polynesian ancestry, partly because of its greater isolation from it. Evidence for this could be the obvious departure from East Polynesian models of religious structure, even though it was settled from there only a thousand years ago. Many of the relevant social concepts arrived in New Zealand, but their material expression was different, and perhaps is to be seen in some 6000 fortified sites or *paa*. Obviously there were many important independent internal changes in East Polynesian islands, but the wider point is worth considering as well.

When prehistory merged with history in West Polynesia and Fiji, elements of political integration and competition were affected by the extra dimension of overseas voyaging of a kind that may have applied to some extent in East Polynesia until late prehistory. However, unlike the model of mutual influence tentatively suggested here for East Polynesia, changes in West Polynesia, which is more compact geographically, are described as being marked by an expanding hegemony of the Tongan maritime chiefdom (Guiart 1963), which Kirch (1988a:257) sees as characterised by prestige-goods exchange between chiefly elites. As an archaeological example of Tongan expansion, he interprets the 'sudden proliferation' of Tongan-style mounds on Niuatoputapu as 'precisely the kind of settlement landscape that would be predicted in the case of conquest and political domination' (Kirch 1988a:260). Similarly, there is clear evidence of the influence of Tongan language on some of its neighbours. The earlier situation in West Polynesia, especially in the first millennium A.D., is a matter of contention (Kirch 1988d; Davidson 1978, 1989), which will need further archaeological evidence to settle. There are some material traces of movement (Best 1984; pers. comm. 1989), and another indication is the linguistic relationship between the Polynesian Outliers, Tuvalu and Samoa, which appears to pre-date the late Tongan phase. In passing, it can be noted that influences of a kind that could be described as 'Tongan' or 'Samoan', would be difficult to attribute archaeologically to those islands, even if, indeed, that is where they came from.

Issues in the study of colonisation and change

Developments in Polynesian prehistory occurred in the range of chiefly Neolithic societies, and scholars such as Terrell (1986) have described factors that made for stability or change. These include adaptation to both new and humanly altered environments, degrees of isolation from external influence, and chance factors such as founder effect. Polynesian prehistory began with empty islands, and progressive changes in population size and economy influenced wider social changes. This study has considered not the causes of change as such, but rather the *context* and *circumstances* in which they took place. It has pointed to the need to distinguish changes that occurred with colonisation from those that followed, and the indications are that they had different patterns.

Exploration preceded colonisation, which itself outran much of the diversification conventionally attributed to it. Some of the signs that prehistorians have used to track the path of Polynesian expansion may actually belong to a later time. This may apply to language, and there are other difficulties of interpretation including a lack of 'effective descriptive case studies and models of how they [languages] diversify in communication' (Terrell 1988:653). Further to this are the various cultural reasons that have been suggested for language differentiation. Until now, the chronology of colonisation has been influenced by presumed rates of linguistic change, but, in the future, improved archaeological dating could calibrate the actual rate of linguistic change. 'Precise association of dates, languages and material cultures connected with a very large and ancient group of [Austronesian] languages will improve our knowledge of the rates of, and variables affecting, linguistic and cultural change' (Pawley and Green 1973:3).

Much the same can be said of biological anthropology. So far, the skeletal material that comes to us directly from the past is sparse, and analysis based on measurement of modern characteristics, whether genetic or other, has to deal with both demographic change in historical times and sampling problems. As in the case of archaeological and linguistic evidence, it requires more explicit models of what colonisation and change were as processes, because measurements of the degree of relatedness between populations do not automatically provide their own explanations.

Studies of social developments in Polynesia, such as Sahlins (1958) and Goldman (1970), sought 'to account for diversity by elements external to the inherent logic of the social and cultural systems with which they were concerned' (Hooper 1985:3) and both studies shared 'a common framework of evolutionism' (Hooper 1985:3–4). More recent anthropological studies have focused on the structural elements of Polynesian society and its transformations in space and time (e.g. Hooper and Huntsman 1985), and these may have archaeological correlates. However, the major contribution of archaeology to the study of cultural change at that level may be in identifying the context in which it took place. One implication of the present study is that although anthropologists usually study people on single islands, in prehistory, communities were commonly connected in a wider social world of moving items and ideas, and were mutually if differentially exposed to changing circumstances.

10

THE REDISCOVERY OF PACIFIC EXPLORATION

A THEORY OF NAVIGATION

This book has presented an account of Pacific colonisation based on an explicit theory of navigation. While it was clear, previously, that ethnographic voyaging was well described, its relationship to the navigation of early exploration was not understood. Vague ideas about colonisation and an inappropriate context for archaeological data were implicated in several arguable interpretations of prehistory. The first part of the book dealt mainly with issues in theory, and the second reviewed them in the detail of archaeological settlement evidence, which fitted well. So far everything was normal: argument and evidence were sitting compatibly in one another's pockets. Some conventional ideas looked a lot less comfortable, but, ultimately, there was no independent proof.

A COMPUTER SIMULATION

Further efforts to build a more tenacious case changed that. One was a computer simulation whose first purpose was to examine general propositions about colonisation and to test many detailed predictions about the order and sequence of settlement. The archaeological outlines of Pacific settlement are tolerably well-known in many island groups and, in so far as computer simulation could imitate them, it identified relevant variables and helped to explain what had happened. In so far as it produced plainly spurious patterns, it could suggest things that had not happened.

Beyond that, because simulation showed what prehistoric explorers were probably able to do, it distinguished things that they *chose* to do, from others that they *chose not* to do. Also, it provided insights into the kinds of navigational knowledge and technique that were appropriate to the colonisation of different parts of the ocean, if it were to proceed with archaeologically implied rates of speed, success and survival. The need for navigational skills to change and improve was well-founded in theory, but the simulation offers a first timetable for it. In other words, these experiments brought us rather closer to the people concerned than the stories that we usually tell one another about them.

ACCESSIBILITY AND DIVERSIFICATION

Pacific voyaging did not end with discovery, or even with colonisation: it continued with relaxed navigational rules in sea-lanes mapped in the mind. Some confusion about colonisation has followed from the lack of distinction between changes that took place with colonisation or afterwards. Both are found to be affected by voyaging considerations in different but systematic ways. This is not to be seen as an intrinsic cause of change, but it is clearly a circumstance. Since settlement, groups of islands have been influenced in generally predictable and similar ways, whatever else happened to them individually, and found to be sensitive indicators of external events and wider communication. These groups include the (former) 'mystery' islands, the marooned margins of Polynesia, the shrinking East Polynesian contact areas, the voyaging spheres of history and the Polynesian Outliers.

The analysis of island accessibility gave another variable to compare with the diversity to be found in biology, language and culture, whose patterns cannot explain themselves any more than they could provide a satisfactory theory of colonisation. It is implied that Polynesian society was commonly less insular than its islands. We should be wary of regarding islands as laboratories in which the inhabitants worked out their human inheritance alone, in a range of different circumstances.

DEVELOPMENT OF NAVIGATIONAL METHODS WITH EXPLORATION

It was suggested that the colonisation of the remote Pacific did not begin until people learned to sail in open ocean and survive. The main element in survival was said to be return voyaging. To confirm the claim, a summary of all of the simulated one-way voyages from Melanesia, is shown in Figure 81. The departure point in Figure 81A, at the eastern end of the main Solomons chain, was the earliest one. For each 10° interval of a 230° segment of the compass rose, the percentage success is shown for the canoes that sailed that course for 15 days and found some other, new land. The higher value, for summer or winter, is taken in each case. Figure

81. A summary of simulated voyages from the Solomon Islands (A), and from Vanuatu, Santa Cruz and New Caledonia generalised as a single origin (B). Both diagrams A and B show a zone of potential settlement as established from simulation, and a zone of actual settlement as established by archaeology. The archaeological zone is smaller than the potential zone and aligned in the same direction in both. Evidently there were directions in which Lapita colonists chose not to sail. Because they sailed upwind, the direction from which they could most easily return, we may conclude that two-way voyaging was part of the repertoire of remote ocean exploration from its beginning.

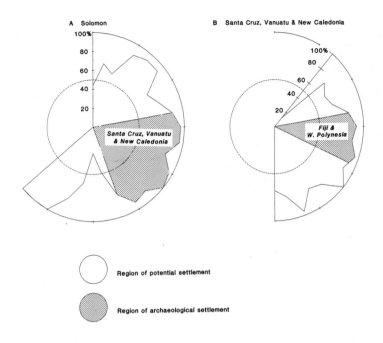

81B generalises the three starting locations of Santa Cruz, Vanuatu and New Caledonia as a single point, and again shows the best score for one-way voyages of 18 days by target angle. However, to be counted, a canoe could not land back in any of these three Melanesian groups. Success rates are seldom less than 50% on courses from the Solomon Islands, and commonly very much more; the same can be said of the Melanesian islands farther east, although canoes do not set out through such a wide arc.

Obviously, new land could have been found through a wide range of target angles from both these starting points by one-way voyaging. But it is also clear that the region of archaeologically demonstrated settlement is much narrower than the region of potential settlement as indicated by simulation. Referring to Figure 81A, no Lapita canoe is known to have reached Australia in the southeast, or any target north of the Reef/Santa Cruz group. For Figure 81B, no known canoe has reached a destination north or south of West Polynesia or Fiji, even though Norfolk, the Kermadecs and New Zealand were just three glaringly obvious targets in the south.

The arcs of the two archaeological regions are aligned in the same general direction. All of the island groups within them have Lapita settlement, while none of those beyond do. The pattern is so clear it could hardly be explained away by a host of independent sampling errors. Voyaging was directed, and the direction was against the prevailing wind. People could not know before they left that there was land to be found, and probably sailed upwind so as to return in the event of finding none. They left a familiar safety screen behind. Simulation has put the case for the negative, which is difficult to do, and it appears that return voyaging was normal from the beginning.

82. A comparison of voyaging strategies simulated by computer, which indicates there was a need for navigational methods to improve. Return voyaging most probably included latitude sailing by the time colonisation reached central East Polynesia. Contact with the more remote islands of Polynesia required an explicit strategy of indirect returns or 'three-way' voyages, as represented by Strategy 5. This became possible as geographic knowledge was added to navigational knowledge.

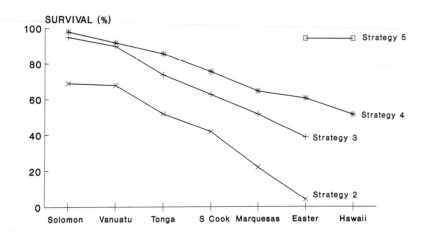

There seems to be no serious alternative. For instance, there is little reason to suppose that sailors particularly wanted to travel east-south-east exclusively, other than for safety, because once they had acquired enough geography to make crosswind voyages safe they began to veer off that line. Far removed from those early explorers, we only have reason to think their starting direction was a relative one.

The issue of improvements in navigation has been raised several times, because there was a need and an opportunity for this to happen. It grew harder to discover more land in the eastern Pacific, but by then explorers had a lot of accumulated experience behind them. The question is examined in Figure 82, a graph that compares survival rates by simulation strategy from a series of starting points from west to east. The graph is arbitrary, because the voyages sent off from each of the starting points were not identical. However, because the diagram summarises tens of thousands of quite realistic simulated voyages, the results are valuable if they are taken only as broad indications of relative difficulty.

Figure 82 shows that return voyages always allowed many more simulated sailors to survive than one-way voyages (had there been many). In the first major crossings from the Solomons to Santa Cruz, Vanuatu and New Caledonia, and from there across to Fiji, there was little difference in the success rates achieved by Strategies 3 and 4. The difference between the two is that returns by Strategy 4 used latitude sailing that required the ability to estimate latitude from the stars, as described in chapter 4. This result supports an earlier suggestion that the survival value of sailing upwind was a much more simple and obvious technique than sailing up-latitude, and that the more esoteric skills of celestial navigation and position-finding could be expected to be acquired and refined more gradually. Figure 82 implies that these would not need to be especially sophisticated for Lapita to cross Melanesia.

Results shown for Tonga refer to success rates in crossing from there to the closer groups of East Polynesia. Firstly, it can be seen that there is no sharp drop in survival rates to support arguments for the West

Polynesian pause. Some 74% of return voyagers could expect to survive, and, if latitude sailing had been added to the repertoire of skills, the rate climbs to 86%. No particular difficulties are encountered in spreading through the Societies, Australs and Tuamotus.

Results for voyages from the Marquesas show a further drop in all success rates, and, indeed, this applies to all voyaging out from central East Polynesia. A concept equivalent to latitude sailing must have existed by this stage, if not before. Contact with several islands on the fringes of central East Polynesia is scarcely feasible without it, yet archaeology shows it did happen.

Success rates fall still further in voyages in the margins of Polynesia. Values in Figure 82 include ones both to and from Easter Island and Hawaii. On many return passages, Strategy 4 voyages no longer work. By this time, if not before, there was a clear need for indirect returns through intermediary island groups. The massive screen of the Tuamotus made contacts with the tropical Polynesian margins possible, and this includes many of the voyages involving Hawaii, Easter Island and the Pitcairn group. Simulated voyages by indirect return are shown as Strategy 5 in Figure 82. Controlled 'three-way' voyaging among known islands was found to be very successful, just as it is known to be for small sailing boats today. Values for New Zealand are not considered in this analysis, because it lies so far outside the tropics, and latitude is not taken into account in this exercise.

It is not imagined that the strategies employed here were ever used in prehistory precisely as described, but they do summarise techniques essential to navigate successfully in sailing boats and the different strategies used do equate with different general levels of skill. The case seems to be made that colonists learned as they went. There is also a good fit with the esoteric skills of navigation described or implied by ethnography.

Cultural discontinuities long proposed for West Polynesia and central East Polynesia do not stand out in this evidence. The original case for them argued from consequence to cause, but now it may be time to turn these around. The order and elapsed time of settlement should be influenced by patterns of island accessibility and weather. In the case of West Polynesia this could mean that in the few centuries that were required to find and then to establish colonies in East Polynesia, perceptible cultural changes had time to occur. Therefore, it is not the case that the need to make various changes in language and culture arrested colonisation in some unknown manner, while they took place: that smacks of rationalisation after the event. Nor is there independent calibration of the speed of change here, and the rate was quite possibly faster than envisaged, given the dynamic state of the small communities scattered through the archipelagos of Fiji and West Polynesia at the time.

But as old discontinuities fade in cultural significance, new ones appear. Sampling error seems to have taken time off the first colonisation of Belau and Yap. The absence of settlement in Australia, and of earlier settlement of New Zealand, the high islands of Micronesia, Nauru, Banaba, Norfolk and the Kermadecs, among others, are new discontinuities definitely of a cultural kind. They were not settled earlier because people chose not to sail in their directions.

MECHANICAL AND PHYSICAL EXPLANATIONS FOR COLONISATION

Much of what is inferred about early exploration and settlement points to rationality – to reason and understanding – in its own cultural context. We see it not least in exploration being directed to safety, not speed, and with return voyaging as the norm. This must surely count against mechanical theories such as settlement by the anomalous westerlies of El Niño, which has problems of its own, as discussed; the main one being the absence of Lapita throughout East Polynesia.

Recently, Houghton (1990; Houghton in press) has noted that the large body size and strong musculature of Polynesians and Micronesians is unusual for tropical latitudes, and proposes they developed in Island Melanesia from the selective pressure of cold and exposure in a marine environment: larger-bodied individuals had a crucial advantage in maintaining body temperature. The suggestion is not that the Pacific was settled simply because those who did it were large, but rather that only large people could survive it, and that selection operated as people spread into an oceanic environment. However, Howells (1979:283) presumed that 'before colonization of the area the parental Polynesian group was already large bodied'. It could be argued that they were large because they came originally from a cold place, such as Japan, as suggested by Brace *et al.* (1990). Another consideration is that because stature and body bulk are polygenic, selection would take longer than the time available in this case (J. Meaney, pers. comm. 1990). Houghton's theory may be at odds with the argument that ocean explorers returned when they were stressed and normally survived at sea. Further, if discovery went ahead of settlement, then groups of colonists did not have to endure long and arduous ocean searches.

LAPITA

Lapita is an uncertain category, but, for all that, it is conspicuously associated with the settlement of a large part of the world. Its origins were discussed in chapter 3, and one of the few conclusions prehistorians can hold with confidence is that in Near Oceania, where the earliest Lapita appeared, being Lapita did not always mean the same thing. However, a case was made for a Lapita 'people' in the remote Pacific who belonged to a voyaging tradition and shared an episode of exploration. Their methods were so alike, they all avoided searching in particular directions. This, especially, makes the possibility of a number of disparate groups, who shared Lapita material culture, but otherwise were buzzing around the ocean independently, an unlikely one.

Related communities dispersed over a wide area at low population densities. In archaeological time, Lapita exploded apart in Remote Oceania, yet, given that this was no involuntary response to pressure but involved common ideas, it was an orderly separation. If colonisation was continuous and based on return voyaging, then interaction held Lapita together as it flew apart in this rather drastic episode of social reproduction. The distinctive and intricate design system of Lapita pottery is a conspicuous element of integration among dispersed communities. The few centuries the most richly decorated Lapita ware lasted in several regions coincide with the spread and consolidation of communities.

Exchange was no reason to colonise empty islands (Irwin 1981), but as Hunt (1989:31-2) remarks, 'many scholars have regarded participation in inter-island exchange and/or communication as a contributing causal factor in the speed and success of the colonization of Island Oceania'. Kirch (1988d:104) has argued that 'long-distance exchange was an essential component of the Lapita dispersal and colonization strategy'. He sees formal exchange of non-critical resources as possibly a social mechanism for successful settlement, a kind of 'lifeline' back to parent communities (Kirch 1988d). Hunt refers to the interaction between small communities, which is regarded 'as an important mechanism in reducing the probability of extinction' (1989:47).

These are most interesting suggestions; however, if colonisation was by return voyaging, then exchange would be incidental to it and there would be less need for exchange to operate more independently as described. We can expect to see differences in the transport of material during the first generation or two of settlement from later on: the difference is between 'coloniser' and 'exchange' modes. The ceramic settlement of the Massim and south Papuan coast 2000 years ago may provide a model for Lapita (Irwin in press a). Early colonisation evidently carried a 'pulse' of imported obsidian farther than it travelled again, and in the lowest levels of sites with data, it was abundant and occurred in larger size than later. Links among the daughter colonies were apparently open at the time. A parallel example in Lapita could be the two pieces of Talasea obsidian found at Naigani, Fiji, believed on the basis of pottery style to be an early site (Best 1981). It will be interesting to compare the size distribution of obsidian between basal and later levels of Lapita sites when the information is published, and to look for other evidence of change occurring after communities were established.

A general observation is that the spatial extent of exchange involving any volume of items in no way matches the extent of colonisation.

WHY COLONISATION BEGAN AND ENDED

The question of human motives is the most tantalising one of all, and there has been no shortage of possible answers. Among those suggested are adventure, curiosity, the joy of discovery, wanderlust, prestige, exile and shame. Other standards are the search for prized resources, raw materials or trade; the search for empty lands to relieve overpopulation, and possibly warfare. Another common theme is stress between senior and junior siblings or branches of a descent group, and this ties in with linguistic suggestions of ranking in proto-Oceanic society. A typical example follows:

> It may also be that now and then ambitious younger sons or chiefs, discontented at not being able to attain higher rank within the community, organized expeditions and left home in order to acquire new lands and there found their own chiefdoms. [Akerblom 1968:92-3]

Taking a different tack, Terrell (1986:65-6) said that the motives of Pacific expansion could have been as mixed as those of the later European maritime exploration.

Some questions are answerable archaeologically, but motive is probably one that is not. However, it can be approached by a process of elimination. For example, we can jettison the idea that the Pacific was settled because those who did it misunderstood their environment. The explanation that people were forced to go casts colonisation in the role of reaction rather than action: it avoids the issue by saying there was no choice. The opposite case has been put (Irwin 1980:328). First, the people who left took large capital items such as canoes and stores: expensive voyages can only have been supported by surplus production. Second, voyages left island groups much earlier than the stress of numbers is attested archaeologically, and did not continue until large islands had been filled by successive groups of migrants. Third, small populations sailed much farther than they had to, if they were just looking for more land. To these reasons we can now add another. Figure 81 showed that land was to be found in a much wider range of directions than people searched. This implies that they were very selective and by no means desperate.

Colonisation of the remote Pacific was not one unique episode, and the motivation must have been general enough to accommodate at least two starts: the spread of Lapita through Melanesia to Polynesia, and the separate settlement of western Micronesia from Island Southeast Asia. While there may have been contact between these ancestral groups in the voyaging corridor, this was indirect enough for them to have different archaeological identities.

Continuity of method suggests that Pacific settlement was broadly related rather than a disconnected series of events. It is appropriate to see it as a tradition embracing a multitude of individuals, events and transformations, played out on island after island. As many scholars have suggested, much of the motivation could have been internal and related to resources and competition. Some motivation may have been external, and exchange could have added another dimension to internal competition. We cannot reject the idea of some quest, even if that is more typical, perhaps, of prehistorians than their silent subjects.

The question of motive is commonly asked out of context and it helps to relate it to technology. It is sometimes suggested that people settled the Pacific because they had the canoes, but this does not distinguish means from ends. A better suggestion is that they did it because they had already been doing it and it was part of their structure of ideas. Ocean exploration did not have a cold start. It could not have been done unless very similar sailing was being done in safer circumstances in the voyaging corridor. The reasons could have been diverse and might have already included colonisation of specialised marine habitats not occupied by co-existing populations. While there may be different kinds of Lapita sites in Near Oceania, some could have been prototypes of ones offshore. For example, the Talepakemalai site on Mussau (Kirch 1988c) could be an early colony rather than a homeland site. It has many points in common with sites in the Reef Islands (Green 1979) in settlement, economy and exchange. Whatever the precise circumstances, interaction systems were broadening and intensifying in Near Oceania, along with their social correlates. This may already have included an impetus for colonisation. The remote Pacific offered a wide field without competition and became accessible when the navigational threshold of survival sailing was crossed.

As for the question of why voyaging stopped, the short answer is that it did not. It continued in settled areas after colonisation. Exploration went on for 2000 years after the first groups were settled and as colonisation spread. To find the land there was, a huge area of empty ocean was traversed as well, and there was feedback of information with returning canoes. Failure to find land was no new or sudden thing, it was increasingly part of the colonisation process. Explorers were used to it, and could not be expected to keep searching the same empty places. Eventually, all of the Pacific that lay within technological range was used up. In a sense, this included the continental boundaries with which slight contact is demonstrated. Oceanic people could hardly have competed with the inhabitants at such great range, which may be a case parallel to Vikings in North America (Keegan and Diamond 1987).

A better question is why did voyaging continue? Most of the motives raised for colonisation apply as well to post-settlement voyaging. To this I would add one other, which is that Oceanic society was wider than its islands and this has implications for how we do research there.

Some time after settlement, for reasons beyond the scope of this book, the frequency of voyaging began to fall away in many regions. It happened gradually and systematically as islands were affected according to their accessibility. Additional archaeological evidence for the time of abandonment of the so-called mystery islands will neatly calibrate the process. We have evidence of occupied groups losing contact with one another. Voyaging survived until Western contact in three main areas. One of these may have been still in decline (the Society Islands and Tuamotus), one was fairly stable (Micronesia), while the third (West Polynesia, Fiji and their neighbours) was expanding, but in a different social context.

The question of why the colonisation of the remote Pacific began and ended is an arbitrary one. Paradoxically, the answer is that it did neither, abruptly.

SOME CONCLUDING REMARKS ON COLONISATION

While the settlement of the Pacific was undoubtedly a remarkable episode in human prehistory, it has been unnecessary to see it as romantic or, at the opposite extreme, mechanical. It was systematic to the extent that settlement order and chronology are predictable within broad limits.

It was done by competent sailors who undertook safer voyages first. Knowledge of geography, as it was acquired, relaxed the stringent rules of survival sailing into the unknown. The ability to navigate offshore persisted in many places until the whole Pacific was settled and, in the case of the Chatham Islands, this may have been only a few centuries before the arrival of the first Europeans in this hemisphere. Voyaging was a tradition that has lasted for more than 3000 years to this day.

Whatever the motivation, geographical expansion is something humans have done for two million years. Technological innovations are associated with the occupation of certain environments. Oceania was the last part of the Earth to be settled (apart from the ice-caps). The colonists of the remote Pacific showed that small founder populations, no bigger than can be carried in an ocean-going canoe, could reproduce themselves and their society. As Levison, Ward and Webb (1973:4) put it: 'In the first and second millennia B.C. the ocean to the east, north, and south of eastern Melanesia was a space frontier as the solar system is today.' Several prehistorians have since raised the implications of Pacific colonisation for space.

This book has emphasised rationality and the practical skills of navigation to counter previous theories (and in spite of the danger of applying such assumptions to other cultures). But the argument is not meant to exclude all haphazard and accidental elements. Yet these may have increased through time, as voyaging declined, and, certainly, it is the recent period to which most accounts of accidental deaths at sea belong.

A SUMMARY OF SETTLEMENT ORDER AND TENTATIVE CHRONOLOGY

The Pleistocene settlement of the voyaging corridor between mainland Asia and the Solomons generally followed the trends of island intervisibility, accessibility and the weather. The rafts or boats used were substantial enough to carry five or six people or more, but still unsophisticated.

Some 25,000 years afterwards, two archaeologically identified groups of settlers came out of the region into the deep Pacific, but their appearance in the evidence is abrupt. For them, the corridor was a voyaging nursery, a sphere of contact, and a safety screen behind.

One-way, preceramic voyagers could have reached the Melanesian groups of Santa Cruz, Vanuatu and New Caledonia, because the islands were there to be found by any who sailed towards them. At present, though, there is barely a suggestion of evidence for it. When Lapita arrived, it was by an exploration method that entailed return voyaging. From the Solomons it was scarcely feasible to sail directly beyond Santa Cruz, Vanuatu or New Caledonia to islands farther east, but all made good origins for a crossing to Fiji, from Santa Cruz and Vanuatu in summer and New Caledonia in the tropical winter. Lapita stayed within the safest arc of exploration for this crossing as well as the one before. According to expectations based on simulated voyaging, evidence for Lapita on Tikopia suggests that actual outward voyages were made from Santa Cruz and Vanuatu. If outward voyages were also made from New Caledonia, there could be signs of it on outlying Hunter, Matthew and Walpole Islands, which were well placed to intercept them, although hardly worth landing on.

Fiji must have been first reached between 1500 and 1000 B.C., allowing for different interpretations of the dates: my preference is for the middle rather than the ends of this range. A scatter of settlement through West Polynesia would have followed soon afterwards. Both Samoa and Tonga were navigationally suitable sources for central East Polynesia, which is the greatest sampling hole in settlement at the time of writing. The Cook Islands were most probably the first to be found, and this could have happened any time after Lapita reached West Polynesia, but scarcely later than 500 B.C. I believe this would have taken a few centuries to achieve, and prefer an average date of c.700 B.C. However, these islands need not have been settled as soon as they were found (Davidson 1989) and archaeological sites are less visible on the Pacific Plate.

The best targets farther east were the Society Islands, Tuamotus and Australs. Mangareva was probably reached via the Tuamotus rather than directly from the Southern Cooks or Australs. Outlying islands, such as Rapa, the Pitcairn group and the Marquesas, were more difficult and later than central groups. The Marquesas were most accessible by an indirect route through the Tuamotus; if they were settled by c. A.D. 0, which seems possible, then the Society Islands, Tuamotus and Australs can be expected to fall between that age and the date for the Southern Cooks, whatever that proves to be. A conservative method of estimation is to count back from the settlement of Hawaii c. A.D. 400.

A form of latitude sailing was probably already in use by this time, and exploratory voyages involving indirect returns were needed to sail safely beyond the cluster of groups in central East Polynesia. Hawaii was more likely to have been reached from the Marquesas than anywhere else, but the Tuamotus were another possibility, and the Society Islands a more remote one: this could have been in summer or winter. Pitcairn and Easter Island were easiest to reach from a source in the southern tropics such as Mangareva, and the best time was winter. Easter Island was a suitable source for return voyages to South America.

New Zealand could have been discovered from New Caledonia, Fiji, Tonga or the Southern Cooks, at any time after they were first settled. However, archaeology, the logic of survival sailing and simulation all suggest it was probably from East Polynesia at quite a late date. The Chatham Islands were probably settled only from New Zealand. Finally, the Line Islands, the Kermadecs and Norfolk Island appear to have been implicated in the settlement of Hawaii and New Zealand, at about the same respective times. The Pitcairn group may have a similar relationship with Easter Island.

The settlement periods of many islands and groups in the Pacific Ocean remain undated or unexamined. However, the data we have, in the context of this theory of colonisation, produce such a coherence that unknown

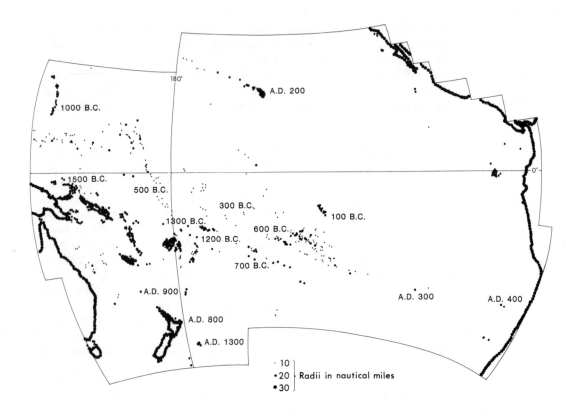

83. A pattern of approximate real and/or predicted dates for the colonisation of the remote Pacific, which follows from the theory of systematic voyaging. Discovery probably preceded settlement, but the two events will be difficult to distinguish even where they were a few centuries apart, which may be the case sometimes, especially as colonisation crossed on to the Pacific Plate. The areas of greatest archaeological uncertainty are currently Micronesia and East Polynesia. (Adapted from Irwin 1989, Figure 14, but a more conservative interpretation of the same data.)

cases are generally predictable in order, if not in years. Among these, Micronesia is the most difficult. It was probably settled independently from west and east, but the first episodes are missing archaeologically from both sides. Another millennium is likely in the far west, in Belau and Yap. High islands in eastern Micronesia could have been settled as early as the Cook Islands, but the settlement of atolls there rather depends upon geological history.

Various age estimates are shown in Figure 83. However, as shown, these do not take account of the delayed and intermittent settlement that we can expect to be a feature among the islands of most groups.

POST-DISCOVERY AND TRADITIONAL NAVIGATION

It now remains only to provide a sketch of navigation as it was at the time of Western contact and as it is today, and to comment upon its development.

After the fifteenth century A.D., when Europeans finally spread into the Pacific Ocean, perhaps the most telling innovation they brought was writing.

Thereafter, eye-witnesses, within the limitations of their point of view, could record what they saw there. But the great episode of Oceanic colonisation was over, unwitnessed, and changes in navigation had occurred in the intervening period. The first difference is that early colonists had explored unknown ocean as they expanded; they sailed with the knowledge of what was behind but not what lay ahead. In contrast, all recent and historic European descriptions are of navigation in seas that are already known. While it is still necessary to search for land, one knows it is there.

Traditional voyagers go to sea with models of navigation that are entirely memorised. A Western navigator carries a chart that shows islands in their correct relative positions and Mercator's projection allows any straight line (rhumbline) to represent a line that can be followed by compass between places on the curved earth. The chart is orientated to north and has compass roses from which one can find any course. Variations between true and magnetic directions are known for every part of the Earth, and further corrections can be made for any compass deviation caused by the magnetic field of the boat itself. The derived compass course can be followed and adjusted, as necessary, to allow for current and leeway. The chart allows easy measurement of distance between islands, and the ship's log monitors progress during a passage. Any departure from the dead-reckoned position is controlled by the intersection of position lines found by celestial navigation. For all of these elements, traditional navigators had different, equivalent or alternative models, which, together, amounted to an integrated navigational system carried in the mind and did not require instruments. It is little wonder that the training of navigators was long and their prestige high (Thomas 1987).

A traditional concept widespread in Oceania and expressed in various forms was 'compasses' whose points were directed to stars, the sun, winds and swells. These are thought to be earlier and independent of the magnetic mariner's compass and in some respects incompatible with it. The star compass of the Carolines has 32 named points on most islands, marked by the rising and setting positions of stars. Altair, the 'Big Bird' is the cardinal point. It has a celestial latitude of 8.5° N. and passes through the zenith of the Carolines, so the system is not quite an east/west one (Lewis 1972:62). There is a north/south axis from the Pole Star to the upright Southern Cross, which, slanting in other attitudes to the east and west, marks four other star points in the south. Navigators knew the star courses leading out to other islands and the reciprocal bearings. Obviously, the star paths were different from different islands, and all had to be memorised. To give an idea of the amount of information required, Alkire's informants had learned the courses radiating out from 18 islands (Lewis 1972:68) to, typically, up to a dozen other named islands in each case.

Thomas (1987:76) says Caroline navigators 'are taught to recognise eight "waves" – one from each octet of the compass', the most dominant being the swells from the north, northeast and east in the northern winter trade wind season. Later, in the voyaging season, south and southeasterly swells mark the southern winter trade winds, while, in late summer, when there are westerly winds, swells come from that quarter. Commonly, two or more swells run across each other and sailors orientate themselves by the way the waves interact and how the canoe is felt to move as it passes through them. Various mnemonic aids and 'stick charts' showing swell patterns as they relate to islands were most elaborate in the atolls of the Marshall Islands, and are believed to be pre-contact.

Lewis (1972:74) reports wind compasses in the Southern Cook Islands with 32 points, Tokelau (12 points), Pukapuka (16 points) and Tahiti, which also has a sun-oriented scheme of 16 points; he thinks the Cook Islands may have been similarly sun-oriented. Navigators needed to use both the sun by day and stars at night, and Lewis finds circumstantial evidence that Polynesia once had a star-based orientation to its navigation, now lost, except perhaps for remnants of a system in Tonga.

The point about finding islands by following star paths, etc., is that such relationships between islands could not have been learned until the paths had been traversed.

The traditional system of orientation and dead-reckoning in the Caroline Islands is called *etak*, in which the canoe's progress is conceptualised by picturing a reference island lying well off to one side of the track, actually moving under star points on the horizon behind it. No such system survives in Polynesia, but it is known that Tupaia was able to point back to his Society Islands home from wherever in the Pacific he travelled with Cook, but it is not known how he was able to do it. Lewis (1972:127) reports that in Polynesia, as well as being able to steer by the stars, navigators were able to point to the islands around them at any time. This ability was also demonstrated by the Reef Islands navigator Tevake on an experimental voyage with him.

Carolinian voyages are preferably divided into approximately 10 equal *etak* units of 10–20 miles, but this varies according to available stars and islands (Lewis 1972:134). The first and last *etaks* are those of sighting and are subdivided on Satawal into more than 20 sections, according to how much island can be seen (Thomas 1987:243). The second and second-to-last are *etak* of the birds, which extend some 20 miles offshore as far as the range of species of noddies and terns that return to roost on land at night. These expand the island target and indicate its direction in the early morning and evening. On only some inter-island journeys do the star points precisely coincide with the range of these seabirds.

While accurate dead-reckoning depends upon estimates of a canoe's speed through the water, one point emphasised is that *etak* is a dynamic model in which the canoe is held to be stationary, while the islands move under the stars around it. 'The Carolinian voyager keeps thinking like this about objects he cannot see, and does not switch to the map concept, or "eye of God" method as we do' (Finney *et al.* 1986:46). '*Etak* is perfectly adapted for its use by navigators who have no instruments, charts, or even a dry place in which to spread a chart if they had one' (Thomas 1987:82). Thus, as Lewis puts it (1972:134), *etak* is a system that integrates all of the known information of rate, time, geography and astronomy.

Sailing directions for each voyage take account of all of the conditions of wind and current that one could expect to meet, and, when the winds are contrary or the current strong, *etak* strategies become complex. For example, to allow for current, navigators back-sight as they reach the end of the sighting *etak*, to see how far they have been displaced, and adjust their star course accordingly. At sea, corrections can be made for changing circumstances. One point laboured by Sharp (1963) is that navigators could not control lateral displacement, but ethnographic evidence tells against him. Leeway is a characteristic of the canoe, not of the place, and is something sailors can estimate for various points of sail. Currents can be detected sometimes out of sight of land in the pattern of ripples on the surface and, with more breeze, in the way that whitecaps fall as the waves break. When tacking into head winds, Lewis reports that the destination can become the *etak* island itself, and it moves sideways and back with each tack, and these become shorter as land approaches (1972:138).

Traditional navigation systems require memorising vast amounts of information and then applying it at sea. Much of the lore is embedded in chants (Goodenough and Thomas 1987:13). In the Carolines it includes names for each individual seaway between islands, and there is an associated system of 'brother seaways', which are similarly aligned, so that if a navigator forgets the star under which an island lies, he can remember it through its brothers. Then there is a series of distinctive sea creatures, known as *pookof* on Satawal, which are believed to keep their station around islands. Various birds, fish, turtles, whales, etc., with known idiosyncrasies might be seen occasionally or searched for when one is lost. Thomas (1987:268) also recorded a combined calendar and weather forecasting system, which he translates as the 'fighting of stars'. In any month there may be one or two stars, which, in the first or last five days of the moon's cycle, will 'fight' or storm, although quite how these relate to recorded weather patterns is unknown. These are supplemented by a detailed lore of other weather signs.

A point that emerges is that from the body of memorised information, experienced navigators have the ability to construct their own detailed sailing directions for particular voyages and then to apply these at sea. In a striking experimental example, the Satawal navigator, Mau Piailug, showed that it is possible to apply indigenous navigation even far beyond one's familiar region, and make a successful landfall. On the 1976 voyage of the *Hokule'a* south from Hawaii to Tahiti, Mau used the Marshalls, far to the west of the track, as *etak* islands for the northern part of the route and the Marquesas, to the east, for the southern part (Finney *et al.* 1986:50).

Because more than 1000 years of offshore experience preceded the settlement of any of the more distant islands of Polynesia, it seems very probable that a developing integrated system of orientation and dead-reckoning gradually expanded into unknown ocean. This could have included a form of star compass that is believed to have been widespread. The sky does not change with longitude and, according to Lewis' calculations, bearings on stars can accommodate some movement in latitude, without introducing undue error. He concludes that the star compass has considerable scope in unfamiliar latitudes (Lewis 1972:71-2). He notes that the Pole Star and Southern Cross and east-west bearings of Orion are unaffected, but that other stars of high declination (celestial latitude) are most affected. Yet, for a star with a declination of 45°, if an observer is anywhere between 18° north or south of the equator – which accommodates much of tropical Polynesia – the error in the bearing will not exceed 3°. For a star of declination 30°, the same error accommodates observers between 23° north or south. However, the example of a star of high declination, which Lewis gives, is for one of 75° and, in this case, the range of 3° error in its bearing is confined within 9° north or south. Few islands in the Pacific present target angles of less than 3°, and it seems possible that the developing concept of a star compass could have accompanied later stages of the colonisation of the remote Pacific. The true relative positions of islands could be learned by return voyages between them.

Thomas's recent account of Satawal navigators, and especially Mau Piailug, brings out some personal qualities of the *palu* or navigator:

> The *palu* had only his senses and his memory. So critical was memory to navigation that it defined [Mau's] notion of courage. (Thomas 1987:83)
> *Uurupa* stressed that the ability to track the movements of the islands beneath the stars in any sea condition, even when tired, cold, and hungry, was the most critical skill in navigation. [Thomas 1987:83]

'To be a *palu* you must have three qualities: fierceness, strength, and wisdom. The knowledge of navigation brings all three'. This was how it was put by Piailug, perhaps one of the last of the traditional navigators in the Pacific (Thomas 1987: front paper).

Lewis (1972) discusses the confidence of navigators to make their landfall:

> Rafe the Tikopian, for example, was not being obtuse when he failed to understand a question about what he would do if he should miss his home landfall. 'I know the way my island is', he said. 'It is my island. It is where I follow the stars where to go – I cannot miss *my* island!' His certainty was reinforced because, in addition to guiding stars he knew signs such as reflected waves and seabirds that would guide him to Tikopia. [Lewis 1972:232]

Needless to say, the navigator, whether of chiefly birth or not, is an expert with responsibility and status in an island society. His skills in building and sailing canoes help maintain the inter-island links that make small island communities such as those in Micronesia viable. Even in the matter of regularly providing food from the sea and bringing extra supplies from small, neighbouring, uninhabited islands, the role of the navigator has been crucial.

It is no surprise that Oceanic ethnographies document a ritual context to voyaging. For instance, Micronesian navigators were separated traditionally from women and children for some time before and after sailing. The building, sailing and repair of canoes was attended by magic. Much information was kept secret, partly as a protection against sorcery. A religious context to voyaging must have been general in the Pacific from early times. Even when I was about to leave the Louisiade Archipelago of Papua New Guinea in my yacht *Rhumbline*, the boat was given traditional magic of the Tubetube, who are famous sailors and traders of the Massim. The boat was given magic to fly and to avoid bouncing rocks. The crew were given magic to stay alert and to see and to be strong to sail. We were protected from the *mulukwausi* or flying witches, who are known to home in on sailors in distress. And I have to report that the magic was not unsuccessful. In the first leg of the return journey to New Zealand, the *Rhumbline* sailed so fast across the Coral Sea that we had to work during the last night to slow her down to avoid arriving at the Great Barrier Reef on the coast of Australia too early, and before it was light.

BIBLIOGRAPHY

Akerblom, K. 1968. *Astronomy and navigation in Polynesia and Micronesia*. Monograph, no. 14. Stockholm: Ethnographical Museum.

Alkire, W. H. 1965. *Lamotrek Atoll and inter-island socio-economic ties*. Illinois Studies in Anthropology, no. 5, Urbana, Ill.: University of Illinois Press.

Allen, J. 1984. In search of the Lapita homeland. *Journal of Pacific History* 19: 186-201.

— 1989. When did humans first colonize Australia? *Search* 20: 149-54.

Allen, J., Gosden, C., Jones, R., and White, J. P., 1988. Pleistocene dates for the human occupation of New Ireland, northern Melanesia. *Nature* 331: 707-9.

Allen, J., Gosden, C., and White, J. P. 1989. Human Pleistocene adaptations in the tropical island Pacific: recent evidence from New Ireland, a Greater Australian outlier. *Antiquity* 63: 548-61.

Allen, J. and White, J. P. 1989. The Lapita homeland: some new data and an interpretation. *Journal of the Polynesian Society* 98: 129-46.

Ambrose, W. R. 1988. An early bronze artefact from Papua New Guinea. *Antiquity* 62: 483-91.

Anderson, A. J. 1980. The archaeology of Raoul Island (Kermadecs) and its place in the settlement history of Polynesia. *Archaeology and Physical Anthropology in Oceania* 15: 131-41.

— 1982. A review of economic patterns during the Archaic Phase in southern New Zealand. *New Zealand Journal of Archaeology* 4: 45-75.

Anderson, A. J., and McGovern-Wilson, R. 1990. The pattern of prehistoric Polynesian colonisation in New Zealand. *Journal of the Royal Society of New Zealand* 20: 41-63.

Anson, D. 1983. Lapita pottery of the Bismarck Archipelago and its affinities. Ph.D. thesis, University of Sydney.

Athens, J. S. 1987. Early settlement on Kosrae: where is the pottery? Paper presented to the Indo-Pacific Prehistory Association Conference, Guam, 1987.

Ayres, W. S. 1987. Pohnpei's position in eastern Micronesian prehistory. Paper presented to the Indo-Pacific Prehistory Association Conference, Guam, 1987.

Ayres, W. S., and Bryson, R. 1989. Micronesian pottery: the view from Pohnpei. Paper presented to the Circum-Pacific Prehistory Conference, Seattle, August 1989.

Babayan, C., Finney, B., Kilonsky, B., and Thompson, N. 1987. Voyage to Aotearoa. *Journal of the Polynesian Society* 96: 161-200.

Banks, J. 1962. *The Endeavour Journal, vols. 1 and II, 1768-1771*. ed. J. C. Beaglehole. Sydney: Angus & Robertson.

Barnett, T., Graham, N., Cane, M., Zebiak, S., Dolan, S., O'Brien, J., and Legler, D. 1988. On the prediction of the El Niño of 1986-1987. *Science* 241: 194-6.

Bayard, D. 1976. *The cultural relationships of the Polynesian Outliers*. University of Otago Studies in Prehistoric Anthropology, 9. Dunedin, New Zealand: Department of Anthropology, University of Otago.

Beaglehole, J. C. (ed.) 1967. *The Journals of Captain James Cook on his voyages of discovery*. vol. III. *The voyage of the* Resolution *and* Discovery, *1776-1780*. Cambridge: Hakluyt Society.

— 1968. *The Journals of Captain James Cook on his voyages of discovery*. vol. I. *The voyage of the* Endeavour, *1768-1771*. Cambridge: Hakluyt Society.

Bellwood, P. S. 1970. Dispersal centers in East Polynesia, with specific reference to the Society and Marquesas Islands. In *Studies in Oceanic culture history*, vol. 3, ed. R. C. Green and M. Kelly, pp. 93-104. Pacific Anthropological Records, no. 11. Honolulu: Bernice P. Bishop Museum.

— 1978. *Man's conquest of the Pacific*. Auckland: Collins.

— 1985. *Prehistory of the Indo-Malaysian archipelago*. Sydney: Academic Press.

— 1986. From late Pleistocene to early Holocene in Sundaland. Paper presented to the World Archaeological Congress, Southampton.

— 1988. A hypothesis for Austronesian origins. *Asian Perspectives* 26: 107-17.

— 1989. The colonization of the Pacific: some current hypotheses. In *The colonization of the Pacific: A genetic trail*, ed. A. V. S. Hill and S. W. Serjeantson, pp. 1-59. Oxford: Clarendon Press.

Bellwood, P., and Koon, P. 1989. 'Lapita colonists leave boats unburned!' The question of Lapita links with Southeast Asia. *Antiquity* 63: 613-22.

Best, Elsdon. 1923. *Polynesian voyagers*. Monograph, no. 5. Wellington: Dominion Museum.

Best, S. B. 1977. The Maori adze: an explanation for change. *Journal of the Polynesian Society* 86: 307-37.

— 1981. *Excavations at Site VL 21/5, Naigani Island, Fiji. A preliminary report.* Department of Anthropology, University of Auckland.

— 1984. Lakeba: the prehistory of a Fijian island. Ph.D. thesis, University of Auckland.

— 1988. Tokelau archaeology: a preliminary report of an initial survey and excavations. *Indo-Pacific Prehistory Association Bulletin* 8: 104-18.

— 1989. Fiji; the first millennium. Paper presented to the Circum-Pacific Prehistory Conference, Seattle, August 1989.

Biggs. B. G. 1972. Implications of linguistic subgrouping with special reference to Polynesia. In *Studies in Oceanic culture history*, vol. 3, ed. R. C. Green and M. Kelly, pp. 143-60. Pacific Anthropological Records, no. 13, Honolulu: Bernice P. Bishop Museum.

Birdsell, J. B. 1977. The recalibration of a paradigm for the first peopling of Greater Australia. In *Sunda and Sahul: prehistoric studies in Southeast Asia, Melanesia and Australia*, ed. J. Allen, J. Golson and R. Jones, pp. 113-67. Canberra: Australian National University Press.

Blust, R. 1984-5. [1988] The Austronesian homeland: a linguistic perspective. *Asian Perspectives* 26: 45-67.

Bonhomme, T., and Craib, J. L. 1987. Radiocarbon dates from Unai Bapot, Saipan – implications for the prehistory of the Mariana Islands. *Journal of the Polynesian Society* 96: 95-106.

Bowdler, S. 1990. The earliest Australian stone tools and implications for Southeast Asia. Paper presented to the 14th Congress of the Indo-Pacific Prehistory Association, Jogyakarta, August-September 1990.

Brace, C. L., Tracer, D. P., and Hunt, K. D. 1990. Human craniofacial form and the evidence for the peopling of the Pacific. Paper presented to the 14th Congress of the Indo-Pacific Prehistory Association, Jogyakarta, August-September 1990.

Bridgeman, H. A. 1983. Could climatic change have had an influence on the Polynesian migrations? *Palaeogeography, Palaeoclimatology, Palaeoecology* 41: 193-206.

Brierly, K. E. 1985. *Weather for New Zealand sailors.* Auckland: Endeavour Press.

British Admiralty. n.d. Charts Nos. 941B, 942A and 942B. London: Hydrographer of the Navy.

Brown, P. 1987. Pleistocene homogeneity and Holocene size reduction: the Australian human skeletal evidence. *Archaeology in Oceania* 22: 41-67.

Buck, P. H. (Te Rangi Hiroa). 1938. *Vikings of the sunrise.* New York: J. B. Lippincott.

Burrows, E.G. 1938. *Western Polynesia: A study in cultural differentiation*, Ethnologiska Studier, 7. Goteborg.

Butler, B. M., and De Fant, D. G. 1989. Preliminary report on archaeological investigations in the Achugao and Matausa areas of Saipan, Mariana Islands. Center for Archaeological Investigations, Southern Illinois University at Carbondale.

Caughley, G. 1988. The colonisation of New Zealand by the Polynesians. *Journal of the Royal Society of New Zealand* 18: 245-70.

Chester, P. I., 1986. Forest clearance in the Bay of Islands. M.A. thesis, University of Auckland.

Chikamori, M. 1987. Archaeology on Pukapuka Atoll. *Man and Culture in Oceania* 3 (Special Issue): 105-15.

Claridge, G. G. C. 1984. Pottery and the Pacific: the clay factor. *New Zealand Journal of Archaeology* 6: 37-46.

Clark, J. T, 1989. Holocene sea level changes in the South Pacific: implications for human settlement. Paper presented to the Circum-Pacific Prehistory Conference, Seattle, August 1989.

Clark, J. T., and Terrell, J. 1978. Archaeology in Oceania. *Annual Review of Anthropology* 7: 293-319.

Clark, R. 1979. Language. In *The prehistory of Polynesia*, ed. J. D. Jennings, pp. 247-70. Cambridge, Mass.: Harvard University Press.

— 1988. Subgrouping in Central Eastern Polynesia. Paper presented to the New Zealand Archaeological Association Conference, Auckland, May 1988.

Cook, J., and King, J. 1785a-c. *A voyage to the Pacific Ocean . . . in the years 1776-80*, (vols.I and II by Cook; vol.III by King). 2nd edition. London: G. Nicol and T. Cadell.

Cordy, R. H. 1981. *A study of prehistoric social change: the development of complex societies in the Hawaiian Islands.* New York: Academic Press.

Cosgrove, R. 1989. Thirty thousand years of human colonization in Tasmania: new Pleistocene dates. *Science* 243: 1706-8.

Coutts, C. 1981. *Coastal yacht navigation.* Auckland: Methuen New Zealand.

Craib, J. L. 1983. Micronesian prehistory: an archaeological overview. *Science* 219: 922-7.

— 1988a. Searching high and low: investigations into early Micronesian prehistory. Paper presented to the Australian Archaeological Association Conference, Armidale, 1988.

— 1988b. Pottery decorations in Micronesia: implications for prehistory. Paper presented to the Lapita Design Workshop, Canberra, Australian National University, 1988.

Crosby, A. 1988. Beqa: archaeology, structure and history in Fiji. M.A. thesis, University of Auckland.

Dale, W. R. (ed.) 1981. Pacific Islands Water Resources. *DSIR South Pacific Technical Inventory* 2. Wellington.

Davidson, J. M. 1971. *Archaeology on Nukuoro Atoll: a Polynesian outlier in the eastern Caroline Islands.* Bulletin, no. 9. Auckland Institute and Museum.

— 1974. Cultural replacement on small islands: new evidence from Polynesian outliers. *Mankind* 9: 273-7.

— 1978. Western Polynesia and Fiji: the archaeological evidence. *Mankind* 11: 383-90.

— 1979. Samoa and Tonga. In *The prehistory of Polynesia*, ed. J. D. Jennings, pp. 82-109. Cambridge, Mass.: Harvard University Press.

— 1981. The Polynesian foundation. In *The Oxford history of New Zealand*, ed. W. H. Oliver and B. R. Williams, pp. 3-27. Wellington: Oxford University Press.

— 1984. *The prehistory of New Zealand.* Auckland: Longman Paul.

— 1988. Archaeology in Micronesia since 1965: past achievements and future prospects. *New Zealand Journal of Archaeology* 10: 83-100.

— 1989. Lapita colonisation of Polynesia. Paper presented to the Circum-Pacific Prehistory Conference, Seattle, August 1989.

Dening, G. M. 1963. The geographical knowledge of the Polynesians and the nature of inter-island contact. In *Polynesian navigation*, ed. J. Golson, pp. 102-54. Memoir, no. 34. Wellington: The Polynesian Society.

Diamond, J. M. 1985. Why did the Polynesians abandon their mystery islands? *Nature* 317: 764.

— 1988. Express train to Polynesia. *Nature* 336: 307-8.

Doran, Edwin, Jr. 1981. *Wangka: Austronesian canoe origins.* College Station: Texas A & M University Press.

Douglas, G. 1969. *Check List of Pacific Oceanic Islands.* Reprinted from *Micronesia* 5: 327-463. London: International Biological Programme Conservation Section.

Downie, J. E., and White, J. P. 1978. Balof Shelter, New Ireland - report on a small excavation. *Records of the Australian Museum* 31: 762-802.

Duff, R. S. 1956. *The Moa-hunter period of Maori Culture.* Revised edition. Wellington: Government Printer.

Dunn, F. L., and Dunn, D. F. 1977. Maritime adaptations and exploitation of marine resources in Sundaic Southeast Asian prehistory. *Modern Quaternary Research in Southeast Asia* 3: 1-28.

D'urville, M. J. Dumont. 1833. *Voyage de la corvette L'Astrolabe exécuté pendant les années 1826-1827-1828-1829 sans le commandement de M. Jules Dumont D'Urville, capitaine de vaisseau.* Atlas Historique. Paris. J. Tartu.

Dye, T. 1987. *Marshall Islands archaeology.* Pacific Anthropological Records, no. 38. Honolulu: Bernice P. Bishop Museum.

Dyen, I. 1971. The Austronesian languages and proto-Austronesian. In *Current Trends in Linguistics no. 8: Linguistics in Oceania*, ed. T. A. Sebeok, pp. 5-54. The Hague: Mouton.

Earle, T. K. 1980. Prehistoric irrigation on the Hawaiian Islands: an evaluation of evolutionary significance. *Archaeology and Physical Anthropology in Oceania* 15: 1-28.

Edson, S. C. 1973. Human ecology and prehistoric settlement on some offshore islands (East Cape to Cape Reinga), New Zealand. M.A. thesis, University of Auckland.

Ellis, W. 1831. *Polynesian researches during a residence of nearly eight years in the Society and Sandwich Islands.* (4 vols). London: Henry Bohn.

Emory, K. P. 1934. *Archaeology of the Pacific Equatorial Islands.* Bulletin, no. 123. Honolulu: Bernice P. Bishop Museum.

— 1939. *Archaeology of Mangareva.* Bulletin, no. 163. Honolulu: Bernice P. Bishop Museum.

— 1959. Origin of the Hawaiians. *Journal of the Polynesian Society* 68: 29-35.

Enright, N. J., and Osborne, N. M. 1988. Comments on D. G. Sutton's paper 'A paradigmatic shift in Polynesian prehistory: implications for New Zealand'. *New Zealand Journal of Archaeology* 10: 139-46.

Ferdon, E. N. 1963. Polynesian origins. *Science* 141: 499-505.

Finney, Ben R. 1977. Voyaging canoes and the settlement of Polynesia. *Science* 196: 1277-85.

— 1979a. Voyaging. In *The prehistory of Polynesia*, ed. J. D. Jennings, pp. 323-51. Cambridge, Mass.: Harvard University Press.

— 1979b. *Hokule'a: the way to Tahiti.* New York: Dodd, Mead.

— 1985. Anomalous westerlies, El Niño, and the colonization of Polynesia. *American Anthropologist* 87: 9-26.

— 1988. Voyaging against the direction of the trades: a report of an experimental canoe voyage from Samoa to Tahiti. *American Anthropologist* 90: 401-5.

Finney, Ben R., Kilonsky, B. J., Somsen, S., and Stroup, E. D. 1986. Re-learning a vanishing art. *Journal of the Polynesian Society* 95: 41-90.

Finney, Ben R., Frost, P., Rhodes, R., and Thompson, N. 1989. Wait for the west wind. *Journal of the Polynesian Society* 98: 261–302.

Flannery, T. F., Kirch, P. V., Specht, J., and Spriggs, M. 1988. Holocene mammal faunas from archaeological sites in island Melanesia. *Archaeology in Oceania* 23: 89–94.

Flenley, J. R. 1989. Man–vegetation interactions in the Pacific. Report to the British Academy. Geography Department, University of Hull.

Frankel, J. P. 1962. Polynesian navigation. *Navigation* (Journal of the Institute of Navigation, Washington) 9: 35–47.

Friedman, J. 1981. Notes on structure and history in Oceania. *Folk* 23: 275–95.

Gathercole, P. 1964. Preliminary report on archaeological fieldwork on Pitcairn Island. Unpublished ms, University of Otago.

Gatty, H. 1958. *Nature is your guide*. London: Collins.

Gladwin, Thomas. 1970. *East is a Big Bird*. Cambridge, Mass.: Harvard University Press.

Goldman, I. 1970. *Ancient Polynesian Society*. Chicago University Press.

Golson, J. 1961. Report on New Zealand, Western Polynesia, New Caledonia, and Fiji. *Asian Perspectives* 5: 166–80.

— (ed.) 1963. *Polynesian navigation*. Memoir, no. 34. Wellington: The Polynesian Society.

— 1971. Australian Aboriginal food plants: some ecological and culture-historical implications. In *Aboriginal man and environment in Australia*, ed. D. J. Mulvaney and J. Golson, pp. 196–238. Canberra: Australian National University Press.

— 1977. No room at the top: agricultural intensification in the New Guinea highlands. In *Sunda and Sahul: prehistoric studies in Southeast Asia, Melanesia and Australia*, ed. J. Allen, J. Golson and R. Jones, pp. 601–38. London: Academic Press.

Goodenough, W. H. 1957. Oceania and the problem of controls in the study of cultural and human evolution. *Journal of the Polynesian Society* 66: 146–55.

Goodenough, W. H., and Thomas, S. D. 1987. Trobriand navigation in the western Pacific: a search for pattern. *Expedition* 29: 3–14.

Gosden, C., Allen, J., Ambrose, W., Anson, D., Golson, J., Green, R., Kirch, P., Lilley, I., Specht, J., and Spriggs, M. 1989. Lapita sites of the Bismarck Archipelago. *Antiquity* 63: 561–86.

Green, R. C. 1966. Linguistic subgrouping within Polynesia: the implications for prehistoric settlement. *Journal of the Polynesian Society* 75: 6–38.

— 1975. Adaptation and change in Maori culture. In *Biogeography and Ecology in New Zealand*, ed. G. Kuschel, pp. 591–641. The Hague: Dr W. Junk.

— 1978. *New sites with Lapita pottery and their implications for understanding the settlement of the Western Pacific*. Working Papers in Anthropology, Archaeology, Linguistics, and Maori Studies, no. 56. Department of Anthropology, University of Auckland.

— 1979. Lapita. In *The prehistory of Polynesia*, ed. J. D. Jennings, pp. 27–60. Cambridge, Mass.: Harvard University Press.

— 1981. Location of the Polynesian homeland: a continuing problem. In *Studies in Pacific Languages and Cultures in Honour of Bruce Biggs*, ed. J. Hollyman and A. K. Pawley, pp. 133–58. Auckland: Linguistic Society of New Zealand.

— 1982. Models for the Lapita cultural complex: an evaluation of some current proposals. *New Zealand Journal of Archaeology* 4: 7–19.

— 1985. *Subgrouping of the Rapanui language of Easter Island in Polynesian and its implications for East Polynesian prehistory*. Working Papers in Anthropology, Archaeology, Linguistics and Maori Studies, no. 68. Department of Anthropology, University of Auckland.

— 1988. Those mysterious mounds are for the birds. *Archaeology in New Zealand* 31: 153–8.

— in press. Near and Remote Oceania – disestablishing 'Melanesia' in culture history. In *Man and a half: essays in honour of Ralph Bulmer*, ed. A. K. Pawley. Auckland: The Polynesian Society.

Groube, L.M. 1971. Tonga, Lapita pottery, and Polynesian origins. *Journal of the Polynesian Society* 80: 278–316.

Groube, L., Chappell, J., Muke, J., and Price, D. 1986. A 40,000-year-old human occupation site at Huon Peninsula, Papua New Guinea. *Nature* 324: 453–5.

Guiart, J. 1963. Un état palatial Océanien: l'Empire maritime des Tui Tonga. Appendix to *Structure de la Chefferie en Mélanésie du Sud*. Travaux et Mémoires, no. 66. Institut d'Ethnologie: Paris.

Habgood, P. J. 1989. The origin of anatomically-modern humans in Australasia. In *The human revolution: behavioural and biological perspectives on the origins of modern humans*, ed. P. Mellars and C. Stringer, pp. 245–73. Edinburgh University Press.

Halpern, M. 1986. Sidereal compasses: a case for Carolinian-Arab links. *Journal of the Polynesian Society* 95: 441–59.

Hessell, J. W. D. 1981. Climatology of the Southwest Pacific Islands. In Pacific Islands Water Resources. *DSIR South Pacific Technical Inventory* 2. ed. W. R. Dale. Wellington: DSIR.

Heyen, G. H. 1963. Primitive navigation in the Pacific-I. In *Polynesian navigation*, ed. J. Golson, pp. 64–79. Memoir, no. 34. Wellington: The Polynesian Society.

Heyerdahl, Thor. 1952. *American Indians in the Pacific*. Chicago: Rand McNally.

Hilder, B. 1963. Primitive navigation in the Pacific-II. In *Polynesian navigation*, ed. J. Golson, pp. 81–97. Memoir, no. 34. Wellington: The Polynesian Society.

Hill, A. V. and Serjeantson, S. W. (eds) 1989. *The colonization of the Pacific: a genetic trail*. Oxford: Clarendon Press.

Hommon, R. J. 1976. The formation of primitive states in pre-contact Hawaii. Ph.D. thesis, University of Arizona.

Hooper, A. 1985. Introduction in *Transformation of Polynesian culture*, ed. A. Hooper and J. Huntsman, pp. 1–16, Memoir, no. 45, Auckland: The Polynesian Society.

Hooper, A., and Huntsman, J. (eds), 1985. *Transformation of Polynesian culture*. Memoir no. 45. Auckland: The Polynesian Society.

Horridge, A. 1987. *Outrigger canoes of Bali and Madura*. Honolulu: Bishop Museum Press.

Houghton, P. 1989a. Watom: the people. *Records of the Australian Museum* 41: 223–33.

— 1989b. The Lapita-associated human material from Lakeba, Fiji. *Records of the Australian Museum* 41: 327–29.

— 1990. The adaptive significance of Polynesian body form. *Annals of Human Biology* 17: 19–32.

— in press. The early human biology of the Pacific: some considerations. *Journal of the Polynesian Society*.

Howells, W. W. 1973. *The Pacific Islanders*. London: Weidenfeld & Nicolson.

— 1979. Physical anthropology. In *The prehistory of Polynesia*, ed. J. D. Jennings, pp. 271–85. Cambridge, Mass.: Harvard University Press.

Hunt, T. L. 1987. Patterns of human interaction and evolutionary divergence in the Fiji Islands. *Journal of the Polynesian Society* 96: 299–334.

— 1989. Lapita ceramic exchange in the Mussau Islands, Papua New Guinea. Ph.D. thesis, University of Washington.

Hutchings, J. W. 1961. Climatic features of the tropical Southwest Pacific Ocean, *New Zealand Meteorological Service Technical Information Circular*, no. 108. Wellington.

Indonesia Pilot. 1980. Vol. III. 1st edition. Taunton: Hydrographer of the Navy.

Irwin, Geoffrey, 1980. The prehistory of Oceania: colonization and culture change. In *The Cambridge Encyclopedia of Archaeology*, ed. A. Sherratt, pp. 324–32. Cambridge University Press.

— 1981. How Lapita lost its pots: the question of continuity in the colonisation of Oceania. *Journal of the Polynesian Society* 90: 481–94.

— 1987. A view from the sea: the first exploration of the Remote Pacific Islands. Paper presented to the Lapita Homeland Conference, La Trobe University, Melbourne, December 1987.

— 1989. Against, across and down the wind: a case for the systematic exploration of the remote Pacific Islands. *Journal of the Polynesian Society* 98: 167–206.

— 1990. Human colonisation and change in the remote Pacific. *Current Anthropology* 31: 90–4.

— in press a. Themes on the prehistory of coastal Papua and the Massim. In *Man and a half: essays in honour of Ralph Bulmer*, ed. A. K. Pawley. Auckland: The Polynesian Society.

— in press b. Pleistocene voyaging and the settlement of Greater Australia and its Near Oceanic neighbours. In *Report of the Lapita Homeland Project*, (2 vols) ed. J. Allen and C. Gosden. Occasional Papers no. 20. Canberra: Department of Prehistory, Research School of Pacific Studies, Australian National University.

Irwin, G. J., Bickler, S. H., and Quirke, P. 1990. Voyaging by canoe and computer: experiments in the settlement of the Pacific. *Antiquity* 64: 34–50.

Ishikawa, E. 1987. The breadfruit culture complex in Oceania. In *Cultural Uniformity and Diversity in Micronesia*, ed. I. Ushijima and K. Sudo, pp. 9–27. Senri Ethnological Studies, no. 21. Osaka: National Museum of Ethnology.

Jennings, J. D. (ed.) 1979. *The prehistory of Polynesia*. Cambridge, Mass.: Harvard University Press.

Jones, R. 1989. East of Wallace's Line: issues and problems in the colonisation of the Australian continent. In *The human revolution: behavioural and biological perspectives on the origins of modern humans*, ed. P. Mellars and C. Stringer, pp. 743–82. Edinburgh University Press.

— 1990. *Homo sapiens* and the colonization of Southeast Asia and Australia-New Guinea. Paper presented to the 14th Congress of the Indo-Pacific Prehistory Association, Jogyakarta, August–September 1990.

Katayama, K. 1988. Biological affinity between the southern Cook Islanders and New Zealand Maoris, and its implicaton for the settlement of New Zealand. Paper presented to the New Zealand Archaeological Association Conference, Auckland, May 1988.

Keegan, W. F., and Diamond, J. M. 1987. Colonization of islands by humans: a biogeographical perspective. In *Advances in Archaeological Method and Theory* vol. 10, ed. M. Schiffer, pp. 49–92, New York: Academic Press.

Kennedy, J. 1983. On the prehistory of western Melanesia: the significance of new data from the Admiralties. *Australian Archaeology* 16: 115-22.

Kirch, P. V. 1980. The archaeological study of adaptation: theoretical and methodological issues. *Advances in Archaeological Method and Theory* 3: 101-56.

— 1984a. The Polynesian Outliers: continuity, change and replacement. In *Out of Asia: Peopling the Americas and the Pacific*, ed. R. Kirk and E. Szathmary, pp. 206-21. Canberra: *Journal of Pacific History*.

— 1984b. *The evolution of the Polynesian chiefdoms*. Cambridge University Press.

— 1985. *Feathered Gods and fishhooks: an introduction to Hawaiian archaeology and prehistory*. Honolulu: Bishop Museum Press.

— 1986. Rethinking East Polynesian prehistory. *Journal of the Polynesian Society* 95: 9-40.

— 1987. Lapita and Oceanic culture origins: excavations in the Mussau Islands, Bismarck archipelago, 1985. *Journal of Field Archaeology* 14: 163-80.

— 1988a. *Niuatoputapu: The prehistory of an island chiefdom*. Seattle: Burke Museum.

— 1988b. Polynesia's mystery islands. *Archaeology* May/June: 26-31.

— 1988c. The Talepakemalai Lapita site and Oceanic prehistory. *National Geographic Research* 4: 328-42.

— 1988d. Long-distance exchange and island colonization: the Lapita case. *Norwegian Archaeological Review* 21: 103-17.

— 1989. Second millennium B.C. arboriculture in Melanesia: archaeological evidence from the Mussau Islands. *Economic Botany* 43: 225-40.

Kirch, P. V., Allen, M. S., Butler, V. L., and Hunt, T. L. 1987. Is there an early Far Western Lapita province? *Archaeology in Oceania* 22: 123-27.

Kirch, P. V., Dickinson, W. R., and Hunt, T. L. 1988. Polynesian plainware sherds from Hivaoa and their implications for Early Marquesan prehistory. *New Zealand Journal of Archaeology* 10: 101-7.

Kirch, P. V., and Green, R. C. 1987. History, phylogeny, and evolution in Polynesia. *Current Anthropology* 28: 431-56.

Kirch, P. V., and Hunt, T. L. 1988a. The spatial and temporal boundaries of Lapita. In *Archaeology of the Lapita cultural complex: a critical review*, ed. P. V. Kirch and T. L. Hunt, pp. 9-31. Research Report, no. 5. Seattle: Thomas Burke Memorial Washington State Museum.

— (eds) 1988b. *Archaeology of the Lapita cultural complex: a critical review*. Research Report, no. 5. Seattle: Thomas Burke Memorial Washington State Museum.

Kirch, P. V., and Rosendahl, P. H. 1976. Early Anutan settlement and the position of Anuta in the prehistory of the Southwest Pacific. In *Southeast Solomon Islands cultural history*, ed. R. C. Green and M. M. Cresswell, pp. 225-44. Bulletin, no. 11. Wellington: Royal Society of New Zealand.

Kirch, P. V., and Yen, D. E. 1982. *Tikopia: the prehistory and ecology of a Polynesian outlier*. Bulletin, no. 238. Honolulu: Bishop Museum Press.

Kurashina, H. 1987. Results of an interdisciplinary research project at Tarague, Guam. Paper presented to the Indo-Pacific Prehistory Association Conference, Guam, 1987.

Lang, J. D. 1877. *Origin and migrations of the Polynesian Nation*. 2nd edition. Sydney: George Robertson.

Law, R. G. 1988. Probability, order of settlement and multiple settlement: New Zealand, Hawaii and Easter Island. Paper presented to the New Zealand Archaeological Association Conference, Auckland, May 1988.

Leach, B. F., Anderson, A. J., Sutton, D. G., Bird, R., Duerden, P., and Clayton, E. 1986. The origin of prehistoric obsidian artefacts from the Chatham and Kermadec Islands. *New Zealand Journal of Archaeology* 8: 143-70.

Leach, B. F., and Ward, G. 1981. *Archaeology on Kapingamarangi Atoll: a Polynesian Outlier in the eastern Caroline Islands*. University of Otago Studies in Prehistoric Anthropology, no. 16. Dunedin: Department of Anthropology, University of Otago.

Leach, H. M., and Green, R. C. 1989. New information for the Ferry Berth Site, Mulifanua, Western Samoa. *Journal of the Polynesian Society* 98: 319-29.

Lepofsky, D. 1988. The environmental context of Lapita settlement locations. In *Archaeology of the Lapita cultural complex: a critical review*, ed. P. V. Kirch and T. L. Hunt, pp. 33-47. Research Report no. 5. Seattle: Thomas Burke Memorial Washington State Museum.

Levison, M., Ward, R. G., and Webb, J. W. 1973. *The settlement of Polynesia: a computer simulation*. Minneapolis: University of Minnesota Press.

Lewis, David. 1972. *We, the navigators*. Canberra: Australian National University Press.

— 1977. *From Maui to Cook*. Sydney: Doubleday.

— 1978. The Pacific navigators' debt to the ancient seafarers of Asia. In *The Changing Pacific: essays in honour of H. E. Maude*, ed. N. Gunson, pp. 46-66. Melbourne: Oxford University Press.

MacArthur, R. H., and Wilson, E. O. 1967. *The theory of island biogeography*. Princeton University Press.

McArthur, N., Saunders, I. W., and Tweedie, R. L. 1976. Small population isolates: a micro-simulation study. *Journal of the Polynesian Society* 85: 307-26.

McCoy, P. C. 1979. Easter Island. In *The prehistory of Polynesia*, ed. J. D. Jennings, pp. 135-66. Cambridge, Mass.: Harvard University Press.

McCoy, P. C., and Cleghorn, P. L. 1988. Archaeological excavations on Santa Cruz (Nendö), southeast Solomon Islands: summary report. *Archaeology in Oceania* 23: 104-15.

Makemson, M. 1941. *The Morning Star rises. An account of Polynesian astronomy*, New Haven: Yale University Press.

Marck, J. C. 1975. The origin and dispersal of the Proto Nuclear Micronesians. M.A. thesis, University of Iowa.

— 1986. Micronesian dialects and the overnight voyage. *Journal of the Polynesian Society* 95: 253-8.

Masse, W. B. 1987. Radiocarbon dating, sea-level change, and the peopling of Palau. Paper presented to the Indo-Pacific Prehistory Association Conference, Guam, 1987.

Mellars, P., and Stringer, C. (eds) 1989. *The human revolution: behavioural and biological perspectives on the origins of modern humans*. Edinburgh University Press.

Meredith, C. M., Specht, J. R., and Rich, P. V. 1985. A minimum date for Polynesian visitation to Norfolk Island, Southwest Pacific, from faunal evidence. *Search* 16: 304-6.

New Zealand Pilot. 1971. 13th edition. Taunton: Hydrographer of the Navy.

Ocean passages for the world. 1973. 3rd edition. Taunton: Hydrographer of the Navy.

Ottino, P. 1985a. Un site ancien aux îles Marquises: l'abri-sous-roche d'Anapua, à Ua Pou. *Journal de la Société des Océanistes* 80: 33-8.

— 1985b. Archéologie des Iles Marquises: contribution à la connaissance de l'île de Ua Pou. 2 vols. Thèse de 3ème cycle en Ethnologie préhistorique, University of Paris.

Pacific Islands Pilot. 1969. Vol. II. 9th edition. Taunton: Hydrographer of the Navy.

— 1970. Vol. I. 9th edition. Taunton: Hydrographer of the Navy.

— 1982. Vol. III. 10th edition. Taunton: Hydrographer of the Navy.

Parsonson, G. S. 1963. The settlement of Oceania: an examination of the Accidental Voyage theory. In *Polynesian navigation*, ed. J. Golson, pp. 11-63. Memoir, no. 34., Wellington: The Polynesian Society.

Pawley, A. K. 1966. Polynesian languages: a subgrouping based on shared innovations in morphology. *Journal of the Polynesian Society* 75: 39-64.

— 1981. Melanesian diversity and Polynesian homogeneity: a unified explanation for language. In *Studies in Pacific Language and Cultures in Honour of Bruce Biggs*, ed. J. Hollyman and A. K. Pawley, pp. 269-309. Auckland: Linguistic Society of New Zealand.

Pawley, A. K., and Green, R. C. 1973. Dating the dispersal of the Oceanic languages. *Oceanic Linguistics* 12: 1-67.

— 1984. The Proto-Oceanic language community. *Journal of Pacific History* 19: 123-46.

Pietrusewsky, M. 1989a. A study of skeletal and dental remains from Watom Island and comparisons with other Lapita people. *Records of the Australian Museum* 41: 235-92.

— 1989b. A Lapita-associated skeleton from Natunuku Fiji. *Records of the Australian Museum* 41: 297-325.

Pritchard, W. T. 1866. *Polynesian reminiscences: or life in the South Pacific islands*. London: Chapman & Hall.

Ramage, C. 1986. El Niño. *Scientific American* 254: 55-61.

Renfrew, C., and Cherry. J. F. 1986. *Peer polity interaction and socio-political change*. Cambridge University Press.

Renfrew, C., and Sterud, G. 1969. Close-proximity analysis: a rapid method for the ordering of archaeological materials. *American Antiquity* 34: 265-77.

Roberts, R. G., Jones, R., and Smith, M. A. 1990. Thermoluminescence dating of a 50,000-year-old human occupation site in northern Australia. *Nature* 345: 153-56.

Rodman, H. 1927. The sacred calabash. *U.S. Naval Institute Proceedings* 53: 867-72.

Ross, M. D. 1987. Early Oceanic linguistic prehistory. Paper presented to the Lapita Homeland Workshop, La Trobe University, September 1987.

— 1988. *Proto Oceanic and the Austronesian languages of Western Melanesia*. Pacific Linguistics, Series C-no. 98. Canberra: Department of Linguistics, Australian National University.

Routeing Chart of the South Pacific Ocean for February. 1967. London: Hydrographer of the Navy.

Sadler, D., and Parry, D. 1990. Alberto, navigator extraordinary. *Yachting Monthly* February 1990: 90-1.

Sahlins, M. D. 1958. *Social stratification in Polynesia*. Seattle: University of Washington Press.

Serjeantson, S. W., and Hill, A.V. S. 1989. The colonization of the Pacific: the genetic evidence. In *The colonization of the Pacific: A genetic trail*, ed. A.V. S. Hill and S. W. Serjeantson, pp. 286-94. Oxford: Clarendon Press.

Sharp, A. 1957. *Ancient voyagers in the Pacific*. Harmondsworth, Middlesex: Penguin Books.

— 1963. *Ancient voyagers in Polynesia*. Auckland: Pauls Book Arcade.

Shun, K., and Athens, J. S. 1987. Archaeological investigations on Kwajalein Atoll, Marshall Islands,

Micronesia. Paper presented to the Indo-Pacific Prehistory Association Conference, Guam, 1987.

Shutler, R. (jr), and Shutler, M. E. 1975. *Oceanic prehistory.* Menlo Park, Calif.: Cummings.

Siers, J. 1977. *Taratai: a Pacific adventure.* Wellington: Millwood Press.

Sinoto, A. 1973. Fanning Island: preliminary archaeological investigations of sites near the Cable Station. In *Fanning Island Expedition: July and August 1972,* ed. K. E. Chave and E. A. Kay. Report 73-13. Honolulu: Hawaii Institute of Geophysics.

Sinoto, Y. H. 1966. A tentative prehistoric cultural sequence in the Northern Marquesas Islands. *Journal of the Polynesian Society* 75: 287-303.

— 1970. An archaeologically based assessment of the Marquesas Islands as a dispersal center in East Polynesia. In *Studies in Oceanic culture history,* vol. 1, ed. R. C. Green and M. Kelly, pp. 105-30. Pacific Anthropological Records, no. 11. Honolulu: Bernice P. Bishop Museum.

— 1983. An analysis of Polynesian migrations based on the archaeological assessments. *Journal de la Société des Océanistes* 76: 57-67.

Smith, S. P. 1921. *Hawaiki: the original home of the Maori.* Christchurch: Whitcombe & Tombs.

Sorrenson, M. P. K. 1979. *Maori origins and migrations.* Auckland: Auckland University Press/Oxford University Press.

Specht, J. 1984. *The prehistoric archaeology of Norfolk Island.* Pacific Anthropological Records, no. 34. Honolulu: Bernice P. Bishop Museum.

— 1988. A Far-Western Lapita? Paper presented to the Lapita Design Workshop. Canberra: Australian National University, 1988.

Specht, J., Lilley, I., and Normu, J. 1981. Radiocarbon dates from West New Britain, Papua New Guinea. *Australian Archaeology* 12: 13-15.

Spriggs, M. J. T. 1982. Taro-cropping systems in the Southeast Asian-Pacific Region: archaeological evidence. *Archaeology in Oceania* 17: 7-15.

— 1984. The Lapita cultural complex: origins, distribution, contemporaries and successors. *Journal of Pacific History* 19: 202-23.

— 1986. Landscape, land use, and political transformation in southern Melanesia. In *Island Societies: archaeological approaches to evolution and transformation,* ed. P. V. Kirch, pp. 6-19. Cambridge University Press.

— 1989a. The dating of the Island Southeast Asian Neolithic: an attempt at chronometric hygiene and linguistic correlation. *Antiquity* 63: 587-613.

— 1989b. The Solomon Islands as bridge and barrier in the settlement of the Pacific. Paper presented to the Circum-Pacific Prehistory Conference, Seattle, August 1989.

— in press. Dating Lapita: another view. In *Lapita design, form and composition,* ed. M. J. T. Spriggs. Occasional Paper. Canberra: Department of Prehistory, Research School of Pacific Studies, Australian National University.

Steadman, D. W., and Olsen, S. L. 1985. Bird remains from an archaeological site on Henderson Island, South Pacific: man-caused extinction on an 'uninhabited' island. *Proceedings of the National Academy of Sciences USA* 82: 6191-5.

Streck, C. F. 1987. Prehistoric settlement in eastern Micronesia: archaeology on Bikini Atoll, Republic of the Marshall Islands. Paper presented to the Indo-Pacific Prehistory Association Conference, Guam, 1987.

Suggs, R. C. 1960. *The Island civilizations of Polynesia.* New York: Mentor Books.

— 1961. The archaeology of Nuku Hiva, Marquesas Islands, French Polynesia. *Anthropological Papers of the American Museum of Natural History* 49: 1-205.

Sutton, D. G. 1980. A culture history of the Chatham Islands. *Journal of the Polynesian Society* 89: 67-93.

— 1982. The Chatham Islands. In *The first thousand years: regional perspectives in New Zealand archaeology,* ed. N. J. Prickett, pp. 160-78. Palmerston North: Dunmore Press.

— 1987a. A paradigmatic shift in Polynesian prehistory: implications for New Zealand. *New Zealand Journal of Archaeology* 9: 135-55.

— 1987b. Time-place systematics in New Zealand archaeology: the case for a fundamental revision. *Journal de la Société des Océanistes* 84: 23-9.

Swadling, P., Chappell, J., Francis, G., Araho, and Ivuyo, B. 1989. A Late Quaternary inland sea and early pottery in Papua New Guinea. *Archaeology in Oceania* 24: 106-9.

Takayama, J. 1987. The western origin for early Eastern Polynesian fishhooks in light of the excavation of Vaitupu, Tuvalu. *Tezukayama University Review* 57: 16-46.

Takayama, J., Eritaia, B., and Saito, A. 1987. Preliminary observation of the origins of the Vaitupuans in view of the pottery. In *Cultural adaptation to atolls in Micronesia and West Polynesia,* ed. E. Ishikawa, pp. 1-13. Tokyo Metropolitan University.

Takayama, J., and Saito, A. 1987. The discovery of Davidson Type 1a hooks on Vaitupu Island, Tuvalu. *Tezukayama University Review* 55: 29-49.

Takayama, J., and Takasugi, H. 1987. The significance of lure shanks excavated in the Utiroa site of Makin Island in the Gilberts. In *Cultural uniformity and diversity in Micronesia*, ed. I. Ushijima and K. Sudo, pp. 29–41. Senri Ethnological Studies, no. 21. Osaka: National Museum of Ethnology.

Taylor, M. A. 1984. Bone refuse from Twilight Beach. M.A. thesis, University of Auckland.

Terrell, J. E. 1986. *Prehistory in the Pacific Islands*. Cambridge University Press.

— 1988. History as a family tree, history as an entangled bank: constructing images and interpretations of prehistory in the South Pacific. *Antiquity* 62: 642–57.

— 1989. Commentary: what Lapita is and what Lapita isn't. *Antiquity* 63: 623–6.

Terrell, J., and Johnston, R. 1989. Lapita as history and culture hero. Paper presented to the Circum-Pacific Prehistory Conference, Seattle, August 1989.

Thiel, B. 1987. Early settlement of the Philippines, Eastern Indonesia, and Australia-New Guinea: a new hypothesis. *Current Anthropology* 28: 236–41.

Thomas, S. D. 1987. *The last navigator*. New York: Henry Holt & Co.

Thompson, C. S. 1986a. *The climate and weather of the Southern Cook Islands*. Wellington: New Zealand Meteorological Service.

— 1986b. *The climate and weather of the Northern Cook Islands*. Wellington: New Zealand Meteorological Service.

Thorne, A. G. 1990. The later evolution and dispersal of the Javan people. Paper presented to the 14th Congress of the Indo-Pacific Prehistory Association, Jogyakarta, August-September 1990.

Thorne, A. G., and Wolpoff, M. H. 1981. Regional continuity in Australasian Pleistocene hominid evolution. *American Journal of Physical Anthropology* 55: 337–49.

Thorne, R. F., 1963. Biotic distribution patterns in the tropical Pacific. In *Pacific Basin Biogeography*, ed. J. L. Gressitt, pp. 311–54. Honolulu: Bishop Museum Press.

Tregear, E. 1885. *The Aryan Maori*. Wellington: Government Printer.

Trent, R. J., Hertzberg, M., and Mickleson, K. N. P. 1990. Polynesian origins and migration: the story according to nuclear and mitochondrial DNA markers. Paper presented to the 14th Congress of the Indo-Pacific Prehistory Association, Jogyakarta, August-September 1990.

Trotter, M. M., and McCulloch, B. 1984. Moas, men and middens. In *Quaternary Extinctions: a prehistoric revolution*, ed. P. S. Martin and R. G. Klein, pp. 708–23. Tucson: University of Arizona.

Walter, R. 1988. The Cook Islands - New Zealand connection. Paper presented to the New Zealand Archaeological Association Conference, Auckland, May 1988.

— 1990. The Southern Cook Islands in Eastern Polynesian prehistory. Ph.D. thesis, University of Auckland.

Walter, R., and Dickinson, W. 1989. A ceramic sherd from Ma'uke in the southern Cook Islands. *Journal of the Polynesian Society* 98: 465–70.

Ward, R. G., and Moran, W. 1959. Recent population trends in the southwest Pacific. *Tijdschrift voor Economische en Sociale Geografie* 50: 235–40.

White, J. P., and Allen, J. 1980. Melanesian prehistory: some recent advances. *Science* 207: 728–34.

White, J. P., Allen, J., and Specht, J. 1988. Peopling the Pacific: the Lapita Homeland Project. *Australian Natural History* 22: 410–16.

White, J. P., and O'Connell, J. F. 1979. Australian prehistory: new aspects of antiquity. *Science* 203: 21–8.

— 1982. *A prehistory of Australia, New Guinea and Sahul*. Sydney: Academic Press.

Wickler, S., and Spriggs, M. J. T. 1988. Pleistocene human occupation of the Solomon Islands, Melanesia. *Antiquity* 62: 703–6.

Wild, S. 1985. Voyaging to Australia: 30,000 years ago. Ausgraph 85, Third Australasian Conference on Computer Graphics, Brisbane.

Williams, J. 1837. *A narrative of missionary enterprises in the South Seas*. London: J. Snow.

Yen, D. E. 1974. *The sweet potato and Oceania*. Bulletin, no. 236. Honolulu: Bernice P. Bishop Museum.

Yen, D. E., and Gordon, J. (eds) 1973. *Anuta: a Polynesian outlier in the Solomon Islands*. Pacific Anthropological Records, no. 21. Honolulu: Bernice P. Bishop Museum.

INDEX

Numbers in italics indicate numbers of illustrations.